IN or OUT

Gay and Straight Celebrities Talk About Themselves and Each Other

BOZE HADLEIGH

IN *or* OUT

Gay and Straight Celebrities Talk About Themselves and Each Other

BOZE HADLEIGH

Barricade Books • New York
www.barricadebooks.com

Published by Barricade Books Inc.
150 Fifth Avenue
Suite 700
New York, NY 10011

Library of Congress Cataloging-in-Publication Data
Hadleigh, Boze.
In or out : gay and straight celebrities talk about themselves and each other / Boze Hadleigh.
p. cm.
Includes Index.
ISBN 1-56980-158-8
1. Gays–United States–Quotations. 2. Celebrities–United States–Quotations. 3. Homosexuality–United States–Quotations, maxims, etc. I. Title
HQ76.3.U5 H33 2000
305.38'9664–dc21

99-054498

First Printing
Printed in the United States of America.

10 9 8 7 6 5 4 3 2 1

To Ronnie
—two dozen years—

and in memory of
Cousin Gaby

By the same author

THE FILMS OF JANE FONDA

CONVERSATIONS WITH MY ELDERS

HISPANIC HOLLYWOOD

LEADING LADIES

THE LAVENDER SCREEN

HOLLYWOOD BABBLE ON

HOLLYWOOD LESBIANS

BETTE DAVIS SPEAKS

HOLLYWOOD GAYS

SING OUT!

HOLLYWOOD & WHINE

CELEBRITY FEUDS!

Acknowledgments

Thank you, Linda, queen of the clippers and a gem of a sister.

Thanks and appreciation to my publishers, Lyle and Carole Stuart, and my frequent and longtime editor (since 1980), Allan J. Wilson.

Thank you to numerous friends, hosts, facilitators and/or quote collectors around the world, especially: Isabela Alvear, John Peter Brownell, Herb Caen, Michael Callen, Hind Desai, Ken Ferguson, Clifford Gallo, Lee Graham, Garson Kanin, Tomiyoshi Kawabata, Aviva Magenheim, Boyd McDonald, Paul Monette, Dick Sargent, Samuel Steward, Susan Strasberg, and Ron Vawter.

Finally, and always crucially, thanks to Ronnie for helping shape the book's four divisions; umpteen quotes could have fit into one or more chapters, until some thematic unity and logical flow was finally, happily, arrived at.

first words...

Always tell the truth. It will please some people and astonish the rest.

—Mark Twain

Most stars' reel lives have little if anything to do with their real lives.

—screenwriter **Anita Loos**

...she feared wagging tongues, and when I asked her to describe her soul, she detailed her wardrobe.

—Cervantes

(On a movie star's life:) It's only a gilded cage.

—Tyrone Power

Table of Contents

I Playing the Game 11

II Out and Outing 103

III Loving in Private 169

IV Dishing in Public 249

Playing the Game

Seem what you should like to be, and the public will be none the wiser.

—Machiavelli

Be what you would like to seem; that's a man's best shield against tongues.

—Socrates

You can't always be what you want or what the mob approves of, but in Hollywood you can always pretend. That's what publicity's all about, and that's why they call it acting.

—studio publicist turned novelist **Richard Condon**

In America, when a famous movie star is with someone not famous, the public is one of two extremes. They ignore the other one, like he is nothing. Or they stare and stare—they are wondering what the relationship is....

—French movie star **Alain Delon**

Most gay celebrities spend their time and energy—with publicists as their partners in crime—trying to keep the masses from getting the right idea.

—Truman Capote

The only thing worse than being gossiped about is not being gossiped about.

—Oscar Wilde

The word 'gossip' derives from 'god-related.' It meant a close friend, someone who gave you the news....Olde English literature often referred to 'my gossip,' meaning my friend, my friendly informant. Later it came to mean the news or information itself...light news. Why or how it got a negative connotation is hard to say. But I suspect Hollywood had a lot to do with it.

—gossip columnist **Sheilah Graham**

Money and gossip. The two subjects that fascinate the Hollywood community.

—Sammy Davis Jr.

Gossip is news running ahead of itself in a red satin dress.

—columnist **Liz Smith**

I love acting. It is so much more real than life.

—Oscar Wilde, who wed a woman and reproduced twice

As to why so many actors are gay, or gays are drawn to acting. First, we learn to act early—almost every gay kid starts pretending he's straight, to pass. Second, a lot of us don't mind playing other characters, other personalities...some of us on and off the screen.

—Dick Sargent, the second Darrin on *Bewitched*

Somebody declared that the marital knot is the lock in the bolt to the room at the top. I don't remember who said it, but you'd imagine he was speaking about the acting profession.

—Dick Sargent

Most actors are very convincing as husbands. Most actors have to play husbands...some of the homosexual ones even get the idea their screen talent is transferrable into the bedroom (with a wife).

—director **Richard Quine** (*How To Murder Your Wife*)

Until the 1970s, no one asked me (in an interview) why I never married. I think they were afraid of embarrassing me—or my embarrassing them, if I answered truthfully.

—director **George Cukor** (*My Fair Lady*)

I am a 'confirmed bachelor'...where women are concerned.

—Cesar Romero, aka The Joker on TV's *Batman*

When it comes to heroes and role models and movie stars and all that, most people don't believe the truth—they believe what they wish were so.

—columnist **Lee Graham**

I'm gay, but on *My So-Called Life* it was decided my character would be bisexual. Maybe they didn't want to offend Puerto Ricans by admitting to Puerto Rican gays...or maybe they didn't want to lose the female audience. But what happened was, most of the critics then thought my character was 'sexually confused.'

—**Wilson Cruz**, grand marshall for the 1998 Los Angeles Gay & Lesbian Pride Parade

I'm not, as some writers put it, 'sexually ambivalent.' I know who I'm attracted to. If you are definitely gay or definitely straight, then what's ambivalent? Maybe certain bisexuals or celibate priests are ambivalent—I'm not.

—**Boy George**

See, everything is defined in terms of heterosexuality. So if you're not married to a female, you're categorized as 'single.' Never mind that you may be more married—except in the legal sense—than a lot of hetero couples. They still classify you as single, and think of you as being alone and without love....We need new definitions here, and to re-think our concepts of straight-only.

—director **Norman Rene** (*Longtime Companion*)

A (website) bio (from) the Liberace Home Page (in 1996) claimed he died of heart disease and emphysema—but history reports otherwise.

—columnist **Michael Musto** about the closeted pianist who died of AIDS in 1987

The heterosexual dictatorship not only recognizes its enemies but defines them in its own terms. In the last few months I have been singled out not only as the National Fag but as the creator of a new order that means to destroy The Family, The American Empire, Capitalism, and Warm Mature Heterosexual Relationships.

—author **Gore Vidal**

I have never known anyone who took great exception to homosexuals...that there wasn't something drastically wrong with that very person himself.

—**Richard Burton**

God made homosexuals (and) must love them. I love them too.

—**Sophia Loren**

I have a great interest in sexuality, and I don't mean just man-woman sexuality....As an actress, there are many ways open to me to explore this in my work.

—**Faye Dunaway**

I completely enjoyed it, very much so. Very much so. I don't think you could be human and not be attracted to your same sex.

—Oscar-nominated **Elizabeth Shue**, on her same-sex love scene in *Leaving Las Vegas*

I figured it was about time I got a straight role so I could prove it was possible. I'm okay with it. It doesn't feel odd. It feels like work.

—**Wilson Cruz**, on playing hetero in the $60 million *Supernova*

...when I have to do that scene, I'm going to walk over to (David Thewlis), and I'm going to stick my tongue down his fucking throat and probably swerve it around a bit.

—**Leonardo DiCaprio**, on his *Total Eclipse* love scene

Who could possibly object to doing a love scene with Catherine Deneuve?

—**Susan Sarandon**, on her costar in *The Hunger*

(On his best kisser on-screen:) Christian Maelen in *I Think I Do* was great. He's straight, but he was very generous about not being obvious about his discomfort with kissing a guy. Whenever we did it he was into it 100%. He even slipped me the tongue a little now and then.

—gay actor **Alexis Arquette**

I thought it was excellent that Jerry Seinfeld confessed that when he had to kiss another man for his show, it wasn't as awful as he'd previously thought. He still made fun of it, but it's still a big advance from when star actors like John Wayne compared homosexuality to tuberculosis, and men only kissed on the screen in porno movies.

—poet **Allen Ginsberg**

I got uncomfortable with, uh, some of the scenes that, uh, were more physical than others. Between Ellen and her...and her girlfriend.

—ABC network president **Bob Iger**, on the few and brief kissing or handholding scenes in *Ellen*, which ABC then canceled

We're all bombarded with heterosexual kisses, affection and sex 24 hours a day on TV....How will (same-sex kissing) ever seem normal or ordinary if it's never allowed to be seen?

—Ellen DeGeneres

The risk is not being perceived as gay—that would mean I did my job well. The risk is being perceived as a straight actor trying to play gay. And that would be a very bad thing. You've gotta be gay—at least while you're doing the part.

—Jason Alexander (*Seinfeld*), on his role in the film *Love! Valour! Compassion!*

There were two things I was worried about (doing a gay love scene in *Alive And Kicking*). That I couldn't do it and I'd freak out, or equally disturbing, that I'd enjoy it. I didn't want to rethink my (hetero) sexuality at this stage. But it was the most enjoyable love scene I'd ever done.

In every sex scene I've done, with beautiful women or with a man, you lose the 'acting' but the brain is still working. Your body responds passionately, and that feels good.

—UK actor **Jason Flemying** (sic)

I just didn't wear any base.

—Tina Louise (*Gilligan's Island*), on how she prepared to enact a lesbian character

It's shocking, the response I got from people supposedly cool with homosexuality. You know, like, 'I don't judge it, but don't you think America is going to think you guys are lovers?'

—**Laura Dern**, who played Ellen DeGeneres' object of affection in the coming-out episode

A reporter asked me, 'Wasn't Tom Hanks brave to do *Philadelphia*?' I said, 'I think he's great, but I don't think he's brave. I think a gay man playing the part would have been brave.'....Robin Williams has the #1 film (*Mrs. Doubtfire*) in the country by wearing a dress, and when Divine wore one, they wouldn't even show it on the airlines. So things have changed, but not really—because everyone knows Williams has a wife....

—director **John Waters** (*Hairspray*)

I just closed my eyes and thought of England.

—**Peter Finch**, when asked about his *Sunday, Bloody Sunday* love scene with Murray Head

I wrote four scripts and all of them were optioned. One, *Cynara*, got pretty famous. But it was a lesbian love story. Everyone shied away from it....Jodie Foster loved it, said she'd do anything to help get it made, but she couldn't play the lead.

—lesbian filmmaker **Nicole Conn** (*Claire Of The Moon*)

Perhaps they think, 'He played that gay part (in *My Best Friend's Wedding*), let's see what else he will eat.'

—openly gay actor **Rupert Everett**, on being offered several cannibal roles by Hollywood producers

On the set of *The Wedding Singer* people assumed I was just an actor playing, the role. They'd make (anti-gay) jokes and ask me how ridiculous I felt in the outfits. But I was like, 'This was how I dressed in the '80s.'

—gay actor **Alexis Arquette**, on his gay role

Your sleeves are too tight, your voice is too high and precise. You mustn't do it. It closes so many doors. It limits you unnecessarily, and young men with half your intelligence will laugh at you....It's hard, I know. One would like to indulge one's own taste....I take ruthless stock of myself in the mirror before going out. A polo jumper or unfortunate tie exposes one to danger.

—**Noel Coward's** advice to the also-secretly-gay but younger Cecil Beaton

With leading men, everyone wonders is he this, is he that?...A lot of leading men are bi, a lot are straight, a lot are gay, but all are masturbators at heart.

—director **Jean Negulesco** (*How To Marry A Millionaire*)

I form deep attachments to people, to places, to pants. I was attached recently to a pair of pants. I just loved them. And I know I have my closet full and that I have to throw something away. But I can't. I am tormented by this. You see, I can love even objects. I get very passionate about everything. Everything....

—Spaniard **Antonio Banderas**, who enacted Tom Hanks' lifemate (sans a single kiss) in *Philadelphia*

The danger of fame is twofold. You can get too materialistic, with never enough purchases, never enough money...and you can try so hard to fit in that you lose your specialness as an individual and as a member of a minority group...because the more people you appeal to, the less you are a unique self.

—Jewish actor **Sam Levene**, who starred in *Crossfire* (the film was about anti-Semitism, in 1947, but its source was about homophobia)

I remember that in (the telefilm) *The Cat Creature* I had a character who ran an occult shop. It was written for a man, but I told the producer to change it to a...dyke. I thought it would make it more colorful. When the network censors got the script, they sent it back with a memo saying, 'There should be absolutely no suggestion that this woman is a lesbian.' And this was in 1973!

—director **Curtis Harrington**

We wanted to make a (film noir) movie, and we (then) got this idea of the two gay women, and that became the story. A couple of big studios said, 'Change Corky to a man, and it's a deal.'

—**Andy Wachowski**, of the Wachowski Brothers, who made *Bound* (not for a major studio)

We made *Bound* in this very liberal environment, and then we found out that the world outside isn't as liberal as ours! People were uncomfortable with the lesbian idea, and the ratings board said we couldn't show hand-sex stuff, even though it's shown in every heterosexual film—like in *Stealing Beauty*, which had a super close-up under Liv Tyler's panties, like they're kneading dough.

—**Larry Wachowski**

Those ratings people are not only censors—in this day and age—they're homophobes and hypocrites. Like most non-ultra-right bigots, they say they're not anti-gay. But where a girl-boy kiss incurs no censorship at all, a same-sex kiss means an R rating and thus fewer patrons...plus a nude woman is PG or somesuch, and a nude man is an X rating, and most cinemas won't even show an X-rated film.

—gay historian **Martin Greif**

They don't want gay directors for studio gay movies, that is, the few that studios make. And why? They think we'll make them too gay. Like, was a picture ever too straight? It's the same thinking that keeps gay people off juries when the murderer of a gay man is on trial. Like that will ever produce justice!

—director **Richard Benner**, *Outrageous!*

Hollywood's about mass audiences, always has been. When most of the moguls were Jewish, they'd avoid Jewish stories....Today, a gay or lesbian executive is often the first to decline a gay love story, say. They do this to show they're not 'biased' or to pass for straight, or out of basic business sense. But it's a shame as well as a sell-out.

—author **Paul Rosenfield** (*The Club Rules*)

Oh, I know that (some people think he's gay). I act gay, I look gay, I move gay....For years, my friends would tell me, 'Look, you've got to talk this way and walk this way and don't make so many movements with your hands when you talk.' Finally, I just said the hell with it. I'm not gonna try to cover up just to please other people.

When I was a teenager, I remember seeing a poster in a doctor's office that said, 'He who carves himself to suit others will soon whittle himself away.' I decided that wasn't going to happen to me.

—**Andy Dick** (*NewsRadio*)

I wasn't the most masculine child. The words 'sissy' and 'let's get him' were familiar to my ears....Up in my room, I put on my own Broadway routines. I was the only person I knew who danced to the *I Love Lucy* theme.

—**Terry Sweeney**, *Saturday Night Live's* only openly gay cast member ever

Where do these bigots who are forever invoking 'the children' or 'our children' think gay people come from? From *pods*? Every tenth child is gay or lesbian. How can they not care about gay teens, even if they've hardened their hearts against gay adults?

—openly gay Olympic gold medal-winning skater **John Curry**

Some more liberal stars publicly support their gay kids, like Cher, while some keep quieter, like Streisand. But what floors me is the conservatives who know they have a gay son or daughter, and still oppose equal rights for gays and lesbians...people like (general) Colin Powell, Phyllis Schlafly, Sonny Bono, and any number of preachers and ministers....Such people do make money off their anti-gay stands, but how far does love for money or power go with such people?

—openly HIV-positive actor **Keith Christopher** (*Another World, Guiding Light*)

I think relatives of gay people are sometimes the worst.

—**Dack Rambo**, referring to costar Larry Hagman vetoing a lesbian storyline on *Dallas* (Hagman's mother, Mary Martin, was lesbian or bisexual)

My twin brother and I were discovered by Loretta Young. She said we looked like 'double angels.' She discovered us in church. So she put us in her (TV) series, back around 1962. Years later, when word got around to her that we were bisexual, which lots of twins are, she dropped us from her Christmas list like a hot potato. I wonder if she'd have been nicer if I'd said I was a gay priest?

—Dack Rambo

Since we were kids, we all knew that Danny would devote himself to public service. I think the tip-off came when he was 8 and he founded a free legal clinic for the dolls he claimed I illegally evicted from my Barbie Dream House.

—Rosie O'Donnell, on her openly gay brother Daniel, running for the New York state senate in 1998

As a child, I knew I wanted to be a director. On the TV series *The Courtship Of Eddie's Father* when I was 6 years old, Bill Bixby did a couple of episodes where he both acted and directed. I said, Someday that's what I want to do. Then I sort of forgot about it and wanted to be president for a while. But ultimately if you're somebody who loves to make decisions and enjoys the process of being decisive, being at the helm, in control—the leader of a set—it's probably the most enticing job you could ever do.

—Jodie Foster, whose brother Buddy outed her in his 1997 book *Foster Child*

Actors have no power. Stars do. Temporarily. And homosexual actors, if they're perceived as such, are the most vulnerable of anyone. Go *behind* the camera; *then* it's not an issue.

—actor turned screenwriter (*Harold & Maude*) turned director (*Nine To Five*) **Colin Higgins**

One of my first agents said to me, 'I only want to represent actors who have a chance of being really successful.' Guess he never heard of Rock or Tab or Tony....Then he says, very aggressive, 'Are you gay?' I'm ready for that one. I say, 'No, but thanks anyway.' And I winked at him....This was all years before I came out as bi.

—Dack Rambo

There's this one L.A. agent who 'tests' for gayness by throwing a cigarette lighter at you all of a sudden. If you catch it, you're straight. If you don't, you're gay....He's known for this!

—actor turned writer **Dale Reynolds**

I think far more gay kids think about becoming actors or actresses than normal ones. But then reality kicks in. Anyway, from what I hear, (in Hollywood) they try to weed them out at entry level.

—Broadway producer **Richard Barr** (*Who's Afraid Of Virginia Woolf?*)

The most important thing in acting is sincerity. If you can fake that, you've got it made.

—George Burns

If you're truly hetero but seem homo, forget it. For tinseltown, what counts is 'straight-acting.' You can be gay, just be sure you're straight-acting and can keep a secret. Forever.

—singer **Michael Callen**

When it comes to outing, George Michael is typical. They won't come out or admit it when they're outed, but they might, sooner or later, expose themselves.

—openly gay UK singer **Jimmy Somerville**, speaking about, um, big male stars (singers and actors)

You know, they talk about a celebrity's right to privacy, all the while ignoring the fact that these very rich and famous people are role models and have a responsibility to the public....How would it look if every Jewish celebrity denied being Jewish? That would be a terrible message to send out to people, particularly young Jews. But that's precisely the message sent about being gay, and the rich and famous have a terrible influence on how gay men and women are perceived—and *not* perceived.

—Michael Callen

I can't remember a single thing I learned in 9th grade French or Science, but I can still remember how much it cost to fly chili from Chasen's in Beverly Hills to the *Cleopatra* set in Rome (for star Elizabeth Taylor).

—gay author **Paul Monette** (*Borrowed Time*), on Hollywood's influence

You can call it outing. Or you can call it telling the truth, which is what it is....I call it 'equalizing,' because it helps make up for the omissions and the lies routinely spread about gays and lesbians.

—writer **Michelangelo Signorile**, who admitted to being so propagandized in his youth that he beat up other—more obvious—gays

It depends how you say someone is gay, presuming that the object of attention actually is gay. A homophobe will say it with malice, sometimes putting down somebody as gay who isn't—just a way of smearing them. For example, when political opponents were hinting that Clinton was gay, just because he was the first openly pro-gay president....With pro-gay activists who out someone, they're reclaiming that individual as what they really are. Either because the person is cowardly and/or greedy, or because it's, say, a politician who's secretly gay but is harming gay people with bigoted legislation. Bigots like that are a menace; such hypocrisy and cruelty should be exposed.

But outing is not about non-celebrities. It's about people with extra privileges and resources but no integrity. We do not out ordinary gay folk—by 'we' I mean *our* groups fighting for our rights—because in over 40 states, you can be legally fired from your job just for being lesbian, gay or bisexual.

—**Matthew Rushton**, TV, theatre and film (*Mrs. Doubtfire*) producer

I didn't like being outed in the tabloids, but it did push me to decide to come out, which I wish I'd done long ago.

—**Dick Sargent** of *Bewitched*

Outing just doesn't work. Even if the star is gay—as everyone knew Liberace was—if the star says he's not gay, then that's the version the press goes by, at least until he's dead, and it's the version the hardcore fans go by, henceforth.

—tinseltown columnist **Lee Graham**

I hated being outed. There was no dignity to it, and it made me feel powerless. But living a life in the closet is worse.

—**Chastity Bono**, who was outed in the tabloids, denied it, then did come out

My sexual preference is no issue. It's nobody's business. I would never say whether I slept with men or women. I'm just old-fashioned.

—diver **Greg Louganis** in 1988, before he became an author

Who I have sex with, what we do, that's private. And I really don't care to hear the private details of heterosexuals' lives either. However the gender I fall in love with and go to bed with, well, that's public record. If I tried to hide it, that would mean I'm ashamed of it. Straights are never ashamed to admit they're straight. And some of them should be!

—former actor **Sheila James Kuehl** (*Dobie Gillis*), now a member of California's state assembly

I was outed before there was outing. Back in the 1950s, when I was the only guy with guts enough to wear a dress in public (on his TV series). That was enough to get some of my detractors whispering, trying to infer negative things about me. My best defense was my wife and all my girlfriends from before I met my wife.

—**Milton Berle**, admitted heterosexual

If I hear somebody's gay, I don't like them any the less. Unless they make a big production out of denying it.

—Elizabeth Taylor

The real malice isn't in pointing out that someone homosexual is a homosexual, but in pretending that such people don't—or even worse—shouldn't exist.

—Johnny Depp

(Hedda) Hopper had a bee in her bonnet about homosexuals of the male variety...excepting her only son (William, of *Perry Mason*),who didn't count as one (to her). And he was a husband and father....Hedda didn't make the same allowance for the much-married Cary Grant, who she repeatedly kept trying to expose...but he was too big a star, and no one touched that subject then....She did expose Michael Wilding and Stewart Granger's affair, when Elizabeth Taylor was engaged to Wilding....Hopper had no humane motives in revealing all this, nor even the motive of a major scoop—she just wanted to ruin these men, run them out of town.

—**Robert Cummings** (also, Hopper disliked Englishmen)

Ken (Wahl, in *Jinxed*) was unbelievably hateful to me...the first time I met him, the first thing he said was, 'I want you to know I hate niggers and faggots!'....I had no idea why he said that, because we had neither of those in our picture....By that time, of course, I knew what particular terrain I had stumbled on to.

—**Bette Midler**, who assumed all gays were visibly so (Wahl was later rewarded with his own TV series, *Wiseguy*)

Hollywood (male) agents are tough, grabby and greedy...always trying to compromise their female clients, to emasculate or uncloset their male ones....There's a famous joke about a (female) starlet who offered her agent a blow job in return for a small part. He replied, 'Yeah, but what's in it for me?'

—openly gay producer **Jerry B. Wheeler**

All the sincerity in Hollywood you can stuff in a flea's navel and still have room to conceal four caraway seeds and an agent's heart.

—radio star **Fred Allen**

My female clients tell me that after years of dealing with male heterosexuals, they find lesbian advances a piece of cake.

—ICM agent **Eric Shepard**, one of the first openly gay agents

What happens is that agencies like CAA (Creative Artists Agency) control the industry. They package people together. They go to some woman—I'm not saying this is true, because I don't know it for a fact, but this is the way I understand it—they go to (an Australian actress) and say, 'Look, if you marry (an American actor) and participate in this P.R. scam, we'll package you into movies with directors and actors that we represent as well.' So she gets something out of it, (he) is covered, and everybody's happy.

—openly gay actor **Craig Chester** (*Swoon, Grief, Frisk*) in 1994, explaining high-level closeting of male superstars

Suzanne Westenhoefer is this hilarious, blonde, attractive comedienne. Who is also openly lesbian. Her talent should put her in a starring role in a TV series or talk show, a movie...but because she's *openly* gay and isn't playing their game, she won't be given that opportunity. The lesbians and gays who reach those successful positions do so by having kept quiet about it along the way.

At least nowadays they don't have to marry the opposite sex (and) use another human being to fool a once totally bigoted public....However, if you're not heterosexual, Hollywood still insists that you be a liar.

—columnist **Lance Browne** of *The Hollywood Kids*

It's surprising how some people will bitch at Ellen (DeGeneres) for no good reason. Like Chastity Bono saying the sitcom was 'too gay.' No one ever said *L.A. Law* was 'too straight.'....Or people who criticize Ellen for not coming out till her sitcom needed better ratings. A) she wouldn't have *had* a sitcom if she'd come out before, and B) once you're out of the closet, you can't take it back; Ellen has to live with her disclosure the rest of her career...Hollywood's still of a mind that an actor should pretty much be what he plays.

—**k.d. lang**, whose sole big-screen role to date was a lesbian Eskimo

Chastity Bono has (left) G.L.A.A.D. (Gay & Lesbian Alliance Against Defamation, where she served as a media spokesperson) so she can complete and then promote her new book 'Family

Outing.'....Hey, Chas? Don't make it 'too gay,' okay?

—Hollywood columnist **The Shadow**, in the Australian magazine *Lesbians On The Loose*

They do call it acting.

—**Marjorie "Ma Kettle" Main**, who unlike most of her movie characters never reproduced

I can't believe the stir created by panicked, sexually insecure heterosexual homophobes about whether Ann Heche can convincingly play a straight romantic lead (in *Six Days/Seven Nights*). Puleeze! Excuse me, but was she not a credible romantic lead before she came out? Is acting not acting?

—*Lesbian News* critic **Nancy Rosenblum**

She and I are having a ball (filming *Six Days/Seven Nights*). I don't have any concerns about people buying a romance between myself and Anne (Heche). She was the obvious choice....I've never discussed any of my coworkers' personal lives before, and I don't see any reason to start now.

—**Harrison Ford**

Gene Kelly told me I should change my name, to get more mainstream roles as an actor. He said 'Tommy Tune' sounded a bit too fey and way too made-up. But it *is* my real name.

—**Tommy Tune**, of *Hello Dolly!* (directed by Kelly)

The Hollywood movie pattern is to cast a straight actor as a gay character; most gay stars won't play gay, too close to home. But now (late 1997) there's a deep-closeted gay actor playing gay and using it as an excuse to further bolster his straight image! It's a clever switch...not that it has to be awfully clever to convince most of the public.

—TV producer **James Komack** (*Welcome Back, Kotter*)

(Hollywood) doesn't want Jews playing Jews or gays playing gays because they don't want those groups to be 'too' visible and they don't want anyone using a role (during interviews) as a soapbox.

—**Robert Hayes**, *Interview* editor

Did you see *Contact*? I wonder what (the late) Dr. Carl Sagan would think of how they've...sugared down (his novel) and leveled it out....Jodie Foster is *so* intense, she seems so uncomfortable...that jaw, clenched so tight, it looks painful. I surmise that she's much happier and more comfortable directing than acting....

—director **George Schaefer**

If 'hide the sausage' is the straight man's favorite game and preoccupation, then 'hide the queer' is the movie industry's #2 pursuit, after trying to make hit movies.

—actor turned novelist **Tom Tryon**

The image of gay people on the screen has been one of perverts and killers or freaks or grotesques or screaming queens or interior decorators or *La Cage Aux Folles*....(People) can accept *La Cage* because it perpetuates a stereotype. But what happens when you show your brother, son or husband—or the girl next door—as gay? *Diversity*: its simple recognition, and the recognition that diversity is not horrible.

—screenwriter **Barry Sandler** (*Making Love*), on Hollywood's responsibility

I accept this (1997 Emmy award) on behalf of all the people—and the teenagers out there especially—who think there's something wrong with them because they're gay. There's nothing wrong with you, and don't ever let anybody make you feel ashamed of who you are.

—**Ellen DeGeneres**, star, cowriter (Emmy-winning) and coproducer of *Ellen*

I commend Ellen DeGeneres for what she's doing, because as a mother I'm concerned and appalled by the rate of teen suicides for gay and lesbian kids. Saving lives is more important than worrying about what bigots and fundamentalists think—and they wouldn't even be watching *Ellen* anyway.

—**Cybill Shepherd**

The problems homosexuals face in life can be reduced to a single, deadly word: homophobia.

—German director **Rosa Von Praunheim**

I realized long ago that the most vocal opponents of gay men are usually very closeted gay or bisexual men. Not only in Hollywood...especially in politics, in the pulpit and in business.

—Oscar-winning cinematographer **Nestor Almendros**

We'd have most of our civil rights today if we didn't spend far too much time and effort over what non-gays think of us and bitching with each other.

—**Robert LaTourneaux**, actor (*The Boys In The Band*, as "Cowboy")

(Gays) exist everywhere, just as left-handed people are everywhere but are always in the min-ority....They could not be this oppressed and this closeted if they weren't that gullible, that greedy and more willing to befriend their enemies than each other.

—openly gay Monty Python member **Graham Chapman**

Interesting that Liberace, who created the phrase 'I cried all the way to the bank,' chose to lie all the way to his grave.

—director **Tony Richardson** (*The Loved One*), who also lied about not having AIDS

(Eventually) he comes out and (says) that he's only been dating men for the past ten years. I guess that means when I woke up next to (George Michael) in 1985 he confused me with Suzanne Somers....And I guess all those years he thought Andrew Ridgely (of WHAM!) was a woman...?'

—*Fab!* magazine columnist **Billy Masters** in 1997

Though his explanation was vague and debatable, it was brave of George Michael to come out, under the circumstances....He could be denied entry into the U.S. due to the arrest. Fortunately it happened in California, not in one of the states with stricter anti-sodomy laws....The U.S. still tries to keep known homosexuals out.

—gay UK actor **Michael Cashman**

I think Anne Heche was very canny, the way she came out after falling in love with Ellen....There may be some men in her past she is covering for, and if she ever leaves Ellen, she can reclaim her 'heterosexuality.'

—actress turned agent **Connie Clausen**

I was told to shut up about my sexuality, that if I didn't shut up about being gay I wouldn't have a career. I said, 'Well, this is a really fucked-up society. So then I won't have a career.' Everyone thinks superstardom is the greatest thing on the planet to ever desire. But my goal has always been to be in love.

—Anne Heche

It's really none of anyone else's business. I'm not interested in fighting anyone's causes.

—writer-director **Stephan Elliott** (*The Adventures Of Priscilla, Queen Of The Desert*), reluctantly admitting his decade-long relationship with "another bloke"

Anne Heche is the first-ever *out* movie star. If she succeeds despite this supposed drawback, we all succeed a little more.

—Martina Navratilova

Can Anne Heche play a convincing heterosexual? Sure she can. Gay men and women who aren't even actors, who are carpenters or CEOs or K-Mart clerks, pass as straight all the time.

—*Detroit Free Press* columnist **Susan Ager**

In 1995, after Jodie Foster got nominated for another Oscar (having won two), it was said that her publicist 'leaked' the story that she was now living romantically with a young man....No, she did not win again, and he came out as gay later the same year.

—gay archivist **Jim Kepner**

Jodie Foster's Marriage Secret

—cover headline of Australia's *New Weekly* magazine (post-pregnancy news), revealing that Foster and "constant companion" Cydney Bernhard wear identical wedding rings

I prefer the word 'actress' because 'actor' would make me sound like a lesbian.

—heterosexual model turned thespian **Kate Fischer**

Somebody who's not lesbian, though it's been rumored, is Dinah Shore. The reason is that golf tournament (named after her) in Palm Springs—it's grown into the biggest gay women's event around. Dinah's not gay, but...where's the problem?...I think it's k.d. lang who said that it's a myth that all female gym teachers are gay. She said, 'Untrue. It's only 95 percent.'

—gay director **Emile Ardolino** (the telefilm *Gypsy*)

Some people thought I might be lesbian. One said because I'm Swedish, like Garbo! I am not (lesbian), but I don't mind if some people think so....In Scandinavia the attitude is very relaxed toward homosexuality. In the movie business, they panic if the word is mentioned....I would only mind if everyone thought I was lesbian, or if it prevented me from being offered acting roles.

—Viveca Lindfors

For me, it's a lot more difficult to relate to the fact that she's pregnant than she's gay.

—**Nora** "I'm not a real lesbian" **Dunn** on an acting assignment

Sometimes staying young-looking is an aid to one's career. Sometimes it is irrelevant. Roddy McDowall in his 40s could pass for his 30s. But he couldn't *pass* in another sense...and since he works in Hollywood, that relegates him to smaller roles and what some might term more 'eccentric' characters.

—gay UK character actor **Richard Wattis**

All the time—if she's beautiful.

—**Nora Dunn** (*Saturday Night Live, Sisters*), asked if she ever imagined kissing a woman for her character's sake

Rupert Everett

There is such a double standard, tinseltown cannot be believed! At the (1998) Golden Globes, Ellen DeGeneres was nominated, for TV, and Rupert Everett, for that movie (*My Best Friend's Wedding*). Neither won, and each is openly gay, each was playing a gay character. Okay? Everyone expected Rupert Everett to get an Oscar nomination. But he didn't. And Greg Kinnear, who's not supposed to be gay—but notice how he suddenly gets engaged when his movie comes out—*did. He* gets nominated for playing gay *because* he's not gay!

Rupert was robbed...and I did hear Academy members saying it takes more effort to play gay if you're not. Then how come heterosexual actors automatically get nominated for playing straight characters?

—record producer **Ben Bagley**

Back in 1995 Leo(nardo DiCaprio) did *Total Eclipse*, where Leo played (poet and bisexual) Arthur Rimbaud. The film has some graphic sex scenes between DiCaprio and David Thewlis (as Paul Verlaine)....In the past few months rental copies of *Total Eclipse* have been pulled from the shelves of video stores around the country....My sources say that a 'major studio' bought the rights and are trying to bury it—'In the interests of Leo's career, it's best that this film never happened,' is how it was described to me.

—columnist **Billy Masters** in March, 1998, post-*Titanic*

A sex scandal never hurt an actor. So long as it involved a female....When Errol Flynn was charged with rape, he actually got more popular....If Paul Reubens (aka Pee-Wee Herman) had been caught with a girl, like Hugh Hunt (sic; Hugh Grant), he might have still lost his children's TV show but he'd still be working steadily....Hollywood folk aren't fond of do-it-yourselfers either.

—Hollywood host and former actor **Samson DeBrier**

The supposed love of James Dean's life was (actress) Pier Angeli. But Warners arranged their first date, and the gossip columnists took a crumb and made a whole wedding cake out of it....Dean broke it off because he saw everyone was pushing him towards marriage, including Pier, who was mad for publicity....Above all, Warners didn't want it known that James Dean frequently had sex with other boys.

—**Richard Condon**, publicist turned novelist (*Prizzi's Honor*)

It's very far-fetched...hard to believe. Yet in view of the whole movie star system and Jimmy's self-destructiveness, it's not entirely impossible.

—stage costar **Geraldine Page**, on the rumor that Jack Warner had James Dean murdered because his sex life was about to be exposed

As far as can be determined, Tchaikovsky drank cholera-infected water…voluntary suicide, due to the (Russian) government learning that the greatest composer of his day was homosexual (1840-1893).

—gay historian **Martin Greif**

Frances Bergen (Candice's mother) and I are very good *friends*. We are *not* romantically involved.

—actor **Craig Stevens** (Alexis Smith's widower), refuting a Beverly Hills newspaper's 1996 claim that he and Bergen were a "couple"

The (Hollywood) publicity machine is such that if a guy goes out to dinner with his sister, and one of them's a celebrity, the columns or the photo captions will say they're a happy couple out on a cozy date....They always want to do that—they're afraid, somehow, *not* to do that.

—actor **Ron Vawter** (*Philadelphia*)

Merv (Griffin) and I are just very good friends, darling.

—**Eva Gabor**, who after a lawsuit by an alleged lover of Griffin's switched to saying they were "engaged"

It's very show bizzy, that mindset....Some gay actors, at the awards shows, won't wear the red (AIDS) ribbon. Some gay ones with wives do. While straight stars like Jack Nicholson, a few others, always do. Prototypical example: *The Birdcage* (costarring couple), presenting (an Academy Award) together—Robin Williams wears the ribbon and Nathan Lane does not....

—producer **Paul Jarrico**

Nathan Lane did virtually nothing but gay roles. As in *The Birdcage*...but that was a $100 million hit, and a starring role. So his ambitions soared...I heard he wanted to do Jackie Gleason's role in the big-screen *Honeymooners* movie. Suddenly, Nathan Lane had no sexuality, the subject was totally off-limits...and during all this (in 1996 and '97), he's been alienating his gay fans who thought he was honest about or at least comfortable with his real sexuality.

—Hollywood columnist **Harold Fairbanks**

Look, I'm 40, I'm single, and I work in the musical theatre—you do the math....

—**Nathan Lane**, to *US* magazine in 1998

I wanted to be honest. I think honesty is the best policy, even in show business....A friend said to me, 'For a center square, you're very well rounded.'

—**Jim J. Bullock**, formerly of *Hollywood Squares*, revealing his HIV-positive status

There's a bar I used to go to on Sunset Boulevard that was a straight bar that's now a gay bar. I went into it once some years later, and...I still finished my beer....People are threatened by their own insecurity, and if they're insecure about themselves, I think they become homophobic...I think guys who knock around females have the same problem as guys who knock around gay males. They want to feel superior in some way (but) somehow they've developed a vast insecurity.

—**Clint Eastwood**

When people who aren't gay ask me why I make a big 'fuss' about it, I tell them, 'We only make a big deal of it because you do.'....One straight guy at United Air Lines, which is (San Francisco County's) biggest employer, asked me very confidentially, 'What do you gays have in common with lesbians anyway, really?' I said, 'One thing: homophobia.'

—S.F. Supervisor **Harvey Milk**

We have a long way to go, in our society and even in show biz. But what is revolutionary to those of my generation is entertainers—it used to be a given that if you became one, you had to from then on hide or deny being queer. No matter if you were a professional female impersonator or a cameraman's assistant. And now, with pioneers like Melissa, you can be main-event star performers and not have to play that whole cat and mouse game....In the '50s, being labeled gay would have been as lethal as being labeled a communist—to your career and possibly your life.

—openly gay **George Etheridge**, Melissa's uncle

It's easier to be a female bisexual or homosexual in our culture, and I have lesbian relatives whom I love dearly. But the flip side is our bodies are still considered dirty by the censors and other men who run the business. I have wonderful, outrageous stories about censorship I've encountered on TV, and I'm saving most for my inevitable book.

—**Cybill Shepherd**
(*Moonlighting, Cybill*)

Let's face it, penises are funny. In fact, I find penises so funny, I have four. However, when I wanted to tell a joke containing the word 'vagina,' that joke was nixed. The message is clear: penis equals good, vagina equals bad. Excuse me, it's 1994.

—lesbian comedian **Lea DeLaria**

I'm not ashamed about being who I am. But most of my comedy's built around being a pants-chaser. Landing a man is the focus of my routine, not to mention my image. So professionally I'm stuck where I am, and not really by choice.

—an **anonymous** older comedic actress (who is also a mother and was quoted, "I don't think my kid, even as a well-adjusted grown-up, would like it if it was always 'What about your mom the lesbian?'")

Once they can say in print that you're gay, you become a target. They won't admit to hating you for being gay, but that'll be all the excuse they need, and they'll *insinuate* things from then on. They'll never treat you the same again, and you'll wonder if any bad review is due to a bad performance or just their hating you?

—secretly gay film actor **John Dall** (*Spartacus, Rope*)

They're not just reporters, they're marksmen. They aim to injure. I can always tell (reading an interview with himself) if they're going to be vicious. It's *yes* if early on they make a big point of my voice...and several tack on imaginary adjectives such as 'lisping' or 'high-pitched.'....From one fact about you, they can let stereotypes do their writing for them...I'm from Alabama, but I don't have the Southern accent, yet I keep reading that I do.

—Truman Capote

One of Gore Vidal's less attractive aspects is that although Truman is long gone, he keeps referring derisively to his appearance and voice and mannerisms. Which coming from Gore is incredibly inappropriate and hypocritical....Truman was at least as tough as Gore and a lot more generous to friends and foes alike.

—poet **Allen Ginsberg**

The truth is, when Ellen and I met President Clinton and we were all talking, I had my arm around Ellen without realizing it. That's how we are. But we were *not* kissing; we save that for when we're alone...but a lot of the news stories said we were kissing, and I think that stems partially from homophobia and wanting to exaggerate our natural affection, making it seem outrageous or improper. And part of it is that tendency of journalistic exaggeration that can easily run to complete fabrications.

—**Anne Heche**

I think those two blondes really do have more fun.

—**Rodney Dangerfield**, on Ellen and Anne

Everyone thinks that actors and actresses are sex maniacs... promiscuous. Then, the moment 'gay' is tacked on to that image, it goes into the category of sex-machine or perverted or self-destructive, and since nobody gay is gutsy enough to speak up and say otherwise, that's what everyone out there believes...yet a lot of actors are too busy or too scared to have much of a sex life.

—singer **Johnnie Ray** in the 1970s

In 1951 Johnnie Ray was arrested for making an indecent proposal to a plainclothes cop in a public restroom. It wasn't his only such arrest...in 1952 he got married, briefly, for his image....Newspapers mostly ignored such arrest stories, not out of concern for Johnnie, but because anything about homosexuality embarrassed them.

—columnist and Ray friend **Lee Graham**

I think it's important that (George Michael) got caught with his trousers down. I've been telling him to come out for ten years. There's no excuse in this day and age, especially for somebody with $50 million in the bank, to be in the closet.

—**Boy George** in 1998

There was no one else in that Beverly Hills restroom with George Michael except the policeman who had nothing better to do than try and entrap the guy, so what's the crime, so-called? Shouldn't such entrapment be a *crime* by now?

—UK singer **Jimmy Somerville**, who was denied entry into the U.S. (a temporary work permit as a musical opening act) after he was similarly entrapped in London

George Michael's arrest for committing a 'lewd act' in a Beverly Hills park restroom...focused attention on the phenomenon called 'public indecency.'....Except in cases of obvious prostitution, heterosexuals engaged in the kind of public conduct that would guarantee two men at least a ticket, if not a pair of handcuffs and a night in jail, are simply cautioned, told to move along, or even ignored.

—**Michael Stubbs** in *Genre* magazine

The men that I knew—Monty (Clift), and Jimmy (Dean) and Rock (Hudson)—if anything, I helped them get out of the closet. I didn't even know I was doing it. I didn't know that I was more advanced than most people in this town.

—**Elizabeth Taylor** in 1996

There was this biography of Montgomery Clift that aired on A&E, and it astounded me that nowhere did it cite Clift's being gay or bisexual or homosexual...only a few put-down words about his 'torment' and 'sexual ambiguity.' And it had several gay men, some of them known lovers of Clift's, who were presented as merely platonic friends! Where's the disclaimer for semi-fiction in all this?

—**Fred Zinneman**, who directed Clift in *From Here To Eternity*, in 1995

Monty Clift was one of dozens of actors over the years who have been arrested for seeking sex with the 'wrong' gender....In Monty's case, he was caught in the late 1940s soliciting a hustler. As a fast-rising young actor, he hadn't wanted to chance non-anonymous sex, thus the hustler and thus the arrest. The whole system worked against him....In Hollywood, studio executives would warn their young actors against being seen publicly with 'that queer.'

—Clift biographer **Robert LaGuardia**

I have never come across anyone in whom the moral sense was dominant who was not heartless, cruel, vindictive, log-stupid and entirely lacking in the smallest sense of humanity.

—**Oscar Wilde**, who in 1895 was sentenced to two years imprisonment at hard labor for homosexual "offenses" (sic)

We're actually not speaking at all, but I'll always leave the door open to her. My mom has a very difficult time with this—we've had a strange history with gay people in our lives. In order for her to accept me, she's going to have to give up a great big belief system, because we've been taught that it's okay to discriminate against gays.

—openly gay star **Anne Heche**, whose father—a secretly gay Baptist minister—died of AIDS in 1983 when she was 14

When my father learned that I was in Berlin trying to be an actor, not a teacher, he cut off my allowance from home. It made him very unhappy...and angry.

—director **F.W. Murnau** (1888-1931), who dropped his father's surname of Plumpe

You'll never learn to earn a living in a drama class with a bunch of sissies.

—James Dean's father, re the book *Live Fast—Die Young*

(When he arrived in Hollywood in 1960:) All I cared about was, 'Hey, man, there's a lot of broads around, and they're paying me $250 a week.' I thought all those guys that put on makeup were sissies anyway.

—Max Baer Jr. (*The Beverly Hillbillies*), in 1998

Kurt Russell has enjoyed deploying anti-gay humor for some time. Back to his Disney child-star days, according to some...at the latest (1997) Oscar rehearsals, he was lisping and limp-wristing his way through reading the name of a guy named Bruce.

—gay historian **Jim Kepner**

(On playing a gay role in the 1984 NBC mini-series *Celebrity*:) I don't hate gays, but I believe they're awfully unfulfilled....Maybe it would have been better if I hadn't played this role because of my feelings. But to me, it's sad. I know many homosexuals. I feel sorry for them...I have a relative who's homosexual and has been for many years. I'm happy that he has found one lover who has been with him for 35 years.

—Joseph Bottoms

You do get these actors who never make it big. They have to lash out at someone, and it's not acceptable to insult Jews, so they insult the gay men in the industry. Which reminds me of an old Yiddish saying about the girl who's a lousy dancer but she tells everyone the reason that she can't dance better is that the orchestra plays lousy.

—William Morris agent **Stan Kamen**

...the fairies' baseball.

—actor-pianist **Oscar Levant**, describing ballet

Levant was no looker, and more than once he blamed his supporting status as an actor upon his not being attractive to the relatively few homosexual powerbrokers whom he characterized as a 'queer mafia,' rather than upon his limited personality or talent.

—eventually openly gay conductor-composer **Leonard Bernstein**

I know two top casting directors that can make you a star if you perform certain acts to or with them...and it's worse with actresses.

—*Family Ties* actor-hunk **Scott Valentine**

When I was a young actress working in Hollywood, I was always aware of the prostitution of girls in the film business. Today it's all so homosexual—the boys having to sleep around with other guys to get places. At my acting school, I say to my male students, 'It was the girls for a while. Now it's your turn, boys!'

—actor-coach **Nina Foch**, in 1984

Another actor I knew, Charles Bronson, working steadily in smaller movie parts, told me to try the Sloan House YMCA when I got back (to New York City). It's in the middle of town and shouldn't cost much...it's an okay place, if you keep one hand over your crotch and the other on your wallet.

—actor-writer **John Gilmore**, re the early 1950s

I've had my cock sucked by five of the big names in Hollywood.

—**James Dean**

People gave him money, enough to tide him over. I'd try to get him to tell me what he'd been doing—to what extent he'd reciprocate with these different people—they were all gay people. He really didn't want anyone to know about it—his hanging around these predominantly gay social scenes.

—actor **Phil Carey** (aka "Granny Goose"), on friend and aspiring actor Jimmy Dean

Vampira was just one of the girls who claimed after (James Dean) died that she'd been his lover....People are always wanting to say that either they discovered this or that star, or that they were more than friends...and in some actors' cases, no one contradicts these publicity seekers because it's in everyone's interest to have a popular star come across as average, you know, straight, right?

—**Jim Backus**,
Rebel Without A Cause

It was later revealed that (publicist) Russell Birdwell was hired by Paramount to pay an actress an extra $5 to impersonate a mournful lover at Valentino's memorial service. It got lots of press and raised the profits on reissues of Valentino's movies. It also gave a more heterosexual cachet to his image....In time, there were spontaneous 'ladies in black' at these annual services, and a few of them were gentlemen in drag. Which did *not* see the light of print!

—former studio publicist **Richard Condon** (later a best-selling novelist)

No, it was sad though perhaps understandable from the point of view of his generation—he was, what?, almost 90. No one in the cultural orbit would believe it, but middle-America would...not that middle-America would be an avid audience for a book by Hollywood's leading hairdresser.

—literary agent **Connie Clausen**, on Sidney Guilaroff's memoirs, which included fake heterosexual affairs

Mr. Guilaroff seems destined never to come to terms with his own personal life nor with the fact that a hair stylist will never be eligible to win an Academy Award.

—**Sir Cecil Beaton**, three-time Oscar-winning costume and set designer, who had a feud with S.G.

In the arts, be it writers or actors or even producers, gay men feuding with each other are as common as saline implants in the waiting rooms of casting directors' offices.

—**Truman Capote**, who had a decades-long feud with author Gore Vidal

It used to be one gay battling another one, but now you have right-wing homosexual spokespeople who are only on TV a lot because they plug right into the conservative, anti-gay agenda. So you have an embittered open lesbian like Camille Paglia who goes on TV and battles gay rights and gay people in general, saying things like there is no anti-gay discrimination and gay-bashings are brought on by the victims themselves.

And since she's admittedly a homosexual, the TV hosts can pat themselves on the back for seeming inclusive, even while she supports the views of homophobic individuals and groups. But then, every minority has its Uncle Toms, and nowadays being a motor-mouthed conservative woman or dyke or gay or black or other ethnic group confers media access and wealth.

—Hollywood writer turned AIDS activist **Paul Monette**

They must prefer the paycheck to their freedom.

—actress **Piper Laurie**, on why gay actors stay in the closet

With most older Hollywood types it was guilt and shame keeping them silent....Today the primary factors influencing coming out or even speaking up and out or against are mostly one: money.

—archivist **Jim Kepner**

I wrote my book because when I grew up there was no such book, and if mine could help just one kid out there who's secretly gay, then it's worth it.

—Broadway fixture **Tommy Tune**, who never came out until publicizing his book, which served as his coming-out

No, I have no plans to write an autobiography. Not unless they offer me a million dollars...if they did, they'd probably want me to tattle on everybody I knew.

—"confirmed bachelor" **Cesar Romero**, who never officially came out

Perry Mason: Case of the Reckless Romeo—Raymond Burr.

The least insightful or candid biographies of celebrities are the ones by or authorized by relatives of the deceased. Like Cary Grant, or any other star who left behind a kid or a widow, etc....Also those 'behind the scenes' TV bios where the family-of supplies photographs or reminiscences—in return for a guarantee that the late celeb be kept entirely in the closet.

See, if a dead celebrity still has a straight reputation, then he's more marketable to his heirs and the studio or TV outfit. Like Perry Mason (actor Raymond Burr) and all those reruns of the series and then the TV movies where (Burr) played (Mason).

—**Bob Randall**, Emmy-winning writer (the gay-themed *David's Mother*)

Most actors think they have a book in them, and perhaps they do. And there it should usually remain. Because actors act on paper too....

—actor turned politician **Glenda Jackson**

Show business, it's what you choose to show or the press chooses to write about that counts. The rest is beneath the iceberg's tip....If a handsome, virile actor goes to the same gay bar every Saturday night, that's a fact which any periodical has the right to print. Yet you'll only see it in print, now, in the Gay press, and that didn't exist 20 years ago...but the general press won't print that, both to 'protect' the VIP in question and to ignore the issue and not admit that there's sexual variety and that gays, lesbians and bi's are not freaks, are not the faceless 'issue' that the press always makes us out to be.

—**Paul Monette**

Next time you're in Hollywood hoping for a few celeb sightings, visit a strip club. And we're not talking about male stars here. Lesbian chanteuse k.d. lang was recently spotted ogling the women at a local nudie bar along with some of her pals, including *Roseanne* alum Sara Gilbert and actress Ione Skye (best known for *Say Anything* and for being the wife of one of the Beastie Boys).

—*Fab!* magazine columnist **Romeo San Vicente**

Hang around the better known West Hollywood or (San Fernando) Valley gay bars and you may spot the likes of George Michael, Nathan Lane, Mitchell Anderson (*Party Of Five*) and Chad Allen (*Dr. Quinn, Medicine Woman*).

—British columnist **Pat McWilliams**

Every actor has the career of acting. Some have, besides, a second career: self-publicity. These are normally the very ambitious or narcissistic actors and actresses, or the gay ones who wish to seemingly prove themselves otherwise.

—columnist **Lee Graham**

Longtime loves (X & Y) are still very much together, as evidenced by their appearance at the L.A. premiere of (Y's) new flick.

—a 1992 *Globe* **tabloid report** (notice the naive use of the word "evidenced"), on two film stars, both gay or bi, who later contractually married and became parents

There have been a few times when I said 'I am gay,' and I meant the interviewer could use it. And he didn't. Which, for any reporter, is amazing. That was in the States....

—**Boy George**

If someone says the words 'I'm straight,' then that's official. You'll have to challenge that, no matter how gay the person is, the closet version will not change until you, say, produce *photographs*. And even then....The double standard is, you need no proof at all to say someone's straight and be believed.

—**Timothy Patrick Murphy**, who played Charlene Tilton's lover on *Dallas*

The deep-closeted actors are so unhappy. The out ones are happy and out there doing good work for the community, meeting people, and being creative....The closeted ones who trick or talk women into marriage, two of ten get in the habit of wife-beating and, more often, drug addiction....One closeted actor now preaches that marriage and adding to the overpopulation is the only 'natural' way to live! Meanwhile, he beats the little woman and his drug use is getting worse.

—actor **Ron Vawter** (*Philadelphia, Silence Of The Lambs*); the actor in question's drug habit finally landed him in jail

Being in the closet is a lot harder than being out. Of course, you don't know that when you're in the closet....I came out by kissing Geraldo (Rivera) during his show (in 1993). I'd been performing for ten years...and people have since been very supportive, very giving. And I've doubled my income since then too.

—comic **Jason Stuart**

They can cancel *Ellen*. But they can't cancel me.

—**Ellen DeGeneres**

The correct assumption that I was gay was the basic reason that the network wouldn't give me my own spin-off series (from *Dobie Gillis*, where she played Zelda).

—ex-actress **Sheila James Kuehl**, now a California Assemblywoman

(*Murder By Death*) was a popular success, and they might have offered me more (movie) roles, but when you're homosexual and a literary genius, that's how they always think of you.

—**Truman Capote**

All through my career, every time I was on stage, I was scared to death that the audience would figure out that I was gay because I was following some guy who made dyke jokes or fag jokes, and I had to stand on stage and try to act straight to fit in. And so for 15 years doing stand-up, I was scared to death....

—**Ellen DeGeneres**

There's not many people you can still make fun of (doing stand-up). Gays is one group. Yeah, that's okay. No problem there. Maybe just a few, only a couple of, complaints.

—"comic" **Sam Kinison**

You'd simply think that a member of a minority would think twice before insulting another minority member in a comedy routine. But some people are plain stupid, or malicious.

—Monty Python member **Graham Chapman**, referring to Eddie Murphy

Damon Wayans used to do humor based on physical gay-bashings. Now, on *In Living Color*, he's still refusing to apologize for anything anti-gay that he initiates.

—gay composer **Paul Jabara** (in 1998 Wayans was as homophobic as ever at L.A.'s Laugh Factory; see Kinison…)

What's stupid is these closeted actors who are so paranoid and disconnected to their own that they'll only attend fundraisers for *pediatric* AIDS....

—Australian actor **John Hargreaves**

Frank Sinatra, when I contacted him to appear (at the first AIDS fundraiser), he did not want to be associated with this...I don't know what he was afraid of.

—**Elizabeth Taylor**, on the hetero entertainer

A lot of straight white celebrities put in an appearance at, like, a charity against sickle cell anemia or Tay-Sachs. But anything gay or gay-nuanced, they shy away. In spite of the gay people in their families...like Bob Hope's two (openly lesbian) daughters and his nephew (who died of AIDS). These people are either blind or they just don't care.

—**Ron Vawter** (*Sex, Lies & Videotape*)

I knew that I was gay when I was nine....It's hard to justify having worked for black civil rights in the 1960s and not work for my own (gay) civil rights in the 1990s.

—Jewish singer-composer **Janis Ian**, who came out as bi, then as lesbian

I got behind (Janis Ian's) song ("Society's Child") because it had a healing message, about different people—interracial or whatever else—coming together through love and even sex.

—**Leonard Bernstein**

(In a NYC cab, in the middle of stopped traffic, with a van driver staring at him:) The fellow turned to his friend, then leaned out the window and yelled, 'Hey, faggot!' It was really a horrible moment. I just sat there and thought, Well, here's the flip side (of fame).

—**Nathan Lane** in 1996, to *Time* magazine, whose 1998 75th anniversary issue completely overlooked gay people

Animals don't hate, and we're supposed to be better than they are.

—**Terence Stamp**, *The Adventures Of Priscilla, Queen Of The Desert*

...the Christian right talks about homosexuality more than they do down at the Ramrod (gay bar).

—*Politically Incorrect* host **Bill Maher** on June 22, 1998

Just about every other person down there is homosexual or lesbian (sic).

—**Sen. Jesse Helms** (R.-N.C.), on hearing that the *Washington Post* had reviewed a documentary about him by gay filmmaker Tim Kirkman in 1998

At the 1992 Republican convention there was "too much bashing of everyone" because "so many people are gay or go both ways....We can't crap on them."

—**Richard Nixon**, theorizing why Republicans lost the presidency that year, according to *Nixon Off the Record*

I have spoken with my grandson about this...and I believe gays are as capable of serving in the military as anyone else....You don't have to be a straight arrow to shoot straight.

—**Sen. Barry Goldwater**, who has a gay grandson

When you tell your family you're gay, then it's not such a remote issue...maybe they'll think twice before telling a fag joke again, or laughing at one.

—**Wilson Cruz** (*My So-Called Life*)

If I am not for myself, who will be for me? If I am only for myself, what am I?

—**Rabbi Hillel**, ca. 100 B.C.E.

I grew up in Jamestown (N.Y.), where Lucille Ball did....When I came out to my mother, she asked, 'Are you going to be promoting homosexuality?' Like *they* never promote heterosexuality...but I said to her, 'No, I'll be recruiting.'

—**Mitchell Anderson**, aka violin teacher Ross on *Party Of Five*

There were many years (in Hollywood) that I didn't go to a bar, I didn't do anything....After a couple of years...I tried to go into gay bars...I walked into the very first gay bar and the coat check guy said, 'Hey, weren't you in *Space Camp*!?' And I looked at him and said, 'No.'

—**Mitchell Anderson**

Girl Bar is a 'floating' entertainment scene for lesbians...lots of female celebs go there. The location changes, and the mailing list is very private. Obviously the most discreet or careful ones are the movie stars, the biggies, like (a two-time Oscar-winning blonde). Their names aren't usually on the list; they have a close friend or a relative's name and address instead...but she doesn't go anymore, after it got mentioned in a column—just a sentence, was all—in some glossy magazine.

—a **TV** (television, that is) **blonde** who's a regular at L.A.'s Girl Bar

Most gay performers entertain and socialize at home, the better to control the situation...small, intimate, confidential gatherings."

—Edward Betz, talent agent

Important note: please *go* before you come, as all conveniences (restrooms) will be locked, to protect the host.

—note on the 300 invitations to **George Michael's** 35th birthday party at a London restaurant on June 27, 1998

Noel Coward with Alfred Lunt and Lynne Fontanne

Homosexuality in that period (the 1930s, '40s and '50s) had two levels: one, it was held in major contempt, and the other was that...it was the most exclusive club in New York....I mean, no ordinary C.P.A. could get in the Larry Hart, Cole Porter, George Cukor world. That was *the* world. That was W. Somerset Maugham. That was Cole Porter. That was Noel Coward.

That was *it* if you were into that, and I remember those houses on 55th Street, with the butlers and carryings-on....You were king of the golden river! That was it!...On the one hand you said, 'They were homosexual—oh, my, isn't that terrible!' On the other hand you said, 'My God, the other night I was at dinner with Cole Porter!' Immediate reaction: '...what did he have on?

What was he wearing? What did he say? *Were* you at that party? Were you at one of those Sunday brunches?'

—playwright and screenwriter **Leonard Spigelgass** (*Gypsy*, *A Majority Of One*)

People forget that 20 years ago the LAPD could arrest a man in a gay bar—dancing was forbidden anyway—for just touching another man....It's astonishing how many straight people and even some young gay ones think that never existed or that gay civil rights have been won!

—gay historian **Jim Kepner**

New York state laws, up until the late 1960s or so, forbade the depiction of gay characters or themes in plays....Even in Manhattan, it was illegal to serve an alcoholic drink in a bar to a 'known homosexual.'

—gay historian **Martin Greif**

I like the big city. I find the pavements friendly. In the big city, you're safer from bigots, in or out of white hoods....

—gay playwright **John Van Druten** (*I Am A Camera; Bell, Book And Candle*)

I'm from Scotland...their mentality is very much small-town. Somehow, the smaller the town, the smaller the mind—the heart too....I found, afterwards (following a suicide attempt), that big-city life helped my recovery...it's the variety of people and opportunities, of meeting people with common interests—and not just sexual—and the fact that in big cities like London, people are daily faced with others who are different from themselves, so they're not quite so horrified by them.

Small-town people never get the opportunity to get used to people who are 'different,' and so they stay small.

—gay singer and activist **Jimmy Somerville**

I could live in Hollywood, for my career it might have been better. But there, all I would be is an actress, not a person. And now, an *aging* actress...because of my (bisexuality), they would all think of me as one way only...I think to me they would never give a housewife role....In Paris, I am not judged like that, and I am not only an actress here.

—**Maria Schneider**
(*Last Tango In Paris*)

I think it's not only less time-consuming for actors to live in Europe, it's safer. We have less guns and less fans—the people who ask for your signature for their children, the people who stop you just to say they saw your latest picture....

—**Omar Sharif**, who lives in Paris

My hometown (Monroeville, Alabama) was so provincial, if a boy said he wanted to be an actor, that was tantamount to coming out.

—**Truman Capote**

The Disney studio wasn't like other studios. It was just like home—it always had a small-town, family atmosphere.

—**Annette Funicello**

Even more than MGM, [Disney] was the most conservative studio in town....They were growing aware. They weren't stupid. They could add two and two, and I think they were beginning to suspect [homosexuality]. I noticed people in certain quarters were getting less and less friendly.

In 1963 Disney didn't renew my option and let me go. But Walt let me return to do the final Merlin Jones movie, *The Monkey's Uncle*—those were moneymakers for the studio.

—teen star **Tommy Kirk**, for whom "Uncle Walt" arranged publicity dates with Funicello et al.

Brad Pitt is, to my knowledge, heterosexual. But he did live with a gay man, an older man, for a while. A fact that has disappeared from his bio and from his conversation with interviewers....I think in part because any pretty boy is suspected of going either way. Many do, either for fun or for their career. But none of them admit it, later.

—**Wayne Warga**, former head writer for *Entertainment Tonight*

It has nothing to do with me. They see a picture of me or a movie or they see an interview with me, but they don't really know me. If my mother said, 'Rob, you're a hunk,' then it might mean something to me. These editors, they don't know me....I move right on from it.

—**Rob Lowe**, protesting too much on being selected "the sexiest man alive" by a national magazine

Most people in Hollywood admit first impressions are everything. That means your looks and your manner....Pretty girls are sought for roles...pretty boys aren't liked much, and some straight guys—macho crew members as well as executives—are kind of homophobic toward them, even if they aren't gay. I think it's jealousy. However, most pretty boys do get very stereotyped. You're better off if you look more like, say, Dustin Hoffman—but with his talent, luck and persistence to compensate.

—**Tom Tryon**, *The Cardinal*

(Being an openly gay actor in the late '90s is:) relatively benign in terms of the damage that can happen to a person's career. In one respect, people get typecast, but that is more the liability of an actor and not of a gay actor. If you're fat with an Italian, New York accent, you will be typecast as a Mafia thug. They typecast all the time in Hollywood, but it's not particular to being gay.

—**David Marshall Grant** (*Thirtysomething*)

I do not want to be stereotyped as a 'gay director.' I want to be able to direct any kind of motion picture. I'm a director, period. That I'm homosexual has nothing to do with my work, so long as I am able to get hired.

—**Gus Van Sant**, *Good Will Hunting* and the homoerotic *My Own Private Idaho*

I don't want to be 'the lesbian actress,' that's all. I'm proud of who I am, but I don't want to be limited.

—**Ellen DeGeneres**

I will not be co-opted.

—**Lily Tomlin's** response, when a stage audience member tried to get her to say she was lesbian

If you're gay and it's known, then that's part of the package. Just like an actress is always a woman actor and a black actor is always black. But a gay or lesbian performer, some seem more gay than others...some never do seem 'really' gay....The point is, the more honest gays are, the less it's an issue, the more gays are seen as individuals first.

—producer **Jerry B. Wheeler**, who tried to bring the novel *The Front Runner* to the screen

Paul Newman seemed to want to film (*The Front Runner*), though his people tried to scare him off it....In the end, the times (the 1970s and early 1980s) weren't right for a gay protagonist who wasn't a drag queen, a clown or somebody with AIDS.

—**Jerry Wheeler**, who died of AIDS in 1990

It's very easy to get gay characters in Hollywood movies these days (in 1998). But it was very hard to get (*The Opposite Of Sex*) made, because our (lead) gay character wasn't diseased, he wasn't coming out of the closet, he wasn't in a dress and he wasn't the heroine's best friend next door who's colorful and puts people down with cute and clever wisecracks...he was a really tough sell.

The studios didn't want to do it and the actors didn't, 'cause there wasn't anything to hide behind....We lost a lot of actors who did not want to appear to be like themselves except they desired men sexually.

—**Don Roos**, openly gay screenwriter (*Single White Female*, *Boys On The Side*) turned director

I wasn't afraid to play a homosexual. Once.

—**Gene Barry**, of Broadway's *La Cage Aux Folles* (he declined to hold hands with his male costar, though)

People advised me not to play gay. But I loved the script, I loved Toddy (his character). And I don't love following advice.

—Oscar-nominated **Robert Preston**, *Victor/Victoria*

Who could play such women? Do you know what they do?

—**Angela Lansbury** in 1967, on declining a lesbian role

At that time, I just didn't want to play a gay woman. But I think the truth has now filtered down to all of us, over time.

—**Angela Lansbury** in the late 1980s (her first husband, actor Richard Cromwell, was gay)

Charles Laughton as Nero in "Sign of the Cross," 1932.

Charles Laughton played every kind of part but never a homosexual. People knew he was gay, but his public image never betrayed his private reality. So he was safe. I wasn't safe.

— **Robert LaTourneaux** ("Cowboy" in *The Boys In The Band*), who never wed a woman

Before I did (play gay), Sly Stallone (a former costar) told me, 'Don't play no faggots.'....Years later, *TV Guide* misquoted me, made it sound like I regretted it, when in fact I'd do it again in a second...it was my best work ever...I'm proud of it.

—**Perry King,** *A Different Story*

When you get an offer to do a gay character, you're interested in whether it has texture, layers...you don't want to play some joke or caricature.

—**Peggy Feury**, Tom Cruise's acting coach

I was very offended, in *Con Air*, that the only character that was ridiculed was the gay guy....It's like in the early days of movies when they used to do that to black characters.

—**Rosie O'Donnell**

It's understandable why most American actors won't essay homosexual roles. They're all villains and victims...underwritten and undersympathized.

—**Peter Finch**, who won British Oscars for playing gay and an American one, posthumously, for not (*Network*)

I was given this semi, crypto, secretly queer character to do (on TV's *Love, American Style*). And the director said it was written in a hurry. 'You'll have to bring your own intangibles with you,' he said. I wasn't sure what he meant...till I realized he didn't mean those little orange fruits.

—camp icon **Paul Lynde**

I think the less gay men are oppressed, the less funny we will become.

—**Scott Thompson** (*The Kids In The Hall*)

I got gay-bashed when I came out of a theatre that was showing (the gay-themed film) *Cruising*....The assailants said that people watching that movie deserved to be attacked.

—screenwriter **Ron Nyswaner** (*Philadelphia*)

It's a wonder you have any homosexuals in America, because daily the children are bombarded with anti-homosexual propaganda. You even pronounce the word differently than we do—you give it a rather nasty sound.

—apparently heterosexual **Sir Robert Morley**, who enacted Oscar Wilde on stage and on screen

We all expect sooner or later to play a homosexual character. At the very least once.

—British Oscar-winner **Daniel Day-Lewis**

Once *Personal Best* came out, everyone was so curious about my personal life, and did I like guys better than girls? I didn't find it terrible, I just found it surprising. Like they don't give you credit for acting your role.

—**Mariel Hemingway**, who shared with Roseanne the screen kiss that frightened ABC

After I did *Making Love*, most Hollywood producers just wouldn't believe I wasn't gay. If I went out with a girl, many of them would figure it was a camouflage.

—**Harry Hamlin** (*L.A. Law*)

It's rather peculiar, I suppose...when a male and female costar get together socially off the set, the studio and the film's publicists jubilate....Yet when two actors or two actresses doing a homosexually inclined movie meet for lunch or drinks afterward, well, anyway it doesn't even happen. If two actors did that, everyone would be on them, telling them not to see each other at all, because of the rumor potential. Everyone is terrified of that rumor's potential.

—**Charlie Earle**, Paramount publicist

Uh, yeah. We did only two takes, and he wasn't very gentle. And he didn't call me afterward.

—**Matthew Broderick**, on his kissing scene with Brian Kerwin in *Torch Song Trilogy*

I got the offer to do (*6 Days/7 Nights*) before I met Ellen (DeGeneres). And a few days after we met, I wanted to bring her to the *Volcano* premiere in L.A.—as my date. I was told they were going to pull the offer (for *6 Days*) if I did. Turned out, the threat wasn't from the people who'd offered me the part—it was from the people surrounding me who were full of fear.

—**Anne Heche**, who a week later fired her longtime manager and switched agencies

Few people in the industry hate gays. They just don't want the *public* to know. Hide it from the public, at all costs....But casting directors had known about me for years...and so far there's been no negative result in my career.

—**Bill Brochtrup** of *NYPD Blue*, the first TV actor to come out post-Ellen

I couldn't deny it anymore. It was just the right time (post-Ellen) to come out...I'm proud to be gay.

—**Danny Pintauro** (*Who's The Boss*), who came out to the usually homophobic *National Enquirer*

It's insulting. I mean, yeah, (Greg Kinnear) was good in *As Good As It Gets*, but it's like, how many times are we going to have to sit through fucking straight guys playing fags? I mean we are a race of people....I have to congratulate Rupert Everett for: a) coming out finally, and b) for actually getting the gay role in a big film (*My Best Friend's Wedding*), being a gay man.

—**Alexis Arquette**

In the long run, the message of *As Good As It Gets* is here's a lonely, pathetic, victim homo who at the end finds happiness because he learns to draw naked women. What a horrible message!

—**Harvey Fierstein** (*Torch Song Trilogy*, *Mrs. Doubtfire*)

In Mel Gibson's *Braveheart*, the gays are shown as cowards or otherwise rotten, and when one homosexual is thrown to his death, it's for laughs...most of Gibson's audience *would* laugh at that. But aside from this juvenile, cruel message of homophobia, Gibson plays havoc with historical fact in this shallow epic that so impressed the Academy (which voted it Best Picture).

—soap opera actor **Keith Christopher**

I think it is time for a comedy about AIDS, and I applaud *Jeffrey*...I take exception to its inclusion of Mother Teresa as a pro-gay heroine, however. For a fact, she does not believe in sterilized needles, and she does follow the homophobic Church line down the line. She is as motivated by religious fanaticism and dogma as by any feelings of charity or compassion. People have canonized her without even examining her beliefs and prejudices. Her beliefs and practices regarding AIDS prevention and treatment are medieval and catastrophic.

—actor and AIDS activist **Brian Hurley**

The movies went out of their way not to offend groups with power. For instance, the 1949 movie *The Prince Of Foxes*, which starred Orson Welles as Cesare Borgia and included his sister Lucretia but never made any mention of their father. That's because he was the Pope, and Catholics might have been offended if it had been factually noted that the Pope had children. Let alone children like that!

—author **Carlos Clarens**

How far have we come, if showbiz figures are supposed to be symbols of acceptance and sophistication? It's okay if Donna Summer or Anita Bryant or Gloria Gaynor dislike homosexuals and say so, but if someone says he dislikes 'born-again' Christian singers, black or white, that's not okay, somehow. The message is it's okay to put down some minority groups but not others. And yet music is supposed to be the universal language of love....If you want the truth, and I can say this, singers tend to be even dumber than actors, and more bigoted.

—singer **Michael Callen**

Do you know why Chelsea Clinton is so ugly? Because Janet Reno is her father.

—Senator John McCain, at a Republican fundraiser

Barney Fag.

—what Republican **Richard Armey** "mistakenly" called openly gay Democratic Congressman Barney Frank

(Comedy Central host) Craig Kilborn ridiculed a gay man who'd been called a 'faggot' and had his car defaced because he was gay...Kilborn didn't believe any of this was discrimination, and later he made degrading and sexist comments about a female executive on his show....After a half-assed apology, not for his homophobia, but his sexism, Kilborn got a big promotion: he left the cable network for CBS and his own talk show, replacing Tom Snyder

—actor **Mart Dayne McChesny** (*Ragtime*, *Friday The 13th Part 2*)

Charlton Heston denies that the gay historical characters he played were gay (Michelangelo and General Gordon in *Khartoum*). Probably not because they would reflect on him, but because he feels a movie about a gay historical personage has less prestige and detracts from his gallery of celluloid heroes.

—film critic **Boyd McDonald**

There is no evidence that Elizabeth I ever had sex with a man, let alone a raging affair....Traditionally, she's always shown as being in unrequited love with men. But (the 1998 film) *Elizabeth* was designed to maximize sex and violence, and historical accuracy be damned. Today, even British films court the American and youth markets...box office is everything. Alas.

—UK film critic **Ken Ferguson**

I think that Shakespeare is a shit. Absolute shit! He may have been a genius for his time, but I just can't relate to that stuff. "Thee' and 'thou's"—the guy sounds like a faggot.

—rock relic **Gene Simmons** of *KISS*

I mean, the spite in that old faggot's mouth! Oh, man, what an old bitch.

—rock fossil **Keith Richards**, on his feud with Elton John, which ignited when Richards jealously carped about the soon-to-be Sir Elton's tribute song to the late Princess Diana

It's so accepted. That is, it may shock a few people or upset several gays temporarily, but it's just, you know, glossed over. You don't have to apologize, your career never suffers for it...it's really something. You wouldn't think nowadays you could get away with it.

—porn star turned publisher **Scott O'Hara**, on entertainers' verbal homophobia

Look at Gore Vidal, Mr. Officially Bisexual—one foot in each camp. In interviews now, he'll refer to 'fags and blacks.' He doesn't say 'fags and niggers,' and he won't say gays and blacks. He seems rather a mixed up old fag.

—transsexual radio/TV talk show host **Connie Norman**

These elder homosexual men, they go on and on about how they can't stand the word *gay*. Yet they understandably don't want to be always called a homosexual. What's wrong with *gay*? Would they rather be called a 'fag'? Or a 'queer'? Anyway, the word doesn't matter, the attitude does.

—**Paul Monette**

I don't think there's no faggots in the room now.

—so-called comic **Damon Wayans**, performing at the Laugh Factory in L.A. in 1998, after a male couple got up and left, due to his homophobic jokes

Who's the bigot? That Mushnick guy in *TV Guide* said I was bigoted for sounding off on the Mormons! What about how bigoted they are against blacks and gays and all?...It's not all Donny and Marie (Osmond). They go into states like Hawaii and Alaska, and they spend millions of dollars to kill the gay-marriage amendment things, you know.

—athlete/actor **Dennis Rodman**

If you care about animals, and most of the public say they do, you still have to be careful what you say about how vulnerable animals are to human beings. It's very easy for them to make the jump from labeling you an animal rights activist to an animal rights fanatic.

—**Earl Holliman**, a founder of Actors & Others For Animals

It's like with animal rights. If you tolerate hurting animals, you're normal. If you care about them or don't want to eat them, you're an extremist....If you badmouth gays, you're normal. If you believe in equal rights, you're an extremist. Or a closet case.

—CBS vice president **Tim Flack**

Some justice....Sara Jane Moore got life for missing (shooting) President Ford. But Dan White, a white male conservative, got like eight years for killing two liberal politicians—the mayor and a homosexual supervisor (Harvey Milk)....The real irony is that the guy who saved the president was a gay man. Of course the hero was closeted back then, and he didn't come out until years later, when nobody was paying attention.

—Hollywood columnist **Lee Graham**

In the States, they use bumper stickers as personal billboards, to advertise their pet peeves, political affiliations and religion. I always thought the lousier a religion, the more advertising it did....Everyone there wants to stick in their two cents. There's a lot of anger there.

—screenwriter **Frederic Raphael** (*Darling*)

After I played a homosexual character (in *A Man Of No Importance*), an American journalist asked if I'd have a rainbow flag on my car's bumper. I said I don't 'do' bumper stickers, but if I did, I'd be pleased to use that one. After all, everyone's included in the rainbow, aren't they?

—**Albert Finney** (*Tom Jones*, *Murder On The Orient Express*)

Palm Springs is where retired old actors go to die, and it's not exactly gay-friendly. First they had (mayor) Sonny Bono. He refused to be in the gay parade, and when the gay business community said he's supposed to represent them too, he went ballistic. I mean, isn't his daughter (Chastity) gay?...Now it's the city government going after rainbow flags, 'cause so many gay businesses are flying them. So they want to make them illegal. It's always pick-on-the-gays time. Not just in Palm Springs.

—**Mart Dayne McChesny** (*Guiding Light*)

Charles Farrell was a closeted movie star, married to a closeted (female) movie star. He was anti-Semitic, and didn't like that more clubs in Hollywood were letting Jews in, so he and his (heterosexual) pal (actor) Ralph Bellamy went to Palm Springs and started the Racquet Club—which was restricted....Farrell became a sort of TV star (on *My Little Margie*), and also mayor of Palm Springs....No, he never did come out.

—film historian **Carlos Clarens**

It's funny how quite often it's the closeted actors, the ones with wives who in their interviews will be the biggest praise singers for marriage. Which alone should make you wonder, because many or most of the actually straight actors aren't so thrilled to be restricted to one woman, and their marriages don't generally last as long, because they're based in large part on sexual desire.

—producer **Larry Kasha**
(*Knots Landing*)

The network wanted me to meet a different girl each time. I didn't want that. I wanted Ellen Morgan to have a relationship, a committed partner.

—**Ellen DeGeneres**, on her series

Lesbian chic. You know what that is? It's some straight guy's idea of what a lesbian is, or should be.

—**Lea DeLaria**

Will & Grace (on NBC) makes the network happier than *Ellen* did (ABC), because the gay character is played by somebody nongay, so he can never become a spokesperson for a controversial cause.

—**Mart Dayne McChesny**

The character of Will is what mainstream audiences will tolerate, because they know he's make-believe, and he has no private life. He never dates. He's an asexual homosexual. The public likes such contradictions, just like the only female they can really respect is a mother who's also a virgin. So Will is the perfect gay TV character. He really functions as a non-threatening male sister to the female lead character. American TV is ingenious!

—Scottish TV critic **Angus Alsop**

I play Will's first date. He finally has a date—me—and he doesn't want him!...It's a great show.

—actor **Miguel Ferrer**

Disney (which owns ABC) was the next to last studio, before Rupert Murdoch's Fox, to grant domestic-partner financial rights to gay employees (which, however, are not recognized by state or federal government). Even so, in 1997 when Disney re-released *The Little Mermaid*, its publicity press kit *inned* Howard Ashman, the producer and Oscar-winning lyricist. His Academy Award had been accepted, posthumously, by his male life partner. On the other hand, the publicity did mention the legal marital status, plus the parental status—all of it superfluous to the movie, but perhaps a reaction to the Baptist boycott of Disney and Catholic anger over the movie *Priest* (which focused on a gay priest)—for the composer and other producers of *The Little Mermaid*. Howard Ashman, though, was accorded no personal life, and therefore no respect as an individual.

—gay attorney and activist **George Bahnsen**

What's that about? The winners on awards shows, where they're thanking their wives or girlfriends, and then their kids. Winners didn't used to do that...and isn't it just an insecure and easy way of letting everyone know that, presumably, I'm not gay...I'm in show biz but I'm straight, I'm really straight!

—comic/politician **Tom Ammiano**

Now he's a movie superstar, deeply closeted. In the early '80s he was dating an entertainment mogul. It was hush-hush. But now it officially never happened, not since the younger guy hit stardom. And the mogul is one of the biggest, most vocal boosters of the married actor's official heterosexuality....Yes, the mogul is now finally *out*, but not that open...when he went to the Academy Awards show, his date was an actress. Isn't that like a straight man taking an *actor* as his date to the show? Why would he do that?

—singer **Michael Callen**

Rules of the Closet:

- To thine own self be false (the Anthony Perkins rule)
- Thou shalt acquire thyself a willing accomplice of the opposite gender to complete thy ruse (the Randy Travis rule)
- Thou shalt be silent (the Jodie Foster rule)
- Thou shalt vilify thy own kind (the Roy Cohn rule)
- Thou shalt act butch, or feminine, if thou art a lesbian (the Troy Aikman rule)

- •Thou shalt rely on thy own idiocy to feign ignorance (the Keanu Reeves rule)
- •Thou shalt ignore thy past (the Charles Perez rule)
- •Thou shalt kill all ex-lovers lest they blab (the Tom Cruise rule)
- •Thou shalt not let photos be taken of thee whilst in a compromising position with thy own gender (the Chad Allen rule, now)

—***Edge*** magazine (Nov. 13, 1996, after the tabloid outing of *Dr. Quinn, Medicine Woman* costar Chad Allen, photographed in a hot tub kissing his male partner)

Luchino Visconti and Rudolf Nureyev at the Spoleto Festival

I never worked in Hollywood...for several reasons. The paranoia and low taste of the moguls, the bankers, the lawyers who run it....They have two faces. They have never cared who an actress sleeps with if they find her sexually appealing. Garbo, Dietrich...when it became well-kept news that Marilyn Monroe was living with her lesbian dramatic coach (Natasha Lytess), they didn't care...but with the men, they very much care, and they won't push them up to become stars if they don't follow their laws—I remember a beautiful actor, Phillips Holmes, blond, he starred in pictures but they didn't keep him a star, and then he died young (in an accident)....More recently, George Chakiris, very appealing...won the (supporting actor) Academy Award (*West Side Story*). But he did not marry, they said he was not 'tough' enough, so soon they demoted him....Hollywood is for money, not for art...and is run by bullies.

—director **Luchino Visconti**

Dirk Bogarde

After I played one homosexual role too many—meaning one or two—that put an end to any possible career in Hollywood. Not that I ever listened to their siren overtures—the few they sent my way, before.

—**Sir Dirk Bogarde** (*Victim*, *Death In Venice*), who according to an *Advocate* obituary "was preceded in death by his life partner of 40 years, Anthony Forwood" (yet never officially came out)

I'll simply say that what holds my friends' marriage together, isn't passion, it's friendship—which endures. And box office—which one hopes endures.

—**Sir Noel Coward**, on secretly gay Alfred Lunt and apparently lesbian Lynne Fontanne, who achieved success and a lifelong "cover" via matrimony, or matriphony...

I couldn't pay attention to (Hugh Grant) in *Four Weddings And A Funeral*. I was just loving these women, this whole group.

—**Jaime Lee Curtis**, in *Los Angeles* magazine (she and husband Christopher Guest, who have adopted, have been outed as an allegedly gay-lesbian couple; both deny it)

When I (worked) in Hollywood, it was suggested I marry a famous agent or a homosexual movie star. It would make everyone more famous but also, they said, make more 'audience sympathy' for me and the actor....I asked (designer) Edith Head what she thought, and she said she preferred a man for a husband who wasn't what she called a 'sex maniac.'

—French actress **Capucine** (she and Head—who gave great wardrobe—featured in the book *Hollywood Lesbians*)

Costume Designer
Edith Head.

Hollywood has always been of two minds about men costume designers. They love their output but not the men themselves.

—**Edith Head** (due to homophobia as much as AIDS, but also the rise of women designers, Hollywood has fewer top male designers than ever)

I married a designer so I could always look good!

—bisexual movie star **Dolores Del Rio**, whose first gay husband, a Mexican, committed suicide; her second was MGM art director—not costume designer!—Cedric Gibbons; Gibbons' brother Elliott was married off to lesbian costume designer Irene, who later killed herself

When the old folks say one thing but your sexual appetite says something else, who're you eventually going to listen to? I don't always want to be on the straight and narrow.

—bisexual **Ricky Nelson**, who allegedly had a bisexual wife

I stopped listening to what Armistead (Maupin) told us about the (closeted) stars when he came in one morning and said that Paul Newman was gay!

—a female *San Francisco Chronicle* **employee** (Maupin wouldn't have said it, he would have said Newman was allegedly bi)

I think he's going too far this time.

—costar **Robert Redford**, after Paul Newman reportedly approached him about reteaming in the gay love story *The Front Runner*, which Newman tried in vain to film

I've played several varied characters on the stage, but everyone seems to take motion pictures more seriously. They're time capsules, I guess....After *Superman*, a whole bunch of people warned me not to do *Deathtrap*...but I thought it was a great script, end of argument.

—**Christopher Reeve**, who played the lover of Michael Caine, married to Dyan Cannon

Sweetie, he wasn't gay around me.

—**Dyan Cannon**, the only wife with whom Cary Grant had a child

If a man is genuinely bisexual, then his woman knows his heterosexual side and his man knows his homosexual side. But if either says that is his only side, they are deceived or lying....Of course, any wife to a gay or bisexual man feels she is right to present him as being morally and sexually 'straight,' and the more successful the man is, the more she has to protect, socially and financially.

—author and sexpert **John Preston**

In Hollywood, a lot of would-be stars undress for success. Most are heterosexual. And a lot of stars closet for success. All of them not heterosexual.

—UK actor **Christopher Gable** (*The Boyfriend*)

Kids, watch your step around movie producers....When they say, 'Let's chew the fat,' they often mean their own....These guys are not sex symbols—their shoulders may be broad, but so's the rest of them.... If you think business and sex mix—they do, in the porno business. Hollywood loves porno, but strictly behind closed doors. Like, there's a gay porno star named Brad Davis, after the late movie star Brad Davis, who was bi but mostly gay. And if he knew, he'd be flattered. But he'd also be horrified.

—openly gay stand–up comic **Frank Maya**, about a UK porn actor (there's also an American "Brad Davis" in porn)

I gave up comedy back when gay comics couldn't be openly funny about who they dated. Like actors, who can't be openly open....But now (1993), the best thing about having Clinton in office is that Al Gore is right down the hall—and I have a big boner for him. Big nose, big hands, big office. I'd salute his American flag pole anytime, day or night. By the way, I'm gay.

—**Scott Capurro**, actor and comedian

As nicely as they could, the Conan O'Brien (talk show) people said, 'You can't be a homosexual on our show, because we're trying to appeal to a middle-American audience.' Now, it's not like I have to talk about that every time I open my mouth, but you hate for somebody to say you *can't* talk about it. But you see, ten minutes before you go on, they give you a list of things you'll be talking about. (Otherwise) they would kick my ass, basically.

—author **David Sedaris**, on TV censorship of gay people

What is this, propaganda? Every role that (Rosie O'Donnell) plays (in a movie) has to be immediately and clearly established as a straight girl. Fat and butch, but straight, straight, straight. Who's doing this, and why, and why so often? It's like science-fiction.

—**Ben Bagley**, theatrical producer (*The Shoestring Revue*)

I do think it's deliberate, and that the more deeply involved (Rosie) O'Donnell gets with her assorted children's charities and shows and books and what-all, the more sexless or maternal it makes her seem, and the more difficult it makes it for her ever to come out—until, possibly, she's a grandmother, and possibly not even then.

—Toronto columnist **Tony Beeman**

People can consider me whatever they like...lesbian, that's fine with me. I'm certainly not offended by it. I don't find the term offensive. I know who and what I am.

—**Helen Reddy** ("I Am Woman," which she cowrote and sang)

Armistead (Maupin) asked, 'Who's going to read the narration?' And they say, 'Lily Tomlin.' He said, 'No, I'm not going to write for a closeted dyke!' They said, 'No, it's fine. She's going to use this opportunity to come out and be honest.' So Armistead wrote her coming-out speech. And she cut it.

—**Sir Ian McKellen** on *The Celluloid Closet* documentary

If you understand how casting agents work, you know they're looking for reasons to red-light you. 'Nobody will buy him as a lead—he's a fag!' is an excuse for not hiring. Many straight men have been awarded for playing gay guys. Many gay people play straight their whole lives. It's not the hardest job in the world to do. You just make yourself a little less interesting, don't dress quite as well as you usually do, watch your movements—no living large with the gestures—and people think you're straight.

—openly gay **Howard Bragman**, co-owner of Bragman, Nyman & Cafarelli Public Relations

We try not to do that, to fall into that habit of tinseltown behavior....I have known of casting directors who go to a gay bar or disco one night, and the next day at the office or studio they encounter somebody they met there or even took home with them, and act like that other person is a complete stranger, or worse, a strange queer. And the actor never dares to protest or complain, because in this business you can't afford to make a single enemy unless you're a star.

—**Kenneth Joseph Carlson**, who cofounded the casting agency Carlson-Dowd

He wore a wedding band and talked in a register lower than his own. He walked around constantly afraid he'd be found out. I don't think it's healthy for artists to create in self-denial.

—openly gay actor **Michael Kearns** (*The Waltons*, *Cheers*), after observing a closeted gay actor on the set of a detective series

My (male) lover would pick me up, and other people would make crude jokes about it.

—**Rick Henderson**, prop man at Los Angeles' Dorothy Chandler Pavilion and ABC-TV

My client, a gay maintenance man, was harassed by coworkers....He often heard things like, 'Get down on your knees, faggot!' And one day he was sent by his supervisor into a supply room that he usually would not have to enter. Inside, in the dark, he was grabbed from behind and shoved into a closet, then stabbed and locked in.

—gay attorney **Lee Walker**, a specialist in employment law, about a 1984 incident on an ABC-TV lot

...fear and panic is created and stoked by agents and managers. God, I hate them more than the actors' fears. Gay casting directors and agents are the worst, the most homophobic.

—screenwriter **Paul Rudnick** (*Addams Family Values*, *In & Out*)

For goodness sake, open your mouths—don't you people get tired of being stepped on?

—**Bette Midler**, to a gay journalist

It is the spectator, and not life, that art really mirrors.

—**Oscar Wilde**, indirectly noting that created entertainment is typically aimed at the average (male) heterosexual spectator

I don't admire movie stars. I admire brave people with integrity. As far as I know, there's no hard evidence that audiences reject actors when they find out they're gay—it's the closeted actors who think of their fans contemptuously.

—former actor **Keith Curran**, who was in the national touring company of *Annie*

I feel sorry for them. There is no career, there is no success worth having if the price you pay is to lie about something so crucial to your nature. Get another job. Actors are doing a job which involves telling the truth about human nature. How can you do it properly if you can't tell the truth to your next-door neighbor or your employer?

—**Sir Ian McKellen**, first openly gay actor to be knighted, on stars who hide their significant others

If you worry too much about what the public thinks, you are no longer an artist, you are a salesman.

—French movie star **Alain Delon**, who however reportedly sued a newspaper that said he was bisexual

Nearly everyone forgets that show business is by nature artificial. We're not scientists, philosophers, explorers—we specialize in illusions....People are a little more hip today to actors not being exactly like their roles, but for their sex symbols and box office idols, they don't want too much divergence....Show biz and politics and, yeah, religion, these ain't truth games. If you want the truth, read *National Geographic*.

—movie producer **Mark Silverman**

In movies, it's a lot of business, a little art if any, and quite a bit of instruction...and movies used to be America's postschool classroom. They taught everyone who wasn't sure that a guy *ought* to get (heterosexually) married, that a woman could only be happy and liked if she got married and submitted to male authority, and that—during times like the Depression and after World War II—it was wrong for a woman to have a career, 'cause it deprived men of them....For a while, movies taught us to hate the 'Japs,' and for a much longer while, to hate gays, that is, when they once in a blue moon crawled out from under a rock.

—**Benjamin Rubin**, director of talent for MGM

It is a conspiracy of silence.

—author and screenwriter **Christopher Isherwood**, on media invisibilization, misrepresentation and underrepresentation of gay people

American television aired a celebratory tribute to Cameron Mackintosh, the highest-paid man in the United Kingdom...missing from the portrait was the fact that Mr. Mackintosh is not only homosexual, but is openly gay.

—UK critic **Ken Ferguson** (musical-stage producer Mackintosh was responsible for *Cats*, *Les Miserables*, *The Phantom Of The Opera*, etc.)

I was desperate to be outed, but nobody would publish the fact. I think lots of journalists believe they're protecting you by not putting it into their articles. But they weren't!

—actor turned playwright (*The Stand-In*) **Keith Curran**

When he got himself arrested for brawling in a gay bar, he outed himself. Case closed.

—*New York Post* columnist **Richard Johnson**, on 10/4/98, reporting about actor Scott Caan (son of James), who with a male companion allegedly assaulted two other males at a West Hollywood gay bar; contrariwise, the *Chicago Tribune* gave no gender to Caan's "date," while Reuters News Service went so far as to claim the fight was "over a woman" (at last report, RNS was owned by anti-gay televangelist Pat Robertson)

Chad Allen's dilemma is further complicated by religious zealots...(since) *Dr. Quinn, Medicine Woman* has a viewership that skews quite conservative/fundamentalist, and the company that syndicates it is tied in with preacher-businessman Pat Robertson, who could get Allen fired if (Allen) followed his being (photographically) outed by coming out himself....Apparently a compromise has been reached whereby Allen came out to family and close friends but will not come out publicly, at least not (during *Dr. Quinn*'s run). He is said to be 'semi' coming out.

—Toronto columnist **Tony Beeman**

The worst thing that's happened to gay and lesbian actors is video cameras...and videorazzi. Once you're out of the confines of your home, even in your own backyard, and of course out shopping, walking, anything, they can film you and your partner and sell it to *Hard Copy* or whomever....And if you're openly gay, like Ellen and her girlfriend Anne, they'll try and provoke you into photogenic rage by making homophobic comments.

—"concierge to the stars" **James Maderitz**, of the Registry Hotel, Newport Beach, Calif.

No, no, no. Closeted stars are very well protected. Even the semi-closeted ones. You almost have to force a newspaper or magazine, at gun-point, to intimate, much less state, that somebody is gay, lesbian or bi.

—**Lance Browne**, *The Hollywood Kids*

(Homosexuality, including gay romance) is just a topic editors shy away from. It makes them uncomfortable, even the gay ones, and they *don't* want to spread it around. They don't want to be reprimanded for including it.

—editor turned publisher **Martin Greif**

I don't use the word 'gay' because it promotes homosexuality.

—former talk show host **Tom Snyder**, a heterosexual, perhaps unaware that 99.99% of television actively promotes heterosexuality

The first two mainstream movies to receive an X rating were *Midnight Cowboy* and *The Killing Of Sister George*, merely for their homosexual or lesbian content....Today nobody but the Pope or a terminal Protestant would consider them X-rated material.

—Leading Artists agent **Ann Dollard**

Mart Crowley's *The Boys In The Band*...is not a musical, The forbidden ad.

The ad showed a head shot of Leonard Frey as Harold. Below, it said, 'Today is Harold's birthday.' Alongside it, a head shot of Bobby LaTourneaux as Cowboy, and below that it said, 'This is his present.' Which was way too controversial for the 1970s—no regular newspaper would run that ad. I mean, it was the Stone Age!

—**Robert Moore**, director of the play *The Boys In The Band*, discussing the original ad for the film version (which he did not direct)

Virgin Cola's new ad campaign 'Say something!' including one showing a real-life gay male couple's wedding complete with rings and a kiss will not be seen on KNBC Los Angeles (TV). A KNBC spokesperson said the ad was 'felt to be of questionable taste, not suited to air on our station.' A Virgin spokesperson had stated that the (1998) ad had been rejected by stations in Boston, New York, San Diego and Washington, D.C.

—*Fab!* magazine item

It's not 'liberty and justice for all,' it's liberty and justice for some.

—attorney and gay rights spokesman **Tom Stoddard**

'*Billy's Hollywood Screen Kiss*' ad was shut out of the *San Diego Union Tribune* newspaper, the city's only major daily. The management found the widely-published-elsewhere image of two young men *about* to kiss inappropriate for a 'family-oriented' newspaper. The paper did agree to an image showing one man alone....

—*Gay & Lesbian Times* item on a 1998 Stone Age newspaper policy

It is, but it's the 'land of the free'—the free heterosexual, that is.

—**Tom Stoddard**, who lobbied in vain against the military's anti-gay policy

Through no choice of our own, we're born into a family...all too often, the family rejects or kicks out the son or daughter when it's discovered he or she is gay, through no choice—so our only choice is to lie, which is why so many do....And when even your family, your supposed nest, act hatefully, that's when suicide goes from a thought to an attempt. I tried it.

—British singing star **Jimmy Somerville**, formerly of *Bronski Beat*

I don't think anyone who becomes an actor had a happy time in high school...I would (today) tell adults, "Stop telling kids these are the best years of their lives!"—that's a depressing and untrue message....I was actually, literally, I was corporally punished (in school) for being left-handed! You think I was going to add to that by admitting I'm gay? No frigging way! There is nothing on earth wrong with being gay, but you still get punished for it one way or another. If I become a star, which I intend to do, then I'll come out, when it creates maximum impact.

—**male actor**, costarring in a Top Ten TV sitcom

Who rides atop the tiger can never get off.

—a **Chinese proverb**, indicating that most *stars* never come out of the closet

Most actors coming out of the closet in the United States are young television actors...not usually regular cast members, but rather, recurring characters. This makes some sense...for, there's a saying current in Hollywood circles: Once a star, always in the closet.

—UK columnist **Ken Ferguson**

I was conversing with a relative of a Baptist minister at a party one time, and I mentioned that it's good there's at least one country where Jews are the majority. And he frowned, I swear, and he said, 'Yeah, but homosexuals'll never be the majority of any country, and do you know *why*?' He leaned in, and I shrugged uncomfortably, and he said, "Cause *that* ain't natural!' And only later did it come to me that, hey, there's no country where left-handed people are the majority either, and *that's* natural *too*, despite this guy, who I think was from Louisiana or Mississippi, one of those light-hearted states.

—*La Cage Aux Folles* chorus boy **Howard Crabtree**, who became a stage costume designer (*When Pigs Fly*)

Over 2,500 left-handed people a year are killed from using products made for right-handed people.

—"Little Known Facts" **brochure item**, published by The Humane Society of the United States

I wish somebody would write what it's really like to be a (gay) celebrity. People come up and ask me for autographs in airports, and I give them 'cause otherwise I think they'll hit me over the head. On Long Island they drove right into the driveway last summer—the gate didn't stop them—and some car broke (his dog) Maggie's jaw and ripped her stomach open. Celebrity! All it means is that you can cash a small check in a small town. Famous people sometimes become like turtles turned over on their backs. Everybody is picking at the turtle—the media, would-be lovers, everybody—and he can't defend himself. It takes an enormous effort for him to turn over.

—**Truman Capote**

All of a sudden I was punched in the face—and then a second time. I went down to the ground, and then (five men) started kicking me in the head and ribs and face. I just thought, Cover your head and wait for it to stop....I believe it was a hate crime, because it's an area (toward a Bourbon Street nightclub) that's 90% gay.

—openly gay Santa Barbara city councilman **Tom Roberts**, revealing he'd been beaten and robbed in 1999 in New Orleans while attending a professional conference (no arrests were made)

Vice President Al Gore interrupted a question-and-answer session with Fairfax High School students (in Los Angeles) to hug a lesbian teen who broke into tears as she described verbal abuse from former classmates. A crowd of several hundred students broke into applause as Gore crossed the gymnasium to embrace senior Jessie Funes after she told the vice president her belief that 'retaliation against gay youth is sanctioned' in California.

—**item** in 7/99 *Edge* magazine

I'm a celebrity, first off. I'm gay. And I'm a female. Any way you look at it, I'm a target....Men earn more, have more of everything, they're physically stronger. Why don't more of *them* come out? If I wasn't a celebrity, I'd probably be *out*, but as a celebrity, my every move is watched, and as a woman, I'm judged no matter what I do.

—anonymous **TV actress**, at L.A.'s Girl Bar

I look at the sadness of somebody like Tony Hamilton. He was unable to make the difference that someone like him could have made if he'd come out. It's really sad.

—publicist **Howard Bragman**, on the star of TV's *Cover Up* spy series and the 1984 telefilm *Samson And Delilah*, who died of AIDS in 1990

Actors and actresses know all the excuses for not coming out, and from one of them, it normally sounds convincing. But it's gay folk in real life that get victimized far more often....One actor acquaintance told me he would hate nothing more than to lose his privacy. Yet all the *out* stars I know of have retained it—you don't know what k.d. lang does in bed or with whom. And so on. Gays' *private* lives do not get outed; straights' sometimes do like Bill Clinton and Monica Lewinsky, where we learned all the details. No details are exposed when it's said someone is gay or lez, just their general sexual orientation. Which is *not* a *detail*.

—Newport Beach hotel concierge **James Maderitz**, who added, "I don't even know if my favorite openly gay singer is a top, a bottom or both," referring to Elton John

Bashers Carve 'Fag' On California Teen's Stomach: For the second time since September, 17-year-old Adam Colton has been attacked by gay-bashers...resulting in bruises and cuts to his face, chest, abdomen and back. On his forearms and stomach, the word 'fag' had been carved into his flesh with a pen.

The first attack occurred...a week after Colton—who had transferred from Marin Academy to San Marin High School in Novato, near San Francisco—had come out of the closet at school and formed a student group called Gay-Straight Alliance....The day after the first attack, Colton's car was vandalized in the school's parking lot with an anti-gay message written in ketchup on the car's hood. That evening he was grocery shopping and attacked by three teens. The next week, his car got keyed. The week after that, there was another ketchup message on his car. That weekend, someone wrote an epithet in lighter fluid on his family's driveway and tried to ignite it.

Colton says he wishes he'd gotten more support from school principal Rudy Tassano after the first attack. 'I feel like this may not have happened a second time if he had come to the plate and really put his foot down,' he says. The teen's father agrees that the school has failed to create a safe atmosphere for his son....Now, the student is not sure he will ever go back to the school. Because of constant anti-gay taunts and looks, Colton two weeks ago had entered an independent study program—attending San Marin only for his two favorite classes: creative writing and drama.

—11/98 *Edge* magazine **item**; as for local police, they would only state that the second attack "was possibly hate-motivated"

I first viewed your shtick in your first PBS special. For the first few minutes the brash delivery had that certain 'give em hell' appeal. But very quickly I sensed a dark and negative underside. I've paid little attention to your trajectory since then, although it was very illuminating to have it explained on your A&E 'Biography' that your career floundered for years until you were put on just after a Rush Limbaugh feed. Obviously you've learned to master his gimmick and feed off his thunder.

Now it seems that in your search for targets to keep the fire of your gimmick glowing, you've turned your attention to the gay community, likening us to incest practitioners and labeling us as 'deviants' and 'biological mistakes.' Using dogma and dictatorial rhetoric to enforce spirituality has been done since time began....

I hope on some level you know that what you're doing is morally wrong and extraordinarily self-serving....I urge you to immediately stop this hate-mongering. There is no God anywhere in that.

—**Mark Cleveland**, of Aliso Viejo, Calif., in a 7/99 *Frontiers* open letter to orthodox-Jewish Dr. Laura Schlessinger, radio's most popular talk show personality

With the right-wing bias of radio and even TV, particularly cable-TV, today, if Hitler were alive, he'd no doubt have his own show. He'd have to soft-pedal it against the Jews, leave blacks alone, but boy, he could go wild against gays and feminists and...the usual suspects.

—gothic novelist **William Edward Daniel Ross**

My cousin thinks he's a big shot. I think he's a big shit...(and) full of hatred....There is nothing inherently gay about Tinky Winky or the Teletubbies. He's just trying to catapult himself back into the public eye and make more money.

—Jerry Falwell's gay relative **Brett Beasley**

Thank God for those gays. They get me all the publicity I need. If they didn't exist, I'd have to invent them.

—televangelist **Jerry Falwell**, in a conversation recollected by now openly gay Mel White, who had helped write anti-gay books for the likes of Billy Graham, Pat Robertson and Falwell

There is no such thing as a homosexual or heterosexual person. In theory all are bi. In practice some are this, some are that, some exclusively, some part-time. The point is that were it not for the three monotheistic religions that have made a nice hell of all human relations—so that we shall love 'God the father' all the more?—no one would have thought to categorize anyone because of his sexual interests....I suggest we work together to flush Judaism, Christianity and Islam into the Mediterranean and restore the Greco-Roman world where, believe it or not, there was no word for 'fag' or 'dyke,' nor was there any conception that an occasional sexual activity constituted an entire personality.

—screenwriter **Gore Vidal** (*The Left-Handed Gun*; *Suddenly, Last Summer*), in Great Britain in 1999

In January, 1852 (at age 42), unable to bear the guilt over his homosexuality any longer, (Russian writer Nikolai) Gogol confessed to a priest, who told him to abstain from food and sleep in order to purge himself of his 'inner filth.' A month later, Gogol, wasted from starvation, driven mad by sleep deprivation and further weakened by doctors who bled him with leeches, finally shed the skin of his sexual 'sin' by shedding the flesh of his body. He died on February 21.

—author **Robert Drake**, in *The Gay Canon* (doctors, anyway, have come a long way since the 19th century)

...(this) rush to canonize the veneer of Mother Teresa, despite the complicated darkness roiling beneath the surface.

—**Robert Drake**, on the woman who declared, "Love can only be found in the religion founded of Jesus Christ" and "All sex is unholy which is outside of (heterosexual) marriage and which is non-procreative"

I don't agree there was too much coverage of Diana's funeral and too little of Mother Teresa's. To begin with, Diana was robbed of most of her life...her sons were robbed of their mother. Also, Diana was for everyone. Mother Teresa was for one religion, only, echoing all the pope's extreme, outdated and biased views....Finally, I don't think she'd ever have gotten as much publicity if she hadn't been a Christian working in a non-Christian land—and a missionary, trying to convert people who already have a religion. There are Hindu and other people in India who do what she does—and several, unlike her, care about overpopulation there. But they don't get the publicity, because of the West's double standard: they're not light-skinned and Christian.

—rock singer **Michael Hutchence**

They go about it the wrong way. After three synagogues were firebombed (in Sacramento, Calif., in June, 1999), Andrew Cuomo, the H.U.D. Secretary, said, 'The terrible attacks weren't just attacks against Jewish Americans, they were attacks against all Americans.' Untrue. I resent the word 'just,' and they were and are attacks against Jews. The point being, America is made up of assorted and *different* groups, and we have to all make more effort to both acknowledge and *accept* those differences. Pretending we're all the same won't solve anything—we're not all the same, and we *all* have a right to be here and to be left in peace!

—gay, Jewish, Italian-American columnist **Leonardo Rossi**

An actor absolutely had no call to reveal his or her religion (during Hollywood's "golden era"). The studio rightly insisted on maximum popularity for their stars, and if your religion was non-normative, shall we say, you kept it quiet for the sake of your own career and the studio that pushed you.

—gay and Jewish A-list director **George Cukor**

R. W. Fassbinder

I think ethics are more effective than religion...less divisive. Both Catholicism and Protestantism are of the opinion that anyone who disagrees with them is wrong. With ethics, I just try and treat other people the way I wish to be treated. Even in the business world.

—gay German director **Rainer Werner Fassbinder**

I don't push my religion onto others, and I don't appreciate having theirs pushed onto me....I think it's rude when some people keep saying you 'won't be saved,' you'll 'go to hell,' and all those negative concepts of theirs. If you're into that, just keep it to yourself!

—Jewish comedian **Sandra Bernhard**

A fanatic is one who can't change his mind and won't change the subject.

—Prime Minister **Winston Churchill**

A fanatic believes that the entire ocean drains into his private swimming pool.

—Sir Michael Redgrave, bisexual actor

England is more liberated in a certain way. We don't have so much influence and even control of our media, especially TV, by the religious right-wing as in America.

—Boy George

The problem goes back to our very roots, to the founding fathers. And I suppose the founding mothers, who went along with them....It wasn't that the Puritans—who were religious fundamentalists—couldn't be Puritans in England. They could. But they couldn't force others to be Puritans too. And that's what they came here to do, and have tried to do in America ever since.

—gay Professor **Walter Kendrick**, Fordham University

Tweety used to be a baby bird without feathers, until censors made him have feathers because he 'looked naked.'

—Humane Society of the United States **factoid**, about a lingering bit of American sexual puritanism

Donald Duck comics were banned from Finland because he doesn't wear pants.

—HSUS **factoid**, about Finnish sexual Puritanism; on the other hand, in 1999 Finland became the latest nation (and fifth Scandinavian one) to legally recognize gay and lesbian marriage

I feel bad for my gay friends when I hear so-called religious people putting down their life, their so-called lifestyle, even their desire to commit to marriage by quoting 'the word of God.' Whose God, and which version, which book?...And so what? We no longer stone adulterous wives to death....Then there's the word *abomination*—I mean, look how often the Bible is used as a weapon!

The homophobes will throw that word at decent gay people but not admit that in the Bible there are other so-called abominations—such as eating shellfish, wearing clothes made of two materials, shaving, and so forth! But then, bigotry—bigots—are very selective...very cunning.

—pro-gay screenwriter **Steve Tesich** (*Breaking Away*)

First it was almost 2,000 years of almost enforced invisibility, most of them with homosexuality being punishable by death. We were burned at the stake along with witches, but you don't hear about *that*. Then, in the last few decades when we've finally mustered up some small voice, daring to ask for equal treatment under the laws we're also expected to support, our usual enemies see they can't pretend we're each a one-in-a-million freak anymore. So they go the opposite route, and now we're the biggest menace to their dysfunctional homes and shallow lifestyle since communism, I guess....They always try to stir up panic, and try and depict themselves—the judgmental majority—as somehow threatened and even persecuted! It sounds insane, but just read their hate literature and watch their fundraising videos.

Still, their reaction to us is thanks to our gains and progress....But we never can afford the luxury of complacency, with enemies and tormentors like that.

—**Pedro Zamora**, MTV's *The Real World*

We are still kissing up to Big Daddy. We are still apologizing for being who we are. It makes sense, then, that people would file in line for lethal chemo drugs, the way many Jews and homosexuals went willingly to the gas chambers, having no concept of what was truly occurring. There is nothing I want from Big Daddy—I don't want his medicines, his laws, his approval. I need nothing from the church, nor am I interested in anybody's definition of my sexuality....I have declared myself a free agent.

—HIV-positive poet and memoirist **Gavin Geoffrey Dillard**

The most inane are the people who say and possibly believe that AIDS is some sort of divine retribution. What kind of God would that be? And the Black Death, which killed a far bigger percentage of Europe, what was that—God's punishment on people for wearing funny period costumes?

—actor-writer **Stephen Fry**

We...make an idol of our fear—and call it God.

—director **Ingmar Bergman**

Serial Killer—L.A. Man Says He Killed Gays To Stop AIDS

—6/99 **headline** in *Bay Area Reporter*

Origin of HIV Found in Chimps—Scientists have long wondered where HIV originated. Now they know: a subspecies of chimpanzees. Researchers at the University of Alabama announced January 31 (1999)...that they think hunters contracted the virus through blood contact.

—*Advocate* **report**

How do you feel about AIDS as, and they pause, a celebrity? Meaning possibly gay. That's how I feel they're gonna bring it up, and sometimes that's how it comes up. But they don't ask me about AIDS as a black man. They don't make the connection....It all goes round the gay thing, but in times to come, when they look back on AIDS, it won't get remembered for what it did to gays. It'll be remembered for the big chunks of whole nations in Africa and the rest of the Third World that it took. But no one wants to talk about that yet.

—actor **Howard Rollins**, who apparently did not come out before his death from AIDS

You know what gets me? I read about a gay student who was expelled from the college run by a famous TV evangelist because of his sexual orientation—and then he killed himself. Which translates to the discriminated-against victim further and fatally discriminating against himself...the ultimate victim. To me this makes far less sense than, if *somebody* has to be eliminated, going after the villain, the source of the ongoing misery. Is this unique to gays? Do other victimized groups kill themselves so readily? And does no one ever think of bumping off these modern-day Hitlers in pastors' clothing?

—producer **Ben Bagley**

The Mormon church didn't used to accept black members...Jerry Falwell was a very vocal enthusiast for racial segregation. Do you think all this changed because *they* changed it? I think not. Blacks got fed up, and *forced* the change....The fact that gays are such almost-total scapegoats is because, imagine, most members of this minority don't admit to being in it! If we don't get together on this, what's gonna change? We'll get some more token concessions but still be hate and violence targets, still have limited citizenship rights, no sanctioned relationships irregardless, and the closet will still be rewarded and visibility will still be dangerous and punished.

It's true: if we'd spent more time since Stonewall (1969) coming together—other than sexually—instead of arguing, backbiting and obsessing over our looks, clothes and youth, we'd have won half our human rights by now.

—Joseph Miller,
original Stonewall rioter

I'll tell you, if we don't quit being so mean-spirited to one another, we're going to choke on our own bile. And I can think of a lot better things to choke on.

—**Bruce Vilanch,**
Oscars-telecast writer

Here's this old queen (hairdresser Sydney Guilaroff) taking so much time and effort to lie that he's not gay—a *hair*dresser! Bad enough. But in his (memoirs) he also made sure to put down hairdressers who are homosexual, and to try and closet everyone from Garbo to Hepburn, and those *fake affairs* with two dead actresses! Fucking the dead, I call it.

—fellow Hollywood hairdresser **George Masters**

One of the nastiest letters I ever got was from a gay man, one of the actors and creators of that play, *Greater Tuna* and its sequel. I'd written politely, about the negative and stereotypical depiction of the one gay character—how wrong this was from somebody *gay*. I *mean*...and the letter was in part obscene, in total furious, and got read by one of my family members....I wonder if some straight homophobe would have responded so shrilly and vindictively?

—gay archivist **Jim Kepner**

The man who ghostwrote Mae West's autobiography was gay, and yet there was a lengthy and needless passage in that best-selling book that reached so many people, denouncing homosexuality just like something out of the blazing pulpit...even if it was the 1950s, a decade that defined the word 'dreary.'....But when I saw *The Celluloid Closet*, a '90s product, I was beside myself. All these closet cases, on screen, talking about how unfairly gays had been portrayed on the screen! And sex expert, whatever, Susie Bright, crying over the time she discovered she was well and truly lesbian! What were those gay producers trying to do?! That was one case more of the book being far better than the movie.

—director **Emile Ardolino** (*Dirty Dancing, Sister Act*)

Amy Grant, the singer. Miss Bible Belt who refuses to wear the red (AIDS) ribbon—as she explained it, she feels wearing it promotes or condones homosexuality. I wouldn't guess anyone gay or lesbian would go to one of her concerts; then one day, in that paper, *Gay & Lesbian Times* (of San Diego), an article promoting her latest concert! Didn't they *know*? Or *care*? Or *what*? I wrote them a letter....The only thing that surprises me is that I can still be surprised—by my own people.

—*Oliver!* composer **Lionel Bart**

I am not an activist, but my heart is in the right place. I try to 'buy gay' when I can....A friend from America brought me a book, a gift. A novel by Tom Clancy. I didn't know how to say it. I'd read in a newspaper here that Clancy made a statement that, he said, America tolerates homosexuals but takes away the rights of smokers! A very anti-gay gentleman, and his books of course mirror this attitude—I have been informed....I had to let my friend know what I knew. Finally, he said, 'Well, he's entertaining.' I suspect so was Stalin, during a jovial mood.

—Dior shoe designer **Roger Vivier**, who was credited with introducing the stiletto heel

Homosexuals can be the hardest on other homosexuals....One very jealous gay man that I'd known, when I published *Other Voices, Other Rooms*, and had such a great success with it, his comment was, 'I suppose someone had to write the fairy *Huckleberry Finn*.'

—Truman Capote

There's this actor, he costarred in a few A-movies in the '70s, then he became known for saying he was no longer gay. After that, he became so crabby; like they say, sex is like a misdemeanor—de more you miss, de meaner you get. So then the biggest gay periodical, the one that's had all these lawsuits from women because of discrimination—even though they're homosexual women—they asked me to interview this actor, see how his 'post-gay' life was coming along. Well, there's no such thing, I told them, and I declined the assignment—and they never hired me again.

I'd heard rumors that this actor would hire male prostitutes, because he didn't want gay relationships, since he was sticking to his ex-gay story....Then I'm in a movie house in Westwood, and in the back corner—hugging, kissing and making out, 'cause it was mostly empty...a movie from England—was our 'ex-gay' actor, with another man. And *not* a hustler, because he wasn't good-looking enough to get paid. What an urge I had to say hi and call him by name!

—anonymous **Hollywood journalist**

Now, if you can help gay people become not gay, could you help Mr. Clinton become gay and then save the country? I mean, you could really help us out here.

—**David Crosby**, of *Crosby, Stills, Nash & Young*, addressing a heterosexual "expert" on homosexuality, on *Politically Incorrect*

It's missionary madness! The idea that gays can, or even should, become ersatz heterosexuals—the ultimate conversion. Never mind that urging everyone towards bisexuality, straights and gays alike, would be easier, also more practical....The concept is becoming a nationally advertised one (in the USA), via the vastly well-funded religious right...and only recently (in mid-1999) has the Christian Coalition's tax-exempt status been governmentally challenged....Of course, the Yanks don't keep their missionary mania to themselves, and no doubt we shall know more than we wish to about this latest American export, adding to that long if undistinguished list which includes the Mormons, Scientology, out-sized urban motor vehicles, the Titanic and the McCafé.

—Sydney, Australia, columnist **Shirley Vior**

This 'ex-gay' movement is, in a sense, a desperate last-ditch attempt to keep lesbians and gay men from being widely accepted....There are always some homosexuals, or even—reportedly—closet heterosexuals—greedy or self-loathing, attention-craving or religiously extreme enough to claim they have 'changed.'...Obviously, the 'ex-gay' movement hearkens back to the Big Lie, so long believed, that homosexuals but not heterosexuals choose their sexual preference. Which more and more of us straights, to use a dubious term, know just ain't so. The more gays we meet, or discover, the more we know that ain't so. Which is the spur behind that 'ex-gay' movement...I might write a song about that.

—musician **John Orloff**, aka Johnny Anus, one of whose songs was titled "I Wish I Was Gay (So You Would Hate Me)"

(On the members of one "ex-gay" group:) 'Oh, all two of them? Exodus is so moronic that it's actually almost endearing. Especially when they come up with all of these kind of stopgap solutions: 'I've stopped masturbating and thinking about men 15 times a day. I'm down to five!' Or 'I'm married and I'm now able to keep my eyes open during sex.' What a beautiful way to create a child—two people looking in the opposite direction.

—playwright **Paul Rudnick** (*Jeffrey*, *The Most Fabulous Story Ever Told*)

Some people will deplore these ex-homosexual organizations, but not more than a handful will point out that in every case, it's a religious organization. Bible-thumpers, and always to the right of Attila the Hun—I mean, most of these parties consider Catholics beyond the pale....So we're not talking about organizations and—rather—*non*-individuals who would refrain from distortions, myths, propaganda, lies, and, excuse the *expression*, out and out fairy tales.

—**Keith Christopher**, best remembered for his pioneering HIV-positive characters on *Another World* and *Guiding Light*

As a member of the board of the American Foundation for AIDS Research, I have to offer my congratulations. You are the only known human being to be cured of AIDS. You are quite a phenomenon.

—**Sharon Stone**, on Roseanne's talk show, to an "ex-gay" guest who also claimed to have "prayed away" his AIDS

My parents were both Pentecostal preachers....Part of my decision to write about my experience with 'gay conversion therapy' is due to the recent media hoopla surrounding religious fundamentalists and homosexuality. They claim to offer a cure, but it's a complete fraud....The ex-gay ministry I attended was successful, anyway, as a place to meet guys. It was mostly a lot of talk, but one evening the director had us split up—choose a partner to go off and talk and pray together.

Well, the guy I paired off with was really nice, and as we got to baring our souls he told me how attracted he was to me. We ended up in a secluded corner and kissed. When we got back from our 'talk,' the director seemed really annoyed and acted coldly towards us. My friend told me later that the director was probably coming on to him. Turns out he was right; this guy—who had preached to us about saving our souls—came out of the closet a few years later.

—gay playwright **David Williams** (*From Shirley Temple To Aimee Semple*)

What Really Goes On In So-Called Ex-Gay Ministries: Fear, Denial and Hot Sex

—headline in 6/99 *Fab!* magazine

What we are not hearing about in the mainstream (media) is the true stories of *ex*-ex-gays....

—comedian and Broadway actress **Lea DeLaria** (*On The Town*)

I read of a young American homosexual, raised in a severely Christian household in Orange County, California, who went to a meeting of similarly inclined males. He acknowledged to them, 'I am a homosexual, and I am not happy,' then asked, 'What can I do to become straight?' The answer seems clear enough to this occasionally practicing heterosexual: Stop fighting yourself and your potential for happiness, and stop caring so much what a cabal or congregation of judgmental zealots thinks! This is really a non-issue, or should be, by now.

—Oscar-winning cinematographer **Freddie Young** (*Lawrence Of Arabia, Dr. Zhivago, Ryan's Daughter*)

Time magazine, questioning ("ex-lesbian" Anne, wife of "ex-gay" John) Paulk's credibility, reported that (they were) unable to find even one former girlfriend...or a single lesbian lover. *Time* reported that Paulk 'conceded that her ties to women in college years were "more emotional than sexual."' It's not known if Mrs. Paulk was ever really a lesbian....Other sources deplore that *Newsweek*, which put the 'couple' on its cover, and other mainstream periodicals, are down-playing the duo's sponsorship by extremist Christian groups, in an effort to make their ex-gay pitch more reasonable to average Americans.

—Israeli L.A. columnist **Mark Ariel**

Former 'Ex-Gay' Establishes Southern Baptist Bible School For Homosexuals....After struggling through 15 years as a Southern Baptist minister and several years at Coral Ridge Ministries attempting to convert gays to heterosexuality, Rev. Jerry Stephenson, founder of the Grace Institute Bible College, finally admitted that he himself was and always had been gay....Stephenson contends that mainstream fundamentalists' condemnations of homosexuality are the result of misinterpreting the Bible, taking passages out of context, or in some cases mistranslations. 'We believe in the Adam and Eve story,' he said. 'We also believe in the Adam and Steve story.'

—1999 article by A.P. writer **Bill Kaczor**

Sex with a man was a poke without a purpose for me until I found God and stability in my girlfriend's arms....I'm living proof that truth about yourself can set you free.

—**Anne Poker**, former Houston wife and mother "and now proud lesbian" and triathlete, re an article on "The Ex-Straight Ministries" in 4/16/99 *Frontiers*

Good God, did you see (actress Anne Heche) on the Academy Awards? She is so fricking hot. What straight woman on the edge wouldn't want to dive head-first into her lap after that? And for the guys there's Rupert Everett. Did you see him in *My Best Friend's Wedding*?

—**Cody Forrester**, trying to explain "the sudden interest in gay lifestyles" by purported heterosexuals, or bisexuals; Forrester is co-president of *CUMING* (Coming-outers United, in Making It Nice to be Gay), whose San Francisco conference was endorsed by Mayor Willie Brown

You can't spend 40 years eating Cheetos, hating your kids and going without an orgasm and then just expect to embrace a new life overnight.

—*CUMING* copresident **John B. Mary**, on why some heterosexuals have problems "converting to homosexuality"

I'm not gay, but I am a diva, and therefore I thought I should be here.

—**Celine Dion**, who with Elton John headlined a concert in conjunction with *CUMING*'s New York City conference

I know of a plumber, a man with wife and children, who left them for about a year to have an affair with a movie director who is gay....What depressed the man was that everyone was saying he had become homosexual. So he said to Jean, 'Why is it if a heterosexual has sex with a man he is called homosexual, but a homosexual who has sex with a woman is not called heterosexual?' Jean explained that all of these people, real and theoretical, are probably bisexual.

But also it is the pressure of how every man is almost forced to have sex with a woman. But almost no one pressures a man to try it with another man—so if he does try, it is from his own personal curiosity and desire, not from fear or pressure.

—French film star **Jean Marais** (*Beauty & The Beast*), lover of male artist Jean Cocteau

"Well, I think if a man gets oral sex from another man, he's gay."

"Not necessarily. It depends on what he's thinking about, *during*. He could be gay, bi or hetero...and in Hollywood, various gay male stars give in to females who offer them oral sex—which doesn't make them straight or even bi, since they'll later privately admit that during the blow job they were thinking of a guy or men....The point being that erections want satisfaction, not labels."

—hostess/author **exchange**, on Manhattan's *Darian O'Toole* radio show, on May 7, 1998

People were so shocked when that tabloid thing came out about Monica (Lewinsky) and her supposed lesbian fling or fantasy. What is so weird? Virtually every sexually active girl has considered a lesbian interlude, if only for variety...(and) because women are still always being presented as sexual objects, so it can't help but turn women on sometimes. Girls aren't hidden in baggy clothes and pants, or de-sexualized with 'bald' haircuts. Feminine flesh and exposure is encouraged...it's a wonder we don't have more lesbianism in America. We do have more dyke-looking women, but they're usually the first to deny in horror.

And I'll tell you why so many, many girls will try a lesbian affair. Because their self-esteem isn't all wrapped up in avoiding or condemning it, and since women don't have pricks, nobody is symbolically conquering anyone else....It's tender, equal, sisterly, and not just a notch on someone else's belt.

—actor **Susan Strasberg**

Monica Lewinsky has begun early her career as a man's woman. She began at the very top, which leaves for her, one imagines, quantity....It will be interesting to see what, who and how many the future brings her....Ms. Lewinsky reminds me of a famous naughty story based upon the legend of Marilyn Monroe, toward the end of her careers as an actress and a connoisseurs of men: it was said that Marilyn and a confidant, I think her hairdresser, were drinking one night at her home, listening to soft music and reminiscing.

The hairdresser said, 'Marilyn, do you remember the minuet?' Marilyn replied, 'Honey, I can't even remember all the men I fucked.'

—Monte Carlo columnist and radio personality **Delphine Rosay** (the minuet reply has typically been attributed to Tallulah Bankhead)

We gave the world the motto *Liberté, Egolité, Fraternité* (the French Revolution slogan Liberty, Equality, Fraternity). Now, with

France as the first major (i.e., big population) country to move toward gay marriage, we may give the world the more contemporarily appropriate *Liberté, Egalité, Diversité*.

—**Jean Marais** (Germany, with its more liberal government, may get there soon; a survey found 54% of Germans feel gay couples are entitled to the same rights and benefits, and only 37% disapprove)

Defense of Marriage? It's like the old V-8 commercial. As if...heterosexual men all over the country would say (smacking forehead), 'I could've married a guy!'

—Congressman **Barney Frank**, on the so-called Defense of Marriage Act that bans gay marriage

Isn't it strange that California will have a referendum on the recognition of gay marriages performed in other states when no states allow us to marry?

—CA Assemblyperson **Sheila James Kuehl**, on the anti-gay referendum sponsored by a 70-year-old Republican who has an openly gay son and who refused to attend the funeral of his gay brother who died of AIDS

Being gay or pro-gay, so often it's about being punished or limited by others. On the screen, off the screen....I played a straight seismologist in *Volcano*, but my associate in it was a character with short hair and glasses—so she gets killed off. Which is Hollywood, because if you're a strong woman they see you as a bitch or a borderline lesbian.

And Fox doesn't want to work with me, like a boycott, because I went to the premiere of (Fox-produced) *Volcano* with Ellen DeGeneres. They'd have preferred a total stranger—a male one.

—**Anne Heche**

I noticed that the international press kit, at any rate, for *Volcano* was very odd in that its leading lady, Anne Heche, was missing from any close-ups, and almost entirely from all the stills. Supporting actors were featured more than her. What else could it be but homophobia? Yet when I inquired at Fox, the net result was being dropped—and despite their being far from gay-free in terms of employees in the publicity and other departments—from their press kit list. Because I questioned the homophobia that excluded openly lesbian Anne Heche. Nor do I regret questioning it—besides, they'll be dealing with me later.

—anonymous **international journalist**

There are some studios who don't want to work with me because when I do publicity (interviews), I talk about things like AIDS. Whatever—I don't give a fuck. This is a town of desperation, and your chances for desperation increase every time you take a stand....It's much more important to my life and my soul to do my political work than to care if I get a role.

—Kathy Najimy

I don't have to worry, and I would not worry, regardless. I'm an actress second.

—Elizabeth Taylor, on the cost her AIDS activism might have on her acting career

I really think the stuff, the integrity and guts, in this town are mostly in the women. How many men do you see, famous men, involved in battling AIDS? They're too busy battling their sense of shame, if they're gay, or embarrassment, if they're not. In Hollywood, men are only driven to succeed or to prove themselves.

—Roseanne

You asshole! No, the vaginal juices, dear!

—Elizabeth Taylor's stunned retort to a man who insisted that HIV was only transmitted via anal sex

I joke that had I been more emotionally and psychologically stable, I would have won just one (Olympic) gold medal. To win four was compulsive, but diving was what I thought was acceptance and love. A lot of gays are incredibly successful, from the outside looking in, because they are driven.

—athlete turned actor and author **Greg Louganis**

Very early we catch on that we don't belong to the world we're presented, so we fantasize a world we do belong in. That's why so many gays become actors, writers or designers—we get to design the world as we'd like it to be. Every gay five-year-old has to be an artist out of necessity.

—actor turned playwright **Keith Curran**

Actors who enjoy acting, and this means primarily stage actors, are among the happiest people in show biz. Not the stars or the executive species. People who like what they do, and do who they like—without professional and personal satisfaction, what real happiness is there?

—**Dick Sargent** (*Bewitched*)

You can be a straight white male in a pin-stripe suit and still have more pain than a black lesbian single mother. And that's the truth of life. People aren't willing, though, to look beyond the masks.

—**Scott Thompson** (*Brain Candy*)

Do you know how much fear and apprehension goes into cover-ups? The deep-closet, stratospheric stars?...At least one movie superstar was part of an escort service. He serviced a very rich, powerful man in the business who is glad to help him cover up. But the rest of it...the payoffs, the threats, the fears and worries, the tendency of the past to catch up with one....*Not* fun or relaxing, as a stellar lifestyle.

—Hollywood columnist **Lee Graham**

The biggest pieces of 'dirt' I've gotten I couldn't write because they were too hot to be printed. A lot of those stories are blind items in my column. Those are the ones I tell my closest friends at dinner parties. But I'd be scared if they got out, because sometimes your life can be at risk because some of these stories are career-damaging. I know really damaging stuff that I don't dare tell because I know how strong my opponents are.

—*Star* columnist **Janet Charlton**

(Asked if she'd ever been threatened:) Yes....One large, so-called religious organization that I shall not name. And Sylvester Stallone, people like that.

—**Janet Charlton** (SS was upset

over a heterosexual matter; the organization or cult includes at least two male superstars, one of them gay or bi, the other gay—both involved in the "straight" lifestyle)

What well-known married couple (he's in front of the camera, she's in the back) is carrying on with the houseman? What's more interesting is that they are doing it separately and think that the other doesn't know....

—columnist **Sue Cameron** (5/8/99)

I don't know if Margaret Cho is gay. Or bi. Or the more common one....She has this cute thing where she says she asked her parents when she was sixeen what 'gay' meant, and they said it means someone who likes to kiss men. So Margaret figured, 'Oh, I must be gay.' Anyway, then she began talking in public about her boyfriend, Scott Silverman. I *knew* that name...and later I confirmed that he's a stand-up comic too and, as Margaret knew, he is *openly gay.* So what was that about?

—an **associate** from Cho's belated ABC-TV sitcom *All-American Girl*

Star Wars is a fantasy movie set in a galaxy far, far away....To dissect (it) as if it has a direct reference to the world that we know today is absurd.

—**George Lucas**' refutation to the press that *Phantom Menace* character Jar Jar Binks could possibly be gay

Hollywood wants every penny, every customer....In an Australian movie like *Proof*, they left it open as to whether (one of two major male characters) is gay....In *The Cable Guy*—one example—they let you wonder for a bit about Jim Carrey's oddball character; but they don't want to make anyone *too* uncomfortable, so before long they reassure you that, yes, the cable guy, the guy Carrey is playing, is, yes, folks, yes, he is, he's straight. Collective sigh of relief....

—**Olga Constantinides,** Melbourne columnist

...a fascinating play, but Hollywood went to work on it. The Jews are played by non-Jews, the gay roles by non-gays, excepting Patrick Bristow (of *Ellen*) in a virtual cameo, and Rosie O'Donnell plays a man-less, child-less heterosexual pal....Most irritating is the way being gay is never compared to being any other minority, despite the gay hero being part of a Jewish household, or less than a part, due to his parents' prejudice...as well as the missing declaration in the very wordy teleplay that the *problem* won't be having a gay child but, rather, the hurt and discrimination which that child will have to face. And it is the unborn's straight relatives who would help guarantee such a future.

—writer **Allen Ginsberg**, on the cable-TV movie of *Twilight Of The Golds*, about a young couple who find out that they are going to have a child and that it will be a gay son and must therefore decide whether to have an abortion!

They do not value our lives! AZT cost People With AIDS $12,000 a year until ACT UP protesters forced Burroughs Wellcome to lower its prices and to reveal—information held back by them and by the F.D.A.—that half of the recommended dose of that toxic and costly drug was no less effective. And was less dangerous. How very humane.

—actor and activist **Brian Hurley**, who died of AIDS at 49

It's important for me to speak openly about my sexuality to help educate people. Forty years ago, when there was a lot of anti-Semitism, it would have been important for them to know that I'm Jewish....Where there is prejudice, it is important to be open. It is important for gay people to let the rest of society know the fact of discrimination and the pain of discrimination.

—Congressman **Barney Frank**, in *Playboy*

I don't see the big deal about sexual behavior. Why do we need this excuse to hate? It should be a non-issue.

—Cybill Shepherd

It just seems silly to me that something so right and simple has to be fought for at all.

—**Gregory Peck**, on gay rights

The hateful people always, desperately, need an opponent. And we're it, kids.

—CBS-TV V.P. **Tim Flack**

Brad Davis

I love it when Republicans say they're for less government and get believed about it. They're for more government inside people's bedrooms, more laws and surveillance against homosexuals, and more reporting and harassment of People With AIDS....

—**Brad Davis**, who died of AIDS

I've always thought that was just the prelude to group sex—the fag joke in the all-male business world. That's what I think that really is about. 'Let's break the ice a little here and make fun of guys who love guys—then let's all fuck!'

—**Roseanne**

How fascinating, these studies which find that rabidly anti-gay men experience more erections at the sight of male-male pornography than *regular* straight guys! This tells us something significant. Not that it'll be widely disseminated, but it confirms what I've long suspected. If you have *gay* on the brain to that extent, then you have gay in *you*....

—former talk host and author **Virginia Graham**

I started to read up on homosexuality. I had a feeling it was biological, although you can dabble, I guess. I found out that they did a study on men who were in comas. They stimulated them while they were asleep with sexual images of women and sexual images of men. If they were homosexual, they got an erection with the male images. Now, that's not a choice! That's the deepest part of your brain. You can't lie about that.

—**Liza Minnelli**

There is a lack of understanding about gay lives in this country....In our society (gay youth) are not being educated or informed. In fact, they are being threatened and surrounded by shame.

—**Stockard Channing** (*Grease*, *To Wong Foo, Thanks for Everything, Julie Newmar*)

People would walk up to me at parties and whisper, 'Hey, you aren't what they say you are, are you?' And I just wanted to shout to them, 'Yeah, what if I am?'

—**Billy Crystal**, on perceptions that he might be gay because he played gay on *Soap*

Great! They'd have a real good mom. I would give them a lot of support.

—**Cybill Shepherd**, asked about having a gay child

Those 'family values' people ignore the loving families comprised of two gay or lesbian individuals, with or without kids, and they also ignore such straight-family horrors as sexism, wife-beating, child-abuse and incest, divorce, and kicking their own gay or lesbian kids out of the only home they've ever known....In point of fact, traditional families have never been the loving, equitable or all-encompassing havens they pretend.

—**Glenda Jackson**, Member of Parliament

I'm gay and in love.

—*Boyzone* singer **Stephen Gately**, 23, who came out in Europe's largest newspaper after learning a former band member was planning to out him to a German publication; Gately added, "The time has come to be honest and tell everyone I'm gay—I owe it to all Boyzone fans" (the five-member band, little known in the USA, has had 13 Top Five UK hits since 1993 and is currently #1 in

Britain with a greatest-hits collection that sold more copies in one week than the other Top Twenty entries combined)

I am a rich white guy, but I bear the brunt of tremendous injustice and I am angry. Let's say I die in two years. If I'm heterosexual and unhappily married, my spouse would get 37% of a judge's salary in perpetuity. But after 21 happy years, *Michael* would get nothing! That irritates me on a very personal level.

—**Stephen Lachs**, in Los Angeles in 1999, after 20 years as California's first openly gay Superior Court judge

If we're not included, it's not a democracy. And we're not included.

—writer/activist **Larry Kramer**

The bigots want to lie that we're all the same. Like the Nazis did with Jews. One stereotype for all. They dare to try and take away our individuality. Which is all that separates any human beings from animals.

—**Michael Callen**

It's dispiriting and grossly unfair. No PDA's (personal displays of affection) between gay people—hand-holding, a hug that lingers, a caress on the cheek, *any* kind of dry kiss. But personal and public displays of young hetero lust, that's more than tolerated, sometimes even admired....We should *not* be made to feel that we're outsiders in what is also our world too.

—**Peter Allen**

We need to stop asking permission to exist! We do exist, this is it....They'll never completely understand our lives. What they need to do is to take our lives at face value....There's a point where our community has to get to where we just start demanding that our lives be valued.

—**Wilson Cruz**

There's a group of older people out there that will never accept it, but there are a lot of empty cemeteries, and when they're filled, the world will be more tolerant.

—openly gay **Tim Doyle**, executive-producer and head writer of *Ellen*

With gay people, you are either part of the problem—accepting and thus perpetuating homophobia—or you are part of the solution.

—**Harvey Milk**

It's a lot of stress, it takes its toll...and whether it's our industry or the world we live in, it's as if it belongs to others and we merely inhabit it.

—closeted **actor-director**

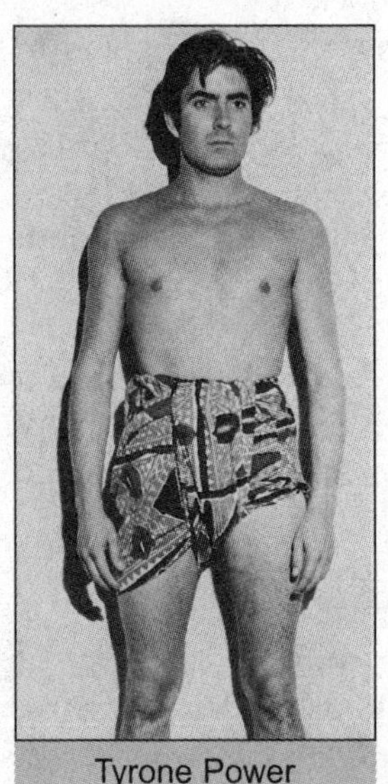

Tyrone Power

It's only a gilded cage.

—**Tyrone Power**, in Argentina, where he traveled in the 1940s on a goodwill tour of Latin America with actor Cesar Romero; the closeted Power, who married three times, died of a heart attack at age 44

(Ramon) Novarro, a man who set female hearts aflutter, was nothing but a queer.

—**defense lawyer**, to the jury, after the movie star was tortured and murdered by two young men in 1968, three decades before Matthew Shepard....

On August 16, 1936, Federico Garcia Lorca was arrested by fascist extremesists. A few days later, the man who was arguably Spain's greatest 20th-century playwright and poet was shot dead—one of the assassins claiming to have fired two extra shots into Lorca's rump because he was a faggot—and buried in a common grave.

—**Robert Drake**, in *The Gay Canon* (in 1999 Drake was almost fatally gay-bashed in Ireland by two men; at this writing he remains in a coma)

When I fly over America on my broomstick, as I often do, I get to feeling what a big country this is—it's big enough for everyone. And despite all the progress that has been made in rights and tolerance, we are still living in a world of hate.

—**Elton John**, to the audience at a benefit concert in Matthew Shepard's hometown of Laramie, Wyoming

Parents teach children to hate, and our—'our?'—or whosoever's institutions make it acceptable and routine. This must be changed; that is, we must change it.

—William S. Burroughs

(Gays) must demand recognition of a culture that isn't just sexual. It's all there—all through history we've been there. But we have to claim it, and identify who was in it, and articulate what's in our minds and hearts and all our creative contributions on this earth.

—Larry Kramer

No one can make you feel inferior without your consent.

—Eleanor Roosevelt

Out & Outing

Don't compromise yourself. You are all you've got.

—Janis Joplin

Did you know that in ancient Greek the word for *actor* is the same word as for *hypocrite*?

—Truman Capote

I'm not gay, but I played a gay man.

—Billy Crystal, on the TV series *Soap*

I'm not a straight man, but I play one on television.

—Dan Butler, *Frasier*

Being *out* is so 'in' now. Especially if you're gay.

—Drew Barrymore

I'm not gay, by the way, if anyone's wondering. But I'm flattered that I may be thought to be so.

—Brendan Fraser

Coming out of the closet is like exhaling...being in it is like constantly inhaling in public.

—Amanda Bearse, *Married With Children*

It's a tremendous sense of relief. At last, to be yourself!

—Elton John, on coming out

Being in the closet is like being a spy for 24 hours of the day. In some cases it means watching everything you say and do, and how you say it and do it.

—Quentin Crisp

As a little girl, I wanted to be somebody. I had no talent, I couldn't play an instrument, I couldn't sing, but I just wanted to be famous. I wanted to be somebody. And on stage I felt like I was somebody. And then I got a TV show and I really felt like somebody. And there was still something missing. And I realized that I had left out one very important word, and that is that I wanted to be somebody *happy*.

And you can't be happy unless you feel proud and you feel good about who you are.

—Ellen DeGeneres

Someone at ABC said that (Etheridge's opening music for *Ellen*) was 'too dykey.' And they did drop it. I think because I'd just come out and they felt it would reflect on Ellen or her show, and neither was out at the time.

—Melissa Etheridge

I was so proud of my niece when she decided to tell the truth about herself...I knew that I was different as a boy, but I've often wondered, were I in Melissa's place, if I'd have the courage to come out. After all, I'm from an older generation...we had no alternative to all the anti-homosexual propaganda we grew up with. Or worse, the silence—the majority's angry silence.

—George R. Etheridge, Melissa's gay uncle, born 1933

I had those (same-sex) feelings of desire when I was about 5 or 6.

—musician **Michael Feinstein**

I feel very fortunate in that I grew up in a family with three out of four children being gay.

—k.d. lang

My siblings were entirely heterosexual, and the fact that I was always being measured against them made my childhood rather a living hell. That is, beyond the hell which childhood already normally is.

—Quentin Crisp

I was afraid, as a teen, that if I acknowledged that I preferred my own kind, my family would stop loving me. We do tend to underrate our families. Sadly, some kids are dead-right about their families, who reject them when they come out. Which indicates that they never really loved the gay child for himself.

—Peter Allen

Since I fell in love with Ellen, my sisters have stopped speaking to me, and my relationship with my mother is very, very cold.

—**Anne Heche**

If you're going to come out, by all means do. But it wouldn't hurt to have a nice nest egg, just in case.

—singer **Michael Callen**

I have certain relatives that if I was sure they'd cut me off if I came out, I'd go back in the closet just to come out to them!

—**Paul Jabara**

What happened to me is exactly the opposite of what closeted people fear. They think they'll lose everything if they come out. This did not happen to me at all. In fact, everything came back tenfold.

—**Melissa Etheridge** in 1995

It is never too late to come out. Never...and I encourage everyone to come out.

—**Leonard Bernstein**, who in vain encouraged his mentor Aaron Copland (in his 80s) to come out

I'd love to come out, but I'm not a lesbian. I really wish I were.

—**Cassandra** "Elvira" **Peterson**

I don't want to be the great lesbian of the western world.

—columnist **Liz Smith**, comparing herself to Sandra Bernhard

I'm willing for people to think I'm gay.

—**Madonna**

If I was Richard Gere, with all those rumors, I'd tell everyone I'm not gay.

—magician **David Copperfield**

I don't care if people think I'm gay, bi, whatever.

—**Richard Gere**, prior to taking out a full-page newspaper ad that stated otherwise

If people want to think I sleep with men, let them. That's their privilege.

—**George Michael**, prior to his 1998 arrest in a Beverly Hills public restroom

It's justice!

—**Boy George**, on George Michael's arrest and subsequent coming out

Stop asking permission from the straight world to be who we are. It has nothing to do with them.

—**Boy George**

Most younger gay people imagine that if they come out, they'll lose all their friends. If they're real friends, you won't. Besides, no gay person should have only straight friends, you know?

—author **Paul Monette**

It's true that success loses you more friends than failure....

—**Truman Capote**

Liberace and Jack Benny

The sad thing is, I just don't have the time to keep up with my old friends from the old neighborhood. And they don't have the financial resources to keep up with me.

—**Liberace**

Some people like me because I'm gay. Some people dislike me because I'm gay....One shouldn't be liked or disliked for their sexuality. It's stupid, it's like being for or against somebody because she's left-handed....If I'm liked, and if someone has to dislike me, it should be on account of my personality.

—**k.d. lang**

I expect people to love or not love my music, my voice. But not *me*. They don't know enough about me to make that decision.

—**Johnny Mathis**, who publicly came out in 1982

I think it's even more troublesome and shameful to come out as bisexual. Both gays and straights are prejudiced against us.

—Jill Sobule

I came out as bi because it just sounded more acceptable, and I wanted to think of myself that way...it doesn't exclude anyone.

—Elton John

I loved Woody Allen's quote that if you come out as bisexual, you double your chances for a hot date on Saturday night. Personally, I think the ambitious ones say they're bisexual. Not everyone's gutsy enough to admit to being gay or being lesbian...I do think if you tell people you're bi, whether it's true or not, they'll tend to think you're promiscuous.

In this business, if you're anything but vague, people will tend to nail you down and limit you....There's always pressure to be specific about your sexuality.

—Peter Allen

I'm as vague as I need to be or want to be, for the time being.

—Rosie O'Donnell, on her sexual orientation

Sally, you ever notice the word 'engaged' has the word 'gag' in the middle of it?

—O'Donnell, to talk host Sally Jessy Raphael's question about why she wasn't married (as in "man and wife")

If I was with a man I wanted to have a child with, I would have gotten pregnant. But that was not the case.

—O'Donnell, explaining why she adopted a son

Single women and lesbians will sometimes adopt. Men in general do not—the male-ego thing....Tom Cruise gets very upset when it's noted that he and Nicole Kidman adopted, though it's natural to wonder why, instead.

—Tim Flack,
CBS VP of Creative Affairs

What do I care? I'm 73 years old. I find it fascinating that people are interested in my sex life at age 73. It's rather complimentary! But...my answer to questions on this subject is simply f*** off. There have to be some private matters left.

—former New York City mayor **Ed Koch**, on whether people think he's gay

I was introduced to (Mayor) Koch at a party in 1982, specifically to talk about (AIDS). And the minute he knew what I wanted to talk about, I was hauled away by police. He was a closeted gay man, and he did not want in any way to be associated with this.

—writer and AIDS activist **Larry Kramer**, in 1998

If it wasn't for career ambitions, particularly in the most public fields, far more gay men would come out....My friend Tom Hulce played Mozart in *Amadeus* and was Oscar-nominated. But even after his niche as more of a character actor than a leading man emerged, Tom was still constantly advised to stay in the closet...and still is told this. He has been out and is something of an activist, but he would be more widely and un-self-consciously out if he wasn't a pretty successful actor.

—writer and activist **Paul Monette**

When I was trying to be a singer, my record label (Geffen) wanted me to stay in the closet, and at that time I thought that's what you had to do to be successful.

—Chastity Bono

My father's respect is worth every single job I may be denied because I came out.

—actor **Mitchell Anderson**, *Party of Five*

It can't be reiterated enough that due to the pervasive homophobia we live in and the lack of role models, the rate of teenage suicide for gay, lesbian and bisexual teens is three times as high as for straight teens.

—Peter Allen

I'm not one of those people who says, 'Why do we have to label?' Openly straight people have no problem being called 'straight.'

The media never call someone an accomplished gay person—they think that's out of line—but they have no problem calling Andrew Cunanan 'the gay murderer.'

—columnist **Michael Musto**

I don't talk about my personal relationships. That is private. But the fact that I am gay, I'm very happy for it to be public knowledge and I don't deny it.

—Sir Ian McKellen

No one wants to be categorized as just one thing. But when it comes to sexuality, you either label yourself or else they do it for you. After all, you are basically one or the other, so 'fess up!'

—British rock star **Marc Bolan**

Why is being outed such a big deal? When I find out that someone's gay, my respect for them increases tenfold.

—Scott Thompson,
The Kids In The Hall

I will not mind being identified as a 'self-avowed gay writer' when John Updike is routinely identified as a 'self-avowed heterosexual writer.'....Also, I look forward to the time when everyone stops asking, What creates homosexuals? That question is relevant only if the question, What creates heterosexuals? is given equal attention.

—novelist **John Rechy**

There hasn't been a studio head I've worked for who hasn't come out and asked me if I'm a lesbian. I say, "Normally this would be none of your business. However, I will answer you....It's possible. I'm not practicing at the moment, but I will not say it will never happen or hasn't happened in my past.'

—Whoopi Goldberg, in the early '90s

A number of celebrities, fairly early on they make rather bold statements and almost come out. Years later, when they're struggling to hold on to the stardom they've got, or trying to resurrect the stardom they had, they backtrack and play it very straight....But I think (David) Bowie is the only example of somebody who came out and later went back in.

—singer **Michael Hutchence**, *INXS*

We've had openly gay stars and singers (in Britain) for years. Now it's beginning in the USA....Have you noticed how since *Ellen* came out, Jodie Foster has been seen wearing dresses more often?

—**Michael Hutchence**

We writers always know who's gay, and we don't point it out. A lot of gay people go out of their way to make up fake romances and even get themselves photographed in magazines just to keep their image together. It's the same as it was 25 years ago, when it comes to celebrities today (1990).

They (the general public) don't mind knowing that Mike Tyson beats his wife. That's something they can identify with. They can't identify with lesbians...it's too scary.

—columnist **Janet Charlton**

One keeps hearing that audiences won't go for this and won't go for that, regarding homosexuality. Well, aren't gay people part of the audience? Don't gays have any say, any presence? It's so behind the times; when will it catch up? Like with blacks—they're not a majority of the audience, but the bigwigs no longer pretend they're not even there....

—football star turned actor **John Matuszak**

Don't compromise your beloved, if you have one. One person you can love and be loved by all your life is more important than any temporary career advantage. Of course if you have no one special in your life, then you can devote yourself body and soul to getting ahead...I think any actress, regardless of her sexual orientation, should never marry...if work is all, then you are married—to your career.

—Oscar and Tony-winner **Sandy Dennis**

It was so important for Ellen and I to tell the truth about our relationship to the press. I did not want anybody thinking this was something they could lie about. Or that I was going to lie because I was more concerned about my career. The first step is demanding truth from yourself. Way too many people don't demand it from other people because they're afraid to get called on their own untruths.

—**Anne Heche**

Closets stand for prisons, not privacy.

—lesbian comedian **Robin Tyler**

Being in the closet takes a terrible toll on your spirit. Every time you change pronouns or stifle a comment about your home life, you cause another microinjury to your soul. When you add up all those bad feelings and all those lies, you damage your self-esteem, your sense of yourself as a valuable human being....Denying reality is not healthy. The damage we fear will come to our career, our lives, and our families from coming out doesn't hold a candle to all the damage we do to ourselves every time we hide in the closet.

—k.d. lang

Take it from me, the first rule of how not to come out to your parents: Do not come out when they are driving. The second rule: Do not come out on a major family holiday when the whole clan is around.

—**Wilson Cruz**, *My So-Called Life*

My parents are very supportive of me...I was never in the closet anyway, but I think that within a family that's heterosexual, you're always going to be an outsider if you're gay. I don't think it's easy to grow up gay anywhere....But I think we've made some big strides now, we don't have to apologize for being gay. I believe we were created this way by God.

—actor **Jason Gould**, son of Barbra Streisand and Elliott Gould

I remember when outing meant a family picnic.

—Rodney Dangerfield

Hollywood is the most closeting place on earth. Europe, less so. A major German director, openly gay there, did some gay films too. Moves to Hollywood, directs and produces mainstream blockbusters, gets himself a wife, and asks a gay magazine to apologize for 'incorrectly' describing him as gay. And they do it! Well, maybe he's truly gone bi, but more likely he's just gone Hollywood—you know, trading truth for dollars.

—historian **Jim Kepner**

Hollywood is like something from the Dark Ages. There is no town more homophobic, at every level of the industry. You go on the sets, they're rednecked. I see actors who I know are gay, who I've seen in a gay bar the night before, who act like they don't know another gay person. They wear wedding bands. It's that devastating here. The gay casting people are the most homophobic of all. They are closeted and they're terrified for their jobs.

—openly gay actor **Michael Kearns**

Most (movie) sets are very straight. Makeup and wardrobe are the only places you see gay people. But half of (the gaffers and lighting men) suck dick anyway. You should see the glory hole in the men's room at Columbia Studios. Jesus! It's big enough to fit half of your body through.

—openly gay actor **Alexis Arquette**

(Asked if he'd ever spoken publicly of his sexual orientation:) No. But only because I don't want to give the critics an extra stick to beat me with. Everybody knows what I do anyway. I don't have many secrets. Once on a television program Groucho Marx asked me if I'd ever been married. I said, 'No, why?' 'Well, I'd marry you anytime,' he answered. I looked him straight in the eye. 'Is that an honest offer or a proposition?' That shut him up.

—**Truman Capote**, in 1972

The stupidest question I was ever asked was on an American TV chat show hosted by a man called Johnny Carson. The (lesbian-themed) film version of *The Killing Of Sister George* had just been released, and he asked me point blank, 'Are you a lesbian?'

—British actress **Beryl Reid**

The dumbest question a magazine like *Rolling Stone* or whoever can ask is, Are you gay? Do they honestly expect an honest answer? Not one in 100 entertainers who do happen to be gay will say Yes. I think such magazines ask, just to seem hip and open-minded, while going along with the conspiracy of silence surrounding the matter. Often hypocritically so. Like *Rolling Stone*, whose head honcho, Jann Wenner, was outed after he left his wife for his longtime male companion!

—former actor **Samson DeBrier** (*Salome*)

I was 17 and I knew immediately that I was not going to live a lie. I enjoy working in films, the money's not bad, but I was never going to compromise. And it is lying, and it soils your soul when you're not honest with yourself or the audience.

—**Alexis Arquette**, brother of Rosanna

It took me my whole life to be as I am now—*free*. I never put my face down or am ashamed. The only joy I have is my work and my life, and I must play until I die. I am an individualist, and that saves me. For the past ten years, I was misunderstood. I cried a lot. But now I don't care anymore. They can give me one star or two or none. People can say what they want. I am honest with myself and my work, and that makes me happy.

What is the point of work if it is not also fun? Life is too short.

—**Gianni Versace**, not long before his 1997 murder

...the idea of her and George Michael having a relationship is about as likely as my having sex with a door.

—**Boy George**, on Michael's official girlfriend at the time

The press tries to make us feel sorry for the selfish actor who earns $5 million or so per movie, who's living a lie and perpetuating the homophobia that pretends all successful actors have to be straight...but I'm not concerned about the closeted, cowardly, greedy movie star who's been outed after earning $20 or $30 million. I'm concerned about the teenager who's gay or lesbian and thinks this means a lifetime of hatred, discrimination and having to keep lying...a teen who's seriously contemplating suicide, thanks to the system of lies perpetuated by, *among* others, that very successful and completely selfish performer.

—**Armistead Maupin**
(*Tales Of The City*)

Good-bye, I said to (the late) Cardinal Cookie, you're out of the closet at last! That s.o.b. hypocrite faggot. Practically every priest I know is gay anyway. The gay baths in New York, half of the clientele are priests....There's a gay bath on Columbus

Avenue in New York that doesn't have any signs. There's a door that has no identification at all. Upstairs is one of the most wild gay baths in the western hemisphere. And the man who runs it told me over a third of its clientele are priests.

—**Truman Capote**, on Terence Cardinal Cook et al.

Here's what my father said when I told him I was gay. 'There's two kinds of people I don't deal with: criminals and queers. You're sick, thwarted and perverted and you're no daughter of mine.' That was 12 years ago and I haven't seen him since.

—writer-director **Nicole Conn** (*Claire Of The Moon*), who is close to her mother and stepfather

I tried to kill myself (because of) all the (anti-gay) hate. I'm glad I survived, and I'm trying to make it better for the kids who come after me. To do this, and to express myself in my music, I had to be *me*, to come out. One can't create anything original or life-affirming from inside the closet.

—**Jimmy Somerville**

If you're going to come out as gay or bi and you live at home, maybe you should wait. Unless your dad's gonna be supportive....If you've got your own income, you can come out to everyone. Except perhaps at work. Unfortunately it does boil down to money, most of the time. Or, in the case of the closeted and affluent in show biz, the desire for *more* money.

—**Dack Rambo** (*Dallas*)

My father was amazed to find out that it is legal to fire somebody just for being gay (in about 40 U.S. states). He said, 'But that's un-Constitutional.'

—**Chastity Bono**, on educating her Congressman father, who then voted anti-gay anyway

It should simply be illegal to vote on whether or not gay people are entitled to equal rights. Or to vote to take them away, after they've been voted in....Can you imagine voting on whether to give equal rights to blacks or Jews or any other group than gays?

—**Peter Allen**

The actors I feel have every right to stay in the closet are the ones who have AIDS. In Hollywood, AIDS-phobia is worse than homophobia....Brad Davis wasn't so much hiding his bisexuality, but his being HIV-positive. He belonged to all those insurance outfits, but still he felt compelled to lie about his health, and I don't blame him a bit.

—Broadway producer **Saint Subber**

Before protease inhibitors, actors in Hollywood really had no incentive to disclose their HIV status. It isn't a question of image...the question really isn't, Should I disclose my status? but, Will the insurance company put up the bond? How many character actors like me can afford to do that?

—**Michael Jeter** (*Evening Shade*) in 1997

I hadn't said I was gay...but I have been living *out*....I've never been to a Hollywood function without a man on my arm. I chose to publicly state I am HIV-positive because that's different...and if it helps people who are too but aren't well known, then I want to help.

But right after my announcement, a reporter from the *National Enquirer* showed up on my doorstep shouting and yelling questions like, 'How long have you been sick? Is that your partner? Is that the guy you caught AIDS from?'...I had to hire a publicist.

—**Michael Jeter**, whose partner, a flight attendant, is HIV-negative

In old Hollywood, if you hired a publicist, it was to get publicity. Today's Hollywood, if you're a big star and gay or lesbian, the publicist is to keep you deep in the closet. That big blonde actress has a big publicist, also a lesbian, who is expert at denials and planting fake straight gossip items in the press and on TV.

—openly gay actor **Craig Chester**

I was part of (a sister-brother team's) Tokyo concert tour as a groupie or friend of their opening act, so I know all about X and his kinky ways and rather slinky body as well...and all the horrors of Y and how he treated her and how all of the troupe awaited the morning's announcement of whether or not—usually not—Y had shit and hence the day and the concert that night was going to be an easy one. They never ate a single bit of any foreign food, and thanks be to the food god that Big Mac was almost everywhere they toured.

—journalist **Forrest G. Hooper** (the singer is deceased, the brother a closeted Republican father of more-than-one)

This question is so direct: Are you gay or not? If somebody excites me, either a man or a woman, then I'm interested.

—German actor **Udo Kier** (*My Own Private Idaho*)

I read where an athlete recently came out and said he was gay. So what? I know 50,000 athletes who are queer as a bat.

—**Johnny Mathis**, who gave up a potential Olympic career to croon

She's been pulling this shit for years. She plays gay for large gay audiences and the rest of the time remains conspicuously silent....Her silence about her sexuality undermines all of her good work (for the lesbian and gay community) and reinforces the notion that homosexuality is something to be tolerated but never discussed. I didn't spend four months of my life writing the script (about gay-themed films) so Lily can sound more enlightened than she really is.

—**Armistead Maupin** in 1996, alleging that Lily Tomlin backed out of an agreement to publicly come out

Let me phrase the question....Here's how I would ask it: Do you find that opposites attract? My own reply would be that I'm the other sort—I find that birds of a feather flock together. (Pause.) *That* answers your question.

—**Nancy Kulp** (*The Beverly Hillbillies*), coming out her way in the book *Hollywood Lesbians*

I have always assumed (sister) Jodie was gay or bisexual, but I wouldn't dare bring it up and risk incurring Mom's wrath.

—former actor **Buddy Foster** (*Mayberry R.F.D.*)

Our mother's lover was like our second parent. We called her Aunt Jo. Her name was Josephine Dominguez Hill. She was called Jo D. for short, and my baby sister was called Jodie in her honor.

—**Buddy Foster**

Brad Davis was bisexual or homosexual, but after starring in a few movies, he felt he could become a real, lasting movie star, and he decided on the closet. To his credit, he's openly pro-gay, which some gay or bi stars are *not*....But the moment a non-straight man gets a wife or has a child, then there are all these interests trying to pretend he's straight and always has been straight.

—Davis pal **Vito Russo** (the Hollywood establishment and Davis' widow-biographer have depicted Davis as a "straight" victim of AIDS)

Notice how villains, if they're gay, are eventually disclosed as being gay. Like J. Edgar Hoover, a paranoid right-wing hypocrite....But the heroes....They keep silent too. Oliver Sipple, the man who saved President Ford's life, who deflected the would-be assassin's bullet, he was gay. But he didn't say so at the time. *Now* he admits it, but now it's no longer news, and no one puts it out there (in print or on TV). So nobody knows. Gay heroes are anonymous—so as a group, we don't get credit for our heroes...or Olympic champs. Unlike other groups. No, we only get the villains, posthumously, and the ones who get caught, as it were, because they have AIDS—you know, Rock Hudson, Liberace, Tony Perkins....

—choreographer **Ulysses Dove**, a regular with the Alvin Ailey Dance Theatre, in 1994

Elvis Presley had a bee in his bonnet about The Beatles. Not just because they dethroned him, musically. He didn't like Englishmen with long hair who might in his view be communists and/or homosexuals. He wrote to J. Edgar Hoover, being an ardent admirer of his, and offered his services toward getting all the 'dirt' he could on the Fab Four, which he once reportedly pronounced—in front of photographers—as the Fag Four.

—UK writer **Anthony Burgess**

Somebody once called me a sissy because I'm polite....There's a 'man' in 'manners.'

—**Elvis Presley**, who was initially thought by the John Birch Society to be "a perverting, communistically inspired menace to the sound morals of American youth"

Anita Bryant should take care of her career and leave her obsession with so-called sodomy alone. If she wants to make a federal issue of 'sodomy,' why doesn't she start at home? I refer to someone who is very close to her *and* I refer to her having her head up her own ass half the time!

—**Allen Ginsberg,**
poet and gay activist

I did know Robert (Reed) was gay. But all of us on *The Brady Bunch* were protective of him....They don't often let actors who are publicly known to be gay play father roles. In spite of the realities of gay actors and other gay men often having kids of their own.

—**Florence Henderson**

Such a foreign subject.

—**Jane Fonda,** on Italian resident Gore Vidal, when he was running for political office against her then-husband, politician Tom Hayden

I remember watching a documentary about Gore Vidal's failed campaign for Senator. Gore and former governor (Jerry) Brown were being introduced by the leader of some professional group, and the emcee said, 'Gore Vidal and Jerry Brown have never before been in the same room together—or even the closet together.' I think Gore smiled smugly...but you should have *seen* Jerry Brown's face....

—**Sandy Dennis** (*The Fox*, *Up The Down Staircase*)

The fun thing about going out to gay nightspots in L.A. is that you're liable to run into celebrities. Like at Love Lounge, which is predominantly gay. George Michael and Chad Allen from *Dr. Quinn, Medicine Woman*, are regulars. And Jason Priestley has been seen there...he says he's straight. I think the rumors began when he and Luke Perry (both from *Beverly Hills 90210*) were rooming together.

—historian **Jim Kepner**

I roomed with (Marlon Brando), and neither of us is exactly shy or afraid of a new experience so long as it doesn't hurt...I once tried to nip his newfound arrogance in the bud. When he had hit it really big. I asked him, 'Is your shadow any longer since you became so famous?' He went back to his old self....Whether or not there's been hanky panky, any two guys that have shared living space get the benefit of the secret-lovers rumor.

—**Wally Cox**, TV star (*Mr. Peepers*)

I was roommates with some future actors when I first landed in Hollywood. So what? That doesn't mean I slept with them. And it doesn't mean that I didn't—though I didn't.

—**Tony Curtis**

I don't know what that is. Two guys live together, everyone assumes they're *doing* it....Two women live together, like live together 40 years, and everyone figures it's just a Boston (sexless) marriage. At least that's how people *used* to think...now, they might suspect you if you live alone with your dog.

—**Phyllis Diller**

Well, they're finally sleeping together.

—Broadway producer **Saint Subber** (Truman Capote's *House Of Flowers*), on Cole Porter and his contractual wife Linda Lee, buried side by side in Peru, Indiana

It happened that because Cole was known to have affairs with chorus boys and other men, Linda's status was questioned. It was rumored that she might be lesbian, of which there was no proof. It occurred to few people to guess that maybe she simply wasn't interested in sex, as a number of ladies are not. No, it sounded juicier to guess that she might be 'that way' herself!

—**Johnnie Ray**, gay hit singer of the 1950s

Whatever the nature of William and Anne Shakespeare's relationship, it is worth noting that in all his canon of works there is not one depiction of a happy marriage.

—historian **Erik Milford**

In Hollywood is the one place, or business, where the average lesbian does get married to a man.

—**Diane Murphy**, one of twins (herself openly gay and no longer acting) who played Tabitha on *Bewitched*

Franklin Pangborn

I once asked (gay character actor) Franklin Pangborn if he'd ever been in love. He replied, 'No, but I have been married.' Interesting, because he had *never* been married, and at the same time he made the remark, he caressed my thigh.

—critic and author **Parker Tyler** (*Screening the Sexes*)

The acting community knows, the public doesn't. This famous actor travels with his wife and his male lover, and the kids stay at home. The lover, seemingly an employee, blends into the background, while everyone comments on the husband and wife's togetherness. Of course they're always together, because the husband is paranoid and takes her everywhere, so the public doesn't get the right idea.

—*Hollywood Studio* magazine columnist **Lee Graham**, longtime (gay) escort to former star Virginia Mayo

The press only reports part of the truth. I've always been very pro-gay....People read that I called a carriage driver a 'faggot.' This came about from a shouting match...I'd been to a hearing...about restricting (New York City's) horse-drawn carriages and about animal cruelty....Then this guy's yelling at me, saying, 'Takin' the food out of our fuckin' mouths—and your nigger-lovin' wife too—you fuckin' faggot.'

So, because of my retarded middle-class upbringing, I turned and yelled back, 'Fuck you, faggot.' The reporters were all there, of course, and not every story included what led up to my using that horrible word, which I later apologized for doing....And I was due to speak at an AIDS rally later that week, but thanks to the incident and thanks to the partial reporting, I got disinvited...and that made it tough for me for a long time after. But it made me so sorry that people who believed I was on their side thought me just like everybody else. I *am* on their side.

—**Alec Baldwin** (whose wife Kim Basinger had dated Prince), considering a switch from acting to politics

I witnessed how the tabloids dealt with gays when a young actor I knew came down with AIDS-related illnesses. Because at the time he was well known for playing a heartthrob on a daytime soap, he became a prime object of tabloid scrutiny. Photographers dogged his every step. Reporters camped outside his door. All this, as he fought and finally succumbed to the terrible deterioration that HIV can bring.

—**Lance Loud**, the openly gay son in the historic TV documentary *An American Family*

Liz Smith says she feels justified in reporting the fake marriages as real ones...because it's not always easy to know if nothing (sexual) goes on behind closed doors and because otherwise she'd 'have to question 80% of the marriages' she writes about.

—screenwriter **Helen Deutsch**, *Valley Of The Dolls*

The problem with most columnists, be they straight or secretly gay themselves, is their biased standards. They'll cover a real straight romance, they'll cover a phony straight romance, but they won't cover a real gay romance—or rather, they'll cover it up.

—New York columnist **Arthur Bell**

The Truth About the Clint Eastwood-Jim Brolin 'Romance'

—the *National Insider* tabloid **headline** of June 17, 1973

Rock Hudson at his home in the hills above Hollywood

In the old days it wasn't called outing. It was called a 'vicious rumor,' and if someone said that, for instance, Rock Hudson was gay, then the reaction was, 'Why do you hate Rock Hudson so?' People didn't think about outing in terms of the truth, they thought about it as a way of harming someone's reputation—which made a vicious circle of continuing the discrimination. Besides, no one believed it back then about a he-man type or about anybody that was married, let alone anyone who was a mother or father.

—**Vito Russo**

In the future, when someone says they're gay or that some celebrity is gay, it won't be such a big deal...and if a (TV) character is gay, that'll just be part of the diversity of real people that characters are supposed to represent.

—**Ellen DeGeneres**

Listen, I remember when if somebody was Jewish and they were in show business and changed their name already, you didn't point them out as Jewish. That was considered to be in bad taste....Even worse was the implication that an actor or singer was part-colored and had Negro ancestors. That didn't even see print—that could hurt an entertainer's career.

—columnist **Sheilah Graham**

The two things that make outing more of a working reality aren't in the hands of the journalists or the fans. It's up to the individual performers. They have to have enough self-esteem to not live their lives in terror of the inevitable, relatively few bigots who the media and the studios think are the average American, and they have to feel they can still make a fair living after coming out.

—CBS Vice President **Tim Flack**

I don't see why it should affect the fan worship I've got. It hasn't hurt David Bowie, and I don't see why it should hurt me.

—**Elton John**, about coming out as bi (he later came out as gay)

"In spirit." and "Probably."

—**Kurt Cobain**'s replies to the questions "Are you gay?" and "Are you bisexual?" (in school his best friend was gay and got gay-bashed, as did Cobain for having a gay friend)

If any of you in any way hate homosexuals, people of different color, or women, please do this one favor for us—leave us the fuck alone!

—**note** on the sleeve of *Nirvana*'s *Insecticide* album

I certainly wasn't real confident with girls. I guess that's what got me started with guys. And small animals.

—rising TV hunk **Jon-Erik Hexum** (1957-1984), to *Playgirl* magazine, which officially claims a readership of heterosexual females

With the extremely handsome or ultra-sexy men, the female fans get so disappointed....The housewife in Des Moines who feels that if a Rock Hudson or a James Dean is gay, then he can no longer be hers. As if such a plain Jane would have a crack at these guys even if they were straight! But then, as Washington Irving put it, nothing is more opulent than a beggar's imagination.

—William Morris agent **Stan Kamen**

Well, Robert (Downey Jr.) loves to say in interviews that everybody is bisexual....His life is such a surprise that if he told me tomorrow that he had had a gay experience, I wouldn't be shocked...I will say this: if Robert is gay, he should be open about it.

—**Sarah Jessica Parker**, who lived with the actor for seven years

Speaking of Jerry (Brown, governor of California), I wonder where his male Indian friend is living now that Jer's Laurel Canyon home went down the hillside during the big rains of two years ago? Just asking!

—columnist **Bill Dakota** in 1981, in the *Hollywood Star*

In the '60s, when people used to ask me 'What's your sexual persuasion?' I'd say, 'Well, I wouldn't throw Mick Jagger out of bed.' But today I would. Just because now he's so fucking ugly.

—former Andy Warhol "superstar" **Joe Dallesandro** in 1993

It's very different now, but you can see why most actors would avoid homosexual roles....After I was in *Death In Venice* (as Tadzio), so many papers in America wrote that I was homosexual. All from one movie! I kept having to say no, no, which makes me sound desperate or prejudiced....Another rumor was about me and Sal Mineo, and I never even met him!...And when (director Luchino) Visconti's lover told the press that I was dead—he said it because he had wanted to play (Tadzio).

So I think for me I'm better being far away from all that.

—former Swedish actor **Bjorn Andresen**

If (gay people) inspire me, those are the people I want around. It took me a while to make that adjustment....I'm very in touch with my feminine side—any good actor is....Freud said that everyone has latent homosexual tendencies....There are a lot of times that people will misconceive me as being gay when they first meet me.

—**Luke Perry**, *Beverly Hills 90210*

Sure! Hasn't everyone?

—hunk actor **Scott Valentine**, when asked if he'd had gay experiences

Guess which young, successful actor is the boyfriend of a big male porn star?

—columnist-novelist **Sue Cameron** in 1993

Last year, Jan-Michael Vincent was charged with assault after causing his two-months-pregnant girlfriend to miscarry after hitting her repeatedly in their home. Then he failed to show up at the trial and got fined $374,000. Now, Hollywood never considers this serious enough to hurt an actor's career or lessen his popularity. Yet they obsess over an actor being labeled as gay or bisexual, even though he's not hurting anyone. But it's not just Hollywood that's sick, it's the whole patriarchal, homophobic society and its laws and institutions that value women and gay men as less than straight men, who can literally get away with murder—and I'm not specifically referring to known wife-beater O.J. Simpson....

—record producer **Ben Bagley** in 1996

That Arab leader with the tablecloth on his head, known to everyone around him as a lifelong homosexual, and an unrepentant terrorist to top it off...afraid that the outside world will learn he's gay, so he marries his secretary or some female, à la Rock Hudson! I mean, the man is a terrorist, for crying out loud, and he's afraid his sex life might reflect poorly on him!

—singer-activist **Michael Callen**

It's not enough if the body's from hunk heaven but the mind's by Mattel or the voice is Milquetoast....The 6'5" Klinton Spilsbury was being dubbed a new Rock Hudson for the expensive *Lone Ranger* remake that flopped big—even after they reportedly dubbed his voice with another actor's....The next we heard from Klinton is in *The Andy Warhol Diaries*, where he's telling Andy that he got drunk one night at Studio 54 and wound up in bed the next morning with (designer) Halston.

—Paul Monette

Yes, I did.

—writer **Armistead Maupin**, asked if he'd really "meant" to out male model and big-titted pitchman Fabio in 1992

When you're an actor, you're yourself and someone else at the same time.

—writer **Gavin Lambert**

I like who I am, but I also like the Latin Lover that some people out there think I am. How could I continue being him for them if they find out all about me?

—**Cesar Romero** ("all" meaning his real sexuality)

If I pretended I'm straight, I'd be slapping my gay fans in the face. Especially someone as flamboyant as me.

—UK singer **Holly Johnson**, formerly of *Frankie Goes To Hollywood*

To be a good-looking actor can always cause a few problems... eventually they will wonder if you are (sexually) normal. But they don't usually print anything like that, unless they have good evidence....But in no other business does a man have to keep announcing how appealing he finds the opposite sex.

—Italian actor **Cesare Danova** (*Cleopatra*)

The true objective of your typical Hollywood Don Juan is not so much the lady's bedroom as a story in the gossip columns.

—writer **Philip Dunne** in *Take Two*

Being an actor and handsome can be a real drag. People get jealous of you just for that, and they can be more suspicious....

—**Guy Madison** (reportedly, there was something to be "suspicious" about)

A narcissist is someone better-looking than you are.

—**Gore Vidal**

Can you imagine the nerve? Some rich and famous star, also seeking our sympathy because he's cursed with good looks?!

—composer **Paul Jabara** (*Enough Is Enough*)

I get hit on by so many guys, but it's no big deal...I see it as a compliment. If I was a gay guy, and I saw someone who was muscular, tattooed, intense, in a band—well, I'd be all over it.

—**Henry Rollins**, who is muscular, tattooed, intense, etc.

I always find men like me to be very desirable. That is all I can tell you or my lady fans.

—**Alejandro Rey** (*The Flying Nun*)

If I wasn't Latino, I'd be a hunk or a cop—in *that* movie, I was a crook. If I was known as a *gay* Latino, I'd get *no* roles, not just lousy ones.

—**anonymous** young actor, who appeared in a box office hit starring a briefly hot Australian actor

I think the public doesn't care.

—**Mitchell Anderson** (*Party Of Five*), on being openly gay

The ones who it (being openly gay) freaks out are the casting directors and all the closeted executives in TV and movieland.

—actor **Michael Kearns** (*The Waltons*, *Cheers*)

When I was in high school, I (hung) out with jocks and some of my gay friends in the drama club....Sexual preference really never did matter much to me. When the guys on the wrestling team said, 'How come you hang out with those queers?' I would say to them, 'What is it about yourself that makes you say that? What fear is it?' I'd turn the tables and have conversations with them. In an hour or so they'd say, 'Hey, you're right.'

—**Stephen Baldwin** (*Threesome*)

I must emphasize that I am purely heterosexual. I die for women! But when (Brad Pitt) first came into my office and his hair was still long and he was wearing an open shirt, I looked at him and could not get over the beauty of this guy. He is extremely handsome.

—*Seven* producer **Arnold Kopelson**

It seems no one in America has heard of bisexuality....

—openly bi actor **Helmut Berger** (*Ludwig, The Damned*)

Forrest Tucker (of *F Troop* and *Auntie Mame*) was an excellent heterosexual lover but a bisexual exhibitionist. Because he was very well endowed, and because it pleased him, he loved to be naked in front of both sexes.

—actor-dancer **Gene Nelson** (*Oklahoma!*)

Reader Phil Aklan of Hollywood asks, 'Why not print cock sizes for all the men you write about? You could just add it to their names with no further comment, like Hugh Hefner 8, Jack Lemmon 6, Sinatra 6, Dean Martin 7, Dave (sic) Letterman 9, John Wayne 4, Johnny Mathis 6, Ed Asner 6, etc. (these are the ones I know about). Also, once and for all, how hung was Jimmy Dean?'

—1981 **letter-to-the-editor** of the *Hollywood Star* tabloid

I don't think he denies being gay...and he didn't marry anyone's secretary, like Rock (Hudson). But I don't think he talks about it to the press...he still wants lead roles.

—**Divine**, on costar Tab Hunter (*Lust In The Dust*)

I'm openly undeclared.

—drag artiste **David Michaels** (*The John Larroquette Show*), re his sexual/affectional orientation

I won't even bother with his name, but here in Britain there's now a rock star who says he defines himself as a bisexual man who's never had a homosexual experience....

—truly gay singer **Jimmy Somerville**

No, I'm not.

—**Valerie Harper**, who unlike *Rhoda* isn't Jewish

Am I gay? Ha, ha, ha, aah...go ahead. Ask me anything you want. Clitoral or vaginal? Both, darling. I'll take anything I can get. Hah!

—**Valerie Harper** (*Rhoda*, *The Mary Tyler Moore Show*)

I saw Oprah the other day—an hour show with Barry Manilow—and she asked him what kind of women he liked. His lover of 15 years was probably annoyed by that. Oprah knows Barry Manilow's (gay).

—writer-activist **Armistead Maupin** in 1992

Olivier is a very virile man, publicly and privately. Honesty is not his forte....Privately, he'll flirt with young actors. On a stage or a set, only with young actresses—and some not so young....The word is he's bisexual. But I think homosexual is more accurate.

—Laurence Olivier's *Spartacus* costar **John Dall**

Tim Curry

Tim Curry (*The Rocky Horror Picture Show*) looked us up in San Francisco. We didn't know to what degree he was in the closet at that point....He was madly in love with some young man there for a while. But when we started pushing him—boom—he was gone. And that's okay, because as sweet as Tim is, if he's not going to be out of the closet, he's perpetuating homophobia and I can't put up with that.

—**Armistead Maupin**

Gay people pay more taxes but have no rights...we are the last minority with no civil rights as individuals or couples....If we have plenty of money—and it's a myth that we're all affluent—then we can cope with the added expenses and hire lawyers to protect us to some extent...while movie stars who are gay can afford to not give a damn about the injustices and financial problems regularly encountered by non-rich-and-famous gays and lesbians.

—**Paul Monette**, former screenwriter

What we have with (closeted actors) who are playing that game is a very cynical way of life that's evolved precisely because they can have gay friends and gay lovers and straight friends who know they're gay and live very comfortable and still lie to the American public. And it's those lies that are killing us.

—**Armistead Maupin**

Mitchell Lichtenstein

I was always out to myself. My dad is very cool about my gayness—supportive, not prejudiced, worldly.

—actor **Mitchell Lichtenstein** (*Streamers*, *The Wedding Banquet*), son of artist Roy Lichtenstein

The more tolerant and educated and loving a household you come from, the easier it is to come out...and generally the more religious the background, the harder it is to be self-affirming rather than self-hating and in denial.

—actor **Casey Donovan**

My good friend Betty Grable would tell some of us this story about Dan Dailey, but she made us promise not to repeat it to civilians (non-actors) until Dan was gone. As fate would have it, Betty died first....Dan was a part-time transvestite, and it seems that at some social function he met a fellow and asked him what he did. 'I'm in ladies' underwear,' said the salesman. Dan smiled that big, wonderful grin of his and slapped the fellow on the back. Then he said, 'Me too! But not in sales.'

—Cesar Romero

Gracie (Allen) loved scandal. I didn't. Those things didn't interest me. I'm not interested in anything that happened yesterday. And how can you deal with Cary Grant's homosexuality?

—comedian and author **George Burns**

Ray (Walston) is heterosexual, so far as I know. He's just not very blatant about it.

—costar **Bill Bixby** (*My Favorite Martian*)

A lot of the comedians in the old days, you'd take them for nellie boys. Humor was broader then, pardon the expression. But most of those funny men were strictly straight...officially they *all* were.

—Richard Deacon (*The Dick Van Dyke Show*), who was gay

It's like this whole litany of adjectives. They've written them all about me: zany, flamboyant, sensitive, quivering, colorful, outrageous, irrepressible, madcap, campy, effervescent, elfin, boyish, nervous, fabulous... get it? Code words. But so long as they think I'm funny....

—comedian **Alan Sues** (*Laugh-In*)

That was a great character, that fag sportscaster on *Laugh-In*. I always cracked up. Just the idea of a fag sportscaster—who would believe it! I loved it!

—hetero sportscaster **Howard Cosell** (Alan Sues' Big Al was the first regular gay character on an American prime-time series)

I play a sportscaster who's straight...and the result is that a lot of people won't believe me at first when I tell them I'm gay. Some think I'm pulling their leg, and why would I want to tell anyone I'm gay?

—**Dan Butler**, *Frasier*

Don't laugh, I was born on a ferry boat...I ruined my mother's green satin dress. She never forgave me...I *hope* that's one of the reasons she never forgave me.

—**Alan Sues**

Yes, I've heard about the closet. It's where anyone different keeps their armor and their disguises. And themselves.

—columnist **Joyce Haber**, who was married to then-closeted TV producer Doug Cramer

We black people can't have closets, man. To have a closet, you got to be able to pass!

—secretly gay actor **Howard Rollins**

All I can volunteer at this time is, Tony Randall's a closet Jew. But so's (designer) Ralph Lauren. So's lots of people outside of the state of Israel and in the state of condemnation.

—**Joe Besser**, the last actor to join The Three Stooges, on the performer born Leonard Rosenberg

(Asked if homophobia in Hollywood has affected his career at all:) Yes! I don't have much of one! I'm on *The Larry Sanders Show* with Garry Shandling, but that was because Garry asked me to do it. But I have had a very hard time trying to get auditions for roles.

—openly gay actor **Scott Thompson** (*The Kids In The Hall*)

(Asked if he minds persistent rumors that he's gay:) It depends on the intent. Some people might look at it as lessening my reputation, others as heightening my reputation.

—John Travolta

Dusty Springfield is going to be on the show. Which will be very good news to my (gay) son Kenny's friends. It was at Kenny's request that I invited Dusty. She's over there in Amsterdam, of course. I don't know much about Holland except the story about the kiddie with his finger in the dyke. I'll be asking Dusty if she knows that story....

—**Barry Humphries** as Dame Edna Everage

It's rather sad that some homosexual cross-dressers have ruined it for those of us who are heterosexual but now and then wear a dress.

—TV star **Benny Hill**

I do hope that people who watch *Ellen* will think I'm gay. I even asked the writers to call my character Emma....If people think I'm gay, that's fine. There is nothing wrong with that. My uncle and godfather were gay, and after I grew up I was shocked to find there was so much bigotry in the outside world. *Ellen* is helping decrease it.

—double-Oscar-winner **Emma Thompson**, guesting on *Ellen*

I grew up in Texas, and I was a ballet dancer, so people thought I had to be gay. To keep from getting beat up, I studied fighting. And I grew my hair long, to be defiant. I became a very angry young man.

—Patrick Swayze (*Dirty Dancing, To Wong Foo*)

I was the Lillie Langtry of the older homosexual set. Everybody wanted me. I had a very bad way of turning these guys off. I thought it would embarrass them if I said I wasn't homosexual, that that would be a rebuke, so I always had a headache. You know, I was like an eternal virgin.

—**Orson Welles**, looking back

(When Richard Dreyfuss was given Italy's Donatello award for *The Goodbye Girl* he went on a European press tour and invited his mother and secretary along:) The press, especially the German press, thought that he must be homosexual. Who else travels with his mother? They gave him a hard time.

—**Gerry Dreyfuss**, in the book *Star Mrothers*

Leonardo DiCaprio, now 23 and following the success of *Titanic*, has moved out of the home he shared with his mother.

—columnist **Arlene Walsh** in January, 1998

My mother told me, 'There are straight people, drag queens, gay people and transvestites in the world. They're not more important than you, and you're not more important than them.' I just can't help but be open-minded!

—Australian actor **Guy Pearce**, who played Felicia in *Priscilla, Queen Of The Desert*, and a cop in *L.A. Confidential*

Is the homophobia in Hollywood generated by agents and studio heads? That's the word about Leonardo DiCaprio: he's very much ready to come out, but his agents and managers won't let him.

—*Genre* magazine in 1994

Someone asked me if I am gay and I said, 'No, but the boy I'm fucking is.' It's a funny little issue that always comes up.

—**Guy Pearce** in 1995, pre-Hollywood, to *Dragazine*

It's kind of amazing, because this hot newcomer, Leonardo DiCaprio, said in *Interview* that he wasn't really sure about his sexuality. That's probably all he dares say, but it's still brave...even if he's not gay like *the* Leonardo (Da Vinci). He could well be bi or gay...they say a picture's worth a thousand words, right? I saw a candid photo of Leonardo with (costar) Mark Wahlberg (at a premiere), and the way Leonardo was holding Mark—who just looks friendly, by comparison—and especially the look on his face—the *eyes* and lips—that confirmed it in my mind.

—former actor **Samson DeBrier**

Has anyone else noticed how much Leonardo DiCaprio and Ellen DeGeneres resemble each other? They could be sisters. Or brothers. Or whatever.

—New York photographer **Brian Weil**

I'm pro-gay because I've seen what gay actors have to go through...some survive it fairly well, but others take to the bottle or worse....If I were gay, which I'm not, I do think I might by now be open about it, because let's face it, I'm in the comedy field and I'm not the standard dreamboat type.

—the late **Phil Hartman**
(*Newsradio*, *Saturday Night Live*)

Little by little, I found out that I might have had some homosexual fantasies and had had what would be considered...homosexual childhood adventures. They were perfectly normal explorations...but a lot of people won't even admit *that*.

—director **Blake Edwards** (*Breakfast At Tiffany's*, *Victor/Victoria*)

Leonardo DiCaprio is trying to squash rumors that he has a French art advisor who is helping him collect art and that there is a hidden relationship brewing. Leonardo has been mentioned with every girl in town and is doing all he can to quell the rumors....Leonardo is very close to his grandmother in Germany....

—**Arlene Walsh** in June, 1998

Black and strong, like Sidney Poitier.

—actor **Woody Strode**'s reply when asked in the 1960s how he liked his coffee

That confirmed it in my mind.

—former actor **Samson DeBrier** on Strode having said his closest companion was his French poodle

Look, Molly, there's the man who killed all of Daddy's friends.

—AIDS activist and former screenwriter **Larry Kramer**, to his dog, when Kramer, who blames the ex-mayor for the spread of AIDS, bumped into his Manhattan neighbor Ed Koch

I remember being impressed by how candid Sammy Davis Jr. was....He loved to watch porno films on video because he enjoyed the sight of girls' big knockers and men's big cockers....He said all this to a *Playboy*-style magazine, I think it was called *Genesis* or *Gallery*.

—Monty Python member **Graham Chapman**

Jann Wenner is more fascinated by my homosexuality than I am!

—**Truman Capote**, on the publisher of *Rolling Stone* and *US*, who in the mid-1990s left his wife and kids for a younger man

Music is a much less uptight arena than movies and TV...but for example *Rolling Stone* persistently closets all singers except the very few who insist on gay pride, most of those being girls or Brits. It just seems like hypocrisy to me.

—Oscar-winning composer and singer **Peter Allen**

Peter (Allen) grew up in a little town in Australia called Tenterfield. He says that at age eight he decided he'd have to depart.

—**Liza Minnelli**, who like her mother Judy Garland had at least one gay husband

Liza and I had a very gay wedding...our best man was Paul Jasmine, an artist who did the voice of Mother in *Psycho* and was Tony Perkins' closest pal...Van Johnson was one of the guests....Oh, yeah, the honeymoon was also rather gay!

—**Peter Allen**, who reportedly spent the wedding night with his boyfriend instead

No one ever asked me.

—dancer-choreographer **Tommy Tune**, on why he didn't come out until his 1997 memoirs (at least one journalist did ask...)

Clive Barker...the openly gay writer and director? The horror guy, right? It's like a lot of celebrities with something to sell. In a gay magazine, he'll say he is gay. On *Tom Snyder*, and I saw it, not a word about being gay. How can you be a part-time 'openly gay' person?

—**Allen Ginsberg**

There are no excuses now. People in the closet—how '70s is *that*? We have to get out as gay people and meet people and be charming. Anne Heche said she wasn't gay until she met Ellen (DeGeneres)—apparently we're overlooking the easiest way to 'make' people gay!

—comedian **Suzanne Westenhoefer**

I was outed as straight in *People* magazine, but some people just assume I'm gay. I'm willing to accept either label.

—actor **Doug Savant**, who played gay on *Melrose Place*

I don't think people understand how traumatic being gay really is. Because there's nothing in our culture that supports you. Even today I find myself having to fight against the desire to have a secret life. I don't want that. I want to merge that destructive impulse into whatever creative life I have. And I think that's still what's driving our subculture. We're taught to have secrets.

—**Michael Jeter**, Broadway, film and TV actor

All actors are liars. I've never met one that wasn't.

—**Truman Capote**

When I began calling him gay publicly...I got a call from my agent, who was also Ron Reagan Jr.'s agent, and he said, 'Ron wants to write to you. Do you mind?' And I said, 'Of course not.' So he wrote me a very long letter, the essence of which was that he said he wasn't gay and was devoted to his wife, that all of this was very hurtful to her, and would I please stop? And I wrote back to him saying that my sources told me he was gay; and indeed I was acquainted with someone who'd been in his class at Yale, who maintained that they had slept together; and there were other stories from other people. I said that if he was prepared to deny these specific allegations I would stop making them. As far as his wife being 'hurt,' I didn't think there was anything so awful about homosexuality and I was tired of that particular argument.

I never got a reply.

—playwright/scenarist/activist **Larry Kramer**

It seems that Nathan Lane's new sitcom, *Encore! Encore!*, is in trouble. One of the biggest problems is said to be Lane, who critics found less than convincing as a womanizing former opera singer. That would be kind of like asking John Goodman to play the lead in *The Kate Moss Story*.

—columnist **Romeo San Vicente**

When I was 22, my father asked me why I was a lesbian, and I replied, 'Because I never met a man who wasn't a man.'

—**Norah Vincent**

If Tony Kushner is an out gay playwright, Martina Navratilova is an out gay tennis pro, David Geffen is an out gay billionaire, Melissa Etheridge is an out gay rocker, Rosie O'Donnell is, um, a daytime TV talk show host.

—columnist **Dan Savage**

I don't have any problems with my sexuality, whatever you wanna think I am. I'll never answer the question. I'd rather have you die wanting to know.

—singer **Dana "Queen Latifah" Owens**

Yes. I am in a relationship with someone (female) who's open privately and with probably three-fourths of the people around, but not totally. Do I like it? No. Do I respect it? Absolutely. I've been there, done that. I think to encourage change is fine, but the reality is that the person has to decide.

—tennis pro **Billie Jean King**, outed in 1981, when she denied it; openly gay by 1998 at age 55

Paul Bartel

I remember when I was 14, my father and I were in the car and somehow the subject of gay men came up. He said, 'I find that really disgusting, don't you?' A little bit of me died inside, but I said, 'Yeah, I really do. It's horrible.' Of course, I'd known since I was 10 that I was gay. But the idea of making openly gay films never occurred to me. You're lucky that you grew up in a much more liberal period in our history. You weren't poisoned by all those attitudes.

—**Paul Bartel**, in 1998, to fellow filmmaker Tommy O'Haver (*Billy's Hollywood Screen Kiss*)

I don't know for a fact—I didn't watch them. I just presumed as much. So did the cats (in the band). One told me he walked in on them one time. I never pressed the issue. It seemed like a given.

—**Mercer Ellington**, on whether father Duke Ellington ever had sex with longtime associate Billy Strayhorn (who was gay)

(Asked if she's had sex with females:) Yeah, I checked it out. You thought I'd say no, right? At the moment, I'm monogamous with my husband of five years, but one of the things he loves about me is that I find a lot of women really attractive. And I *don't* find as many men attractive.

My mother (literary agent Charlotte Sheedy) is gay, and she's been living with a woman for a long, long time. So when somebody says 'lesbian chic' to me, it's like, when did it become chic? I was growing up with it all the *time*.

—**Ally Sheedy**, in 1998, after she played a lesbian character

My main regret is that I was basically frozen out of coaching jobs because I'm gay. I couldn't even get an interview. The other regret is that Jerry Smith isn't here to go through this with me. If he had lived, he and I were going to do this together. I would have had someone to help me deal with Anita Bryant and all that bullshit as a gay athlete. But he took his secret with him to his grave.

—former football star **David Kopay** (Smith, a Redskins tight end, died of AIDS in 1986)

The irony was, I was playing (in the Broadway musical *Grand Hotel*) a man who was dying, and the star of the show, David Carroll, really was dying....I saw the bottle (of AZT in Carroll's hotel room) and just burst into tears. David made me vow not to tell a soul. And I didn't.

—Michael Jeter (*Designing Women, Evening Shade*)

I'm an intelligent man. I knew how to prevent (AIDS)...I was in a real depression (when he didn't have safe sex)....I can handle it. I can't feel bad about having it. I feel no ill will. I'm pretty sure who it was....I understand that fear of being shunned (the other man didn't disclose his HIV status). And if it was the person I think it was, I can't tell you it was an altogether unpleasant experience getting it.

—Michael Jeter, who admitted being HIV-positive

There is some evidence that (for a movie actor) being a fag isn't fatal. Okay, he's no Hugh Grant, but studly British actor Rupert Everett came out years ago, and he still gets roles as raging heterosexuals. He was the womanizing clothing executive in Robert Altman's *Ready To 'Wear* and the priapic Prince of Wales in *The Madness Of King George*. It didn't seem to bother Altman that on camera Everett's character is balling both his movie wife and another model while off screen he's probably making love to the handsome young man I see him working out with at my gym in Hollywood.

—author **Frank Sanello**

Ian McKellen always said I should come out. But why? I make my living playing heterosexuals.

—**Sir Nigel Hawthorne**, who came out anyway

It took me 49 years to be able to say to a stranger like you that I was gay.

—**Sir Ian McKellen**, the second openly gay actor to be nominated for the Best Actor Academy Award (after Hawthorne, as George III)

I think if people want their relationships to be more respected, they shouldn't hide them. I can see why actors do, but writers?…Truman Capote would tell the media about his closest enemies, the ladies he lunched with, the ladies he feuded with, but he said nearly nothing about his longtime better half (Jack Dunphy)...and Gore Vidal has to be encouraged to talk about Howard (Austen); even then he tries to make it sound like college roommates—two men sharing a room rather than a life together.

—screenwriter **Eleanor Perry**

When no girls were around, my best friend in high school and I would make out with each other as a last resort.

—**Robert Downey Jr.**, who finally came out as bi in 1999

Cantinflas

Oh, Rosie, like that's the first time you've seen my boobs!

—openly lesbian comic actress **Lea DeLaria**, on Rosie O'Donnell's talk show after the host exclaimed, "I saw your boobies in the play!"

I like homosexual men, they are usually very nice. But please not to get the wrong idea!

—Mexican comic superstar **Cantinflas**, to reporters; he was in fact gay, but never came out

If you live in northern Europe—Scandinavia, Holland—you can come out. If you live in England, the USA, a few other countries, you *might* come out. If you live in the Third World, you don't come out....It all depends on how socially advanced the country is.

—**Pedro Zamora**, *MTV's The Real World*

I think the toll that the closet takes on a performer shows in someone like George Michael, who I used to have a crush on. It's worn him down from the way he was with Wham!—scenic and perky—to how he is now: a cynic, and sort of quirky. And tired.

—soap actor **Keith Christopher**

The worst is probably when you're not even out to yourself...that inner struggle you hear about. Especially with people from fundamentalist backgrounds, where they'd rather believe religion than reality...where it's gotten all twisted, and instead of helping people, the religion becomes a hindrance, even a torture. When it's religion for religion's sake, it's become a cult...I lost a gay friend to suicide who belonged to a cult.

—**Colleen Dewhurst**

If you're raised in a very uneducated or very religious household, which is often the same thing, chances are you grow up with a very negative attitude toward same-sexuality—heaven help you. Or rather, heaven helps those who help themselves.

—soap star **Joel Crothers**

Some gays say they didn't know, for the longest time, because they're not stereotypically gay. Fine. Many or most gays aren't. But someone who says, 'I never really knew I was gay till I was 30,' or 40 or more, they're lying. Because everybody masturbates, and when you do, you're thinking of someone—so which gender?—or some body part. You know by the gender you fantasize about—no matter what kind of sex you're actually having—who and what you're attracted to.

—**Robert LaTourneaux** (*The Boys In The Band*)

I think my first awareness of homosexuality was when the tackle and the guard on the football team broke down a bed in the dormitory. I was 15 then, so I never had the stereotype.

—**Andrew Young**

I don't know what pisses me off more: the belief that a gay man can't play a straight lover convincingly or that a gay guy is too limp-wristed to operate a machine-gun in an action film. That's the implicit message of the reigning taboo: If you want to kiss Sharon Stone on-screen or blow up a block of downtown Los Angeles for (producer) Joel Silver, stay in the closet.

—gay author **Frank Sanello**

(Author) Jack (Kerouac) felt there was nothing homosexual about being the blowee, only the blower...the distinction was important to Kerouac, who managed to convince himself that he could dig deeply and regularly into homoeroticism and still be a part of society's heterosexual tyranny. The price for living so dishonestly? Ever-increasing amounts of alcohol and drugs.

—Kerouac's final editor and his biographer, **Ellis Amburn**

My father was bisexual...(and) spent an incredible amount of energy creating this totally masculine, martini-mixing, dog-breeding, duck-hunting father of three—the beautiful wife, the whole American masculine patrician dream. Then he got to a point in his life where he realized that it was pointless. Why cover it up? He was who he was.

—**Susan Cheever**, re her writer father, in her memoir *Home Before Dark*

My stepmother had a wonderful line. 'Oh,' she said. 'Thank goodness! I thought you were going to tell me something really dreadful. I've known that for about 35 years.' That's the best thing about coming out: I've discovered that I've got a wonderful old lady who loves me unconditionally.

—**Sir Ian McKellen**

(They) touched, and groped, and tried to achieve orgasm.

—**Anne Heche** (*Volcano*, *Psycho*), in 1998 before a film festival audience, revealing that her anti-gay, fundamentalist mother, who had cut relations with her, had once had a 20-minute homosexual experience

Nathan Lane, who officially stopped being gay when he hit it big in movies and then got his own TV series, is now getting verbal support from establishment-type gays who just don't get it. They say gays dislike that Lane's now playing straights. No, no, no! An actor is entitled to play everyone. But not to go back in the closet the moment he thinks he can be nationally rich and famous by turning his back on the truth, on his true self and on everyone like him. He says only 'angry queens' criticize him. But who's taking the valid criticism like an angry queen?

—actor **Mart Dayne McChesney**

Roddy McDowall

Before I heard it, I knew Roddy McDowall was gay. Duh! But as an actor, I kept hearing that McDowall was also completely closeted, and I never could figure out why. It seemed so needless, but I guess he carried a lot of shame with him....Since he died, I read of people describing him as the Keeper of the Secrets. As if that were something noble! And perhaps he never outed anyone else, okay, but he never outed himself either. He hid the truth...he was like a frontman for Hollywood's homophobia.

—**Mart Dayne McChesney**
(McDowall's diaries are not to be made public until the year 2100 C.E.)

Roddy (McDowall) may have become a U.S. citizen, but in his heart I think he was still an old British queen....He was known as Hollywood's biggest gossip, but with a difference. He collected it, but he didn't like to share it....He puts me in mind of that saying, I think from Benjamin Franklin, that three people can successfully keep a secret if two of them are dead.

—Dublin columnist **Larry Fitzpatrick**

Risk! Risk anything! Care no more for the opinion of others, for those voices. Do the hardest thing on earth for you. Act for yourself. Face the truth.

—New Zealand-born author **Katherine Mansfield**, giving timeless advice (1888-1923)

Truth and freedom are attitudes of the spirit.

—**Truman Capote**

I'm not ashamed of thinking or saying I'm bisexual. I think it's good, or commendable, to explore that aspect...which most people don't. Who does it harm? No one, just society's biased, one-sided rules....I came out in a lesbian magazine, a very public place, because that way I could control the information, and it wasn't a dirty little secret discovered against my will.

—former TV actress **Dana Plato** (*Diff'rent Strokes*) in 1998

Ironically, closeted stars think they maintain their dignity in there...and then a George Michael gets arrested in a toilet, because that's where this closeted superstar goes to meet partners. Some dignity. Some lifestyle! The closet stinks.

—organist **James Holmes** (life partner of openly gay composer Ned Rorem)

People wall off part of their life because there's stigma or shame attached to it. And the price is higher for gays. People can admit having affairs and illegitimate kids or drinking problems, but being gay is still a problem for many Americans.

—**Betty Berzon**, psychotherapist and author of *Setting Them Straight: You Can Do Something About Bigotry and Homophobia In Your Life*

An article about me that was in the *New York Times* was reprinted in my hometown newspaper in Paris, Tennessee. (It) described my personal life, (so) the hometown press received quite a few letters. Some of which read 'Glad for Cherry's success, not her lifestyle....,' along with various biblical quotes and the call for 'the need for Cherry to change.' My family decided to just lay low and let the local community deal with the controversy. As the debate went back and forth in the local paper, I was so glad when one of the final letters read 'Leave Cherry alone, get a life!'

—openly lesbian Tony-winning Broadway star **Cherry Jones**

If my being open(ly gay) is upsetting to a whole bunch of bigots, tough! It would be more than upsetting to me to live a life of hiding and lies...and if enough of us came out, then they'd just have to get over it. Like it or not.... A lot of people are still racist, but they don't say so in public—they know that the majority attitude and the laws no longer support their racism. So *we* have to get to that point where they can like it or lump it....Of course, it's easier in that way for, say, blacks—they don't need to come out as black. They don't need to say the words or decide to say them. Just saying it—'I'm gay'—is intimidating. We have made it intimidating. But it's also very necessary.

—novelist **David Feinberg**

I'm not sure which is more morally heinous, but I think it's not so much staying in the closet yourself as it is closeting other people. I mean, for a gay individual to do so....It's done often in the history books and in literary appreciation, so-called. But one also finds several self-hating, usually but not always older homosexual authors who even closet departed Hollywood figures. So needlessly. I've heard it called the Lamparski syndrome, but there are in fact these authors and co-authors who feel that describing somebody who was homosexual as, well, homosexual, is a sort of 'accusation.' It's amazing to me.

—**Paul Schmidt**, uncloseted poet and translator of Rimbaud and Chekhov

It's so simple to retract a not exactly heterosexual image. Look at (basketball player and actor) Dennis Rodman. Some said he was moving toward coming out...gay or bi. Then he marries this *Baywatch* actress, and much of the mainstream is relieved, while much of it says, 'You see, he was only fooling....'

—**Paul Schmidt**

One thing that, say, *People* or *TV Guide* will do is to label a lesbian mother as a single mom. That'll give the connotation that she's *sans* husband or beau, but not necessarily by choice....Then, usually, they won't say that her child or kids are adopted, and thus the assumption is she had sex with a man....Now, with Paula Poundstone, I read she has two adopted girls and a foster son—what the distinction is, I don't know. And that much detail is unusual, because mainstream publications tend to supply minimal information and maximum connotation and/or coverup.

—Sydney columnist **Shirley Vior**

There's this actor, former movie star. His sister's now a superstar. When he hit L.A., he used to go to gay bars. Soon learned that was a no-no...eventually got a wife. Does not treat her well, but...now he shows up at interviews, closeted as anything, and always brings the wife. Most interviews will refer to 'his wife and business partner.' Most of the interviewers know she's really his cover.

—**Mart Dayne McChesney**, soap actor and activist

Helmut Berger

...but happiness can't buy money.

—uncloseted Austrian actor **Helmut Berger**'s way of stating why Hollywood stars don't come out

Ellen (DeGeneres) came out, and then there was a backlash against her, even some non-supportive queers like Elton John and Chastity Bono, and then her series got canceled. Which again proves that in Hollywood no good deed goes unpunished.

—columnist **Shirley Vior**

They can say what they want. This is me. I can't retract it. It's who I am, and it is part of my life. There is nothing to hide or retract.

—new French tennis sensation **Amelie Mauresmo**, 19, in 1999; after competitor Lindsay Davenport said it was "like playing a guy" and competitor Martina Hingis called her "half a man"

There was a rumor that I used to be male and had a sex change. That's not a bad rumor.

—singer **Annie Lennox**

When Billie Jean King, who had a husband, was outed via a palimony lawsuit by her girlfriend, she denied....Merv Griffin was sued by an alleged ex-lover, and he denied it....Look to youth for honesty. The latest example is (two-time Olympic silver medalist) ice skater Brian Orser. This young Canadian was sued for palimony. Against his will, the details were made public, in Ontario. Not pleasant, but he stood by the reality. Now he is openly gay, and says the public has stood by him to a wonderful extent.

—Toronto columnist **Tony Beeman**

I'm out now. That's what matters.

—**Brian Orser**, in 1999

I'm a gay man, I'm an athlete, a Canadian, I'm several things. Some successful performers in the USA deny being Canadian, and some people do deny being gay. I don't see a need for that. I was honest as an athlete, and I wanted to follow that by being honest as an actor and an individual.

—Olympic gold-medal-winning swimmer **Mark Tewksbury**, in 1999; he went national about being gay after a financial group dropped his six-figure contract as spokesman because he was "too openly gay;" Tewksbury thereafter appeared in a one-man show titled *Out And About*

(Asked what would occur if a major athlete came out:) It takes only one person to break down the barrier. If a major star were to finally come out at the height of his career, it would revolutionize America. It would mean a society with a lot less hatred, a lot less bigotry. He would be under tremendous pressure. But pros are used to performing under pressure anyway.

It would be tough, but the player, if he were the right person, would survive. I've heard some great stories about professional hockey players. Maybe it will happen there, in a sport that's just a little more liberal. It's going to happen. It might take another 50 years, but it's going to happen.

—former football star **Dave Kopay**, in 1998

I think the media enjoys the thrill and the power...they'll sometimes dare themselves to ask about somebody gay or lesbian, in print, Is X Gay? Could it possibly be? And ahead of time they know X is going to say no, he or she is not gay, and they—the media—are going to help continue the coverup. It's an appalling game, because it's all so deliberate.

—heterosexual author **James Michener**, who went on record as being pro gays in the military

You know, this (closeting) isn't so new. It's not a new phenomenon, not even among actors and writers....Bram Stoker, who wrote 'Dracula,' was absolutely devoted to an actor (Henry Irving). The biographers write it up as a strong friendship, but let's face it, the man had at least a major, adult, long-lasting crush on his idol. But he also had a wife and so on, and the widow saw 'Dracula' and its play versions as a moneymaker, and she kept him more closeted in his death than he'd been in his lifetime. It does remind me of the situation now with Cary Grant.

—**Raymond Huntley** (1902-1990), the first actor to play Dracula on stage (the novel was published in 1897)

I was offered the role of Dracula in the American play (in 1928), and I wanted more money than they cared to pay. I'd had quite a success (as Dracula) all over Britain...so they hired a Hungarian for less...Bela Lugosi....Yes, I heard that Lugosi used to use quite homophobic terms when referring to Boris Karloff (who became a star when Lugosi declined the title role in *Frankenstein*). Karloff was also English, so I'm not sure if Lugosi was anglophobic or knew more about Karloff's life than most of us....Karloff did seem almost asexual, in point of fact, but he'd struggled to attain his belated stardom, so whatever his inclinations were, he kept them under wraps. Or as they now say, 'in the closet.'

—**Raymond Huntley** (*Room At The Top*, *Young Winston*)

People didn't examine celebrities' private lives like now. Do they have kids? Did he leave her for a younger, prettier girl?—ah, then he's straight....Only the sex symbols, the leading men, got that kind of scrutiny...and male comics, comedic actors, were ignored. Off the big or little screen....I don't doubt that Lucy's (*The Lucy*

Show) wonderful sidekick, Gale Gordon, was a charming but extremely closeted man—very private, and nothing like his cantankerous image. People who knew him will often confirm it without meaning to, but no one comes out—pardon the expression—and says, Yes, he was gay.

People wouldn't feel comfortable saying that...he was too old, he was married for so long....They're more comfortable saying it about a young guy. Besides, with an older man, it makes him out like he was a lifelong liar, which isn't nice.

—movie writer **David Shipman**

Is Ricky Martin Gay?

—1999 *Globe* **headline**

I don't think anyone much likes to out women. You know? As if it's ungentlemanly or as if it's really putting her down...saying she's unfeminine. The irony is that if she's rather butch, like Martina Navratilova or some of the female comediennes (sic), then they might point her out (as gay), but if she's feminine and good-looking, they hesitate because just to say she's a lesbian, a dyke, etc., is to declare that she's unfeminine—no matter how feminine she is!

—director **Emile Ardolino** (*Sister Act*)

If a man is outed, you usually figure, 'Well, he can take care of himself.' If a girl is outed, it's like, How dare they say that? —are they sure?

—stage producer/director and character actor **William Frankfather** (*Foul Play*, *Death Becomes Her*)

This in or out business is really Nathan Lane's business...I think if this new series (*Encore! Encore!*) flies, then there'll be more of the same (not coming out). But if it flops, then he may well up and decide to come out.

—William Frankfather (*Mouse Hunt*, starring Nathan Lane)

In my opinion, the closet magnets are two: materialism, because it's a shocking fact that if you come out you are for all practical purposes blacklisted, at the very least graylisted; and our Judeo-Christian anti-sex heritage that especially stigmatizes non-procreational sex...they spend their time tyrannizing people's senses instead of enhancing their souls and capacity to explore and to love and accept...so that even younger people, who are normally more daring, hesitate to say they're gay in the same way that they might say they're left-handed or circumcised or, on the negative side, dyslexic or trying to quit smoking.

Our culture sees to it that most people operate out of fear.

—**Clifford Gallo**, *L.A. Reader* theatre editor

I felt forced to talk about my sexuality and, you know, my queerness, just because...uh...I felt like I was being looked on as a coward for not talking about it. And I...I...I abhor that, you know. If anything, I felt like...a...I thought it was dead obvious to everyone all along, you know. I was wearing skirts and mascara in 1981...um...onstage and in photo shoots.

—R.E.M. frontman **Michael Stipe**, in 1998

I can understand the reticence...if you're young, you have the guts to come out but you fear cutting off career opportunities. You tend to wait. And when you're not young, and you've fulfilled most of the opportunities that have come your way, you have less guts and you also feel maybe you've waited too long to come out....I feel lucky as a non-performer; it's much easier for us—those of us, that is, with a healthy degree of self-esteem. Because the insecure *always* have an excuse or two or twenty to remain in the closet.

—director **Norman Rene** (*The Lost Language Of Cranes*)

It's rather ridiculous how some extremely desperate, ultra-right factions are trying to say Hillary Rodham Clinton is gay, which is what that ilk say when a woman is strong and not defined and limited by her husband....You can turn around and far more truthfully say that the other most active First Lady, Eleanor Roosevelt, was gay—was a lesbian, though a wife and a good mother. But no one wants to admit that, oh, no. Because she's admired and by now she's part of history....I have to conclude that conservative heterosexuals don't much care for facts. If they dislike you, you're queer; if they like you, you're straight forever, and facts be damned.

—English professor **Walter Kendrick**,
Fordham University

There are these novels, supposedly written by Elliott Roosevelt (son of FDR and Eleanor), featuring his mother as a kind of American Miss Marple—an amateur sleuth. A whole series....He died (in 1990) but is said to have, conveniently, left behind a whole slew of novels starring Eleanor Roosevelt!...Anyway, as a commercial enterprise, that kind of publishing is going to be far less apt to admit the truth of Mrs. Roosevelt's sexual orientation —for fear of losing elderly mainstream readers and *money*....Truth is typically less profitable than fiction.

—talk show host **Connie Norman**

There's that nearly illiterate Italian actress whose book got its major publicity boost from her claim of an affair with Cary Grant. He flirted—he did not bed her. She gives the impression it was love *and* sex....The murder mystery novels by that prosecutor in the O.J. Simpson case, which I doubt he could have written alone. But then, publishers often supply a ghost writer *and* a plot when a *name*, if not a name author, is thought to be able to sell a book big-time.

Celebrities purportedly writing novels—yeah, sure, all by themselves....Or novels by sons-of...like the Eleanor Roosevelt collection by one of her sons...and I read, though it may or may not be true, that the series of White House murder mysteries by Margaret Truman (daughter of Pres. Harry S. Truman) are sometimes delivered to her complete (in manuscript form), and that, allegedly, that's the first time she sees any such novel, before her name goes on it....All I know is, when money talks, truth often flies out the window.

—novelist **Brian Moore** (*The Lonely Passion of Judith Hearne*)

If you're looking to learn about the real lives of the celebrities profiled in these one-hour programs on A&E or Bravo, the E! channel, and those other cable channels, forget it. They do well enough by straight subjects, but with anybody lesbian, gay or bisexual, it's cover-up, cover-up, cover-up...the few times they allow that someone wasn't straight, it's invariably in negative or stereotypical terms...most of that, it's just TV by bigots and for bigots.

—**Ed Joe Shown**, openly gay founder of Atlanta's leading entertainment magazine, *Off P'tree*

Well, Robert Osborne, of all people, should know better. Whether or not everything he reads about the movies he introduces is prescripted. He's a, uh, confirmed bachelor, a long-longtime columnist for the *Hollywood Reporter*. He *knows* William Haines (silent-screen movie star) was gay, and he *knows* Haines did not, as Osborne told the nation, 'walk away' from his movie career. He was blacklisted, boycotted, for being gay and caught (with another man in his bed at the Y)....People like Osborne only help closet Hollywood's gay actors and to pretend that there was no homophobia in Hollywood's history. It's shameful.

—**Ed Joe Shown**, on the host of Turner Classic Movies, a cable-TV channel

It was disappointing to see Steve Kmetko, the anchor for E! Entertainment, asking Rosie O'Donnell what kind of actor she'd like to do a 'love scene' with. All I can say is, they're both good actors. But not good role models for gay youth.

—**Richard Rouilard**, *Advocate* magazine editor, mid-1990s

I was interviewing Susan Sarandon for *Stepmom* (on E!)...and I'm a sucker for tearjerkers, and she said, 'Chicks dig that, if you can let a woman see that....' So I said, 'But I'm gay,' then she said, 'Oh, well, chicks like that too.' So we went on with (the interview) and it aired. I couldn't sit there and let her tell me how chicks, to use her word, would like me more, etc., because in reality I don't date, uh, chicks. I couldn't be false in that way.

—*E! News Daily* co-anchor **Steve Kmetko**, in 1999

I hope so. We'll find out if I ever get another job.

—**Steve Kmetko**, asked if there'll be a time when coming out in broadcasting will ever "be easy?"

Years ago, I was supposed to be promoted to the primary anchor position in Grand Rapids, Michigan, and the general manager got wind of the fact that I'm gay and called me up to his office. I answered every one of his questions honestly. At the end of the conversation, he said, 'You might as well start looking for a new job because you're not going any further here.' And that was a jolt and, I thought, a good reason to be closeted.

—**Steve Kmetko**, 46

Discrimination against gays and lesbians is still legal in at least four-fifths of these United States. In those states, we must become more litigious. We must challenge these discriminatory laws. We must protect our interests...no one else will. We must vote in and make accountable pro-gay politicians, and vote out homophobic ones....We must end our complacency and our hiding, else we'll always be the scapegoats, the throwaways and the legitimate targets.

—**Jeffrey Lettow**, entertainment editor of Northern California's *Marin Independent Journal*, in 1998

The Defense Department's 'don't ask, don't tell' military policy...acknowledged the existence of gay people in the armed services and then instituted an official method of closeting them...(a supposedly) kinder, gentler version of the closet.

—author **Michael Bronski** (*Culture Clash*)

Wish that there were closets, in more virulently homophobic times, for those men and women unable to 'pass.' The masculine female and the feminine male, though not always homosexual, is one of nature's myriad phenomena, but has been propagandized by most human cultures into a symbol of evil—a reassurance to the average majority....For a variety of reasons, including suicide, 'obvious' members of the sexual minority like Ronald Firbank have tended to live shorter and/or tortured lives...tortured by themselves and by the societies that refused to tolerate or integrate them.

—**Brigid Brophy**, who biographed novelist Firbank and artist Aubrey Beardsley, both short-lived

Outing is an inevitable and even necessary new reality born of a desire to overthrow oppression. It is aimed at oppressors, not at victims. For, there are gay victims—most gays—and there are gay—usually secretly so—oppressors....Outing expanded from political and religious oppressors to anybody rich, famous or culturally influential...outing those who join, as it were, the bigger, richer club by pretending to be like the rest and by continuing the oppression of most of their own kind.

—*Advocate* publisher **David B. Goodstein**

Did This Man Ruin 2,000 Lives, Know About the Suicides, Waste Taxpayers' Millions on Military Witchhunts?

—***Advocate*** cover headline outing Pete Williams, a gay man (who later admitted it) hypocritically employed by the Pentagon

Like niece, like uncle. Grace Kelly was a semi-Anita Bryant, anti-gay though secretly alcoholic, distressed that her only son (Prince Albert of Monaco) never married (and still hasn't)...and her uncle, George Kelly, was a never-wed, ultra-conservative gay playwright....He wrote about unpleasant women, had none of Tennessee Williams' insight into and compassion for women. An unpleasant, me-first character...a social-climber, like his entire clan. Needless to say, (George) Kelly was entirely and paranoiacally in the closet.

—Brigid Brophy

I couldn't believe it when The Princess Grace Foundation sponsored a collection of three plays by George Kelly (in 1999)...the bio and other new material was written by some retired professor who dismissed as 'speculation' any and all evidence that Kelly was a homosexual man...describes him as having 'monastic' tendencies....With these biased and determinedly closeting groups and individuals, all that's changed nowadays is that they can't ignore The Question. So they reluctantly, briefly bring it up, only to ignore the facts and recreate these late gay achievers in their own, straight image.

—Monaco-based book reviewer **Delphine Rosay**

Well, in Germany—West Germany, as it used to be—(director) Wolfgang Petersen was known as openly gay...he did movies on that theme, as well as box office fare....By Hollywood, he got married and now does only the big box office stuff....But what surprised me was that after the *Advocate* described him as a gay producer/director, he took exception to it. And what also surprised me was when that particular magazine gave in and ran an *apology*. For saying he was gay! Even if they didn't say he's straight....Sell-out, sell-out. So sorry.

—*Marin Independent Journal* entertainment editor **Jeffrey Lettow**

Okay, the *Advocate* wants to get celebrities for covers, for interviews. But sometimes this crosses the purposes of good journalism. They won't pin down celebrity interviewees on their bisexuality or their gay relatives or their own, perhaps, past homophobia....Most recently, there was an *Advocate* list of ten, I believe, 'straights we admire.' I literally gasped when I read it, because at least three of them were either bi or in-the-closet gays or lesbians! Is this what the big focus on celebrity journalism has brought us to? Openly gay, pro-gay periodicals in the business of closeting Hollywood gays?

—Jeffrey Lettow

A lot of people say I'm bent....Girls run after me a lot, and it doesn't upset me....I couldn't stand to be thought to be a big, butch lady. But I know I'm perfectly as capable of being swayed by a girl as by a boy. More and more people feel that way, and I don't see why I shouldn't....Being a pop star, I shouldn't even admit that I might think that way.

—**Dusty Springfield**, in 1970, in Britain

Dusty came out as bisexual, and she made some contradictory statements, but it was still very brave of her, at the time. Elton (John) only came out as bi, before revealing he was gay....As she got older and less popular, I think Dusty became more cautious. So she never came out all the way...I think part of that is the way women age, becoming a little heavier, a little deeper-voiced, less feminine. Dusty never wanted to be thought of as butch or unattractive; she sort of froze in her tracks, even after so many younger (female) singers did come out, even as out-and-out lesbians.

—UK actor-producer **Derek Nimmo**

Although several of her female lovers talked to us for this article, only one allowed herself to be named....They feel it's important now that she be remembered fully, as the woman she was and not just the woman we saw.

—**disclaimer** re the *Advocate*'s Dusty Springfield tribute article (April 27, 1999)

Yeah, well, I'm probably going to destroy any mystique I've managed to build up on that subject (seeming heterosexual). Well, if it's out, it's out.

—author **Bret Easton Ellis**, coming out in 1998, in a British newspaper

I remember back in the late '80s, Barbara Howar was a big-time, rather cynical journalist, and she said how the advent of celebrity journalism meant that the media was less loath to reveal what she termed 'the sexual predilections of a Michael Jackson or a Whitney Houston.' And I thought, true. To a degree—to titillate, but not to widen the truth or not uphold the status quo.

Because they're so ready, so happy, to retract anything of that nature the moment a Michael or a Whitney or a Prince Edward gets legally married.

—critic/columnist **Delphine Rosay**

Some men want to have children, some don't, and some don't but do anyway. The problem is that everyone thinks a male-female relationship counts for more than a two-male one, once it's officialized by marriage. And if you want to have children, it's almost a necessity, to get married...it's all rather lop-sided. It isn't meant to be fair, but most people never give it a second thought. Let alone the inequality when it's a two-male couple *or* a male-female couple that doesn't want to have kids. If it were fair, the straight couple with kids would count for more, in official and legal terms, than the straights with no kids. And yet that would be unfair too.

The government ought simply not to get involved in people's relationships and private lives. Because they always want to rate everything 1-2-3....

—bisexual actor **Christopher Gable** (*The Boyfriend*)

To encourage babies and more babies, still, is crazy. In such an overpopulated world, it is crazy! I would have imagined the most overpopulated countries, like India and China, would encourage their homosexuals...that even the less crowded countries, as in Europe and North America, would encourage their people who are 'gay' to come out of their closets and let them live how they are meant to live. It would mean that at least ten percent of a nation could be counted on not to breed overpopulation....It has not happened because still the Stone Age ideas and habits, they die very slowly.

—French director **Jacques Demy** (*The Umbrellas Of Cherbourg*)

It's queer. Or funny, I mean. One reason some people feel Cary Grant must have been straight was all his (five) marriages.

They'll think if he married that often, he had to be straight. Never mind that he was an actor, in show business. They don't figure that if he married that often, he was trying that hard to seem or even become straight. It also indicates he never fell deeply or lastingly in love with any of them...try logic: would Grant's marriages mean he was that much more of a heterosexual than, say, James Stewart? 'Cause Stewart really was straight, and he married once—real thing, for keeps.

—producer **Ben Bagley**

Yeah, this proliferation of biographical TV portraits of famous people, it's an industry now...you can go into bookstores and buy videos from the A&E *Biography* series....They'll compete with each other for 'inside' scoops or photos never before seen or some official endorsement, which means the relatives...like with a Cary Grant *Biography* which boasted that it had exclusive family photos. But they didn't acknowledge how that meant in return for the widow's or daughter's cooperation, the whole gay angle is never brought up. And if a biography, of any kind, isn't factual and impartial, then you know what it's called? A hagiography. Like with the saints—mostly myth and image. Hagiography—it's in the dictionary. Under H, not F....

—**Steve Smith**, award-winning broadcaster and president of the Gay Men's Chorus of Los Angeles

In terms of looks, charm and mid-Atlantic appeal, Rupert Everett is a latter-day Cary Grant. Women desire him and men envy him. Plus he's honest about his sexuality....The (print) ad for his latest movie has him grinning sexily in a tuxedo while three women surround and coo over him. So who says you can't have an openly gay romantic leading man? Though I know *An Ideal Husband* is upscale fare for a smaller, more discerning crowd than goes to see the movies of, for instance, Bruce Willis or Sly Stallone or, uh, Tom Cruise and John Travolta.

—UK reviewer **Ken Ferguson**

One of those establishmentarian columnists in the *Advocate* wrote that it's selfish of gays to *claim* Nathan Lane, whatever that signifies, and that we should *allow* him to play non-gay roles! What a dork! Anyone knows actors play all sorts of roles; Lane's one of the few who's mostly played gay roles. Who could object to anything he plays? The difference between him and Rupert Everett, who plays mostly non-gay roles, is that when he's done acting, he doesn't try to hide behind the roles. As himself, Everett is out, and we respect his guts and integrity.

—actor **Mart Dayne McChesney**

Today if you're gay in Hollywood, you can say you're gay and get on with your job, if you're a producer or director or writer or manager or agent. But if you're an actor, then suddenly all those people—straight or gay—think there's a problem. This is being worked out in front of our eyes—Anne Heche stands as a fascinating historical figure. So far she's giving the lie to all those people who have told young actors who play romantic leads, 'Don't come out, the public won't accept it.'

—Sir Ian McKellen

I'm a lesbian who is a writer. This is the question I always get asked (by the mainstream press), and they ask it because they want me to say I'm literary, not lesbian.

—author **Dorothy Allison**

For reasons unique to herself—or not so unique—Liz Smith told the world in her column that she objected to Harvey Fierstein thanking his lover at the Tony Awards. She said she found 'lover' a less than dignified word, but I suspect no matter what word he might have used, Smith would find it more comfortable all around if everybody stayed in his or her closet. On which I will not, because I cannot, comment further.

—author **Vito Russo**

If Middle America only knew: Grandpa Walton was gay!

—columnist **Boyd McDonald**, on actor Will Geer, who was a lover of gay rights pioneer Harry Hay, before marrying a woman and becoming a father

Who would believe it, but truth is stranger, and queerer, than fiction...Grandma Walton (Ellen Corby) was also gay! The Walton family, like every family, had at least, and in this case at least two, non-straight loved ones in the bunch....Unlike Will Geer, who died in 1978, Corby left behind a loved one of the same sex, a companion of about 40 years duration.

—**obituary** in *Gay News Quarterly*, 1999

Harry Hay

I had him first.

—**Harry Hay**, to Will Geer's widow Herta

I had him longest.

—**Herta Geer**, to Harry Hay

Ellen Corby and her friend (sic) donated a sizable collection of plays to our branch, in Miss Corby's name. But she would also, from time to time discreetly urge us to be sure and keep buying new books with gay and lesbian subject matter. Especially lesbian-interest books, for the young ones, she said.

—**anonymous librarian**, at the West Hollywood public library (Corby began as a script-girl, and was an occasional scriptwriter for *The Waltons*)

Does anyone imagine the widow of Theodore Geisel or the publishers of Dr. Seuss are going to fess up that the man behind Dr. Seuss was gay? The man behind so many delightful, unique and self-affirming children's books?...And the fact that he had no kids of his own, that's so easily passed off by saying he loved all kids and that his books were his children...and at least his books supported him in better style than any real kids would have done.

—Broadway producer **Ben Bagley**

If (ballet dancers) want to, do you say (sic), come out, why not? They should be able. Such men are athletes, but also artists...strong and refined. They shouldn't care what more ignorant men think.

—ballet star **Rudolf Nureyev**, who never came out himself

What would it have hurt, really? He was older, campy, he starred in horror movies, for heaven's sake! If he had love scenes, they'd be with ghouls or corpses, vampiresses, I don't know....But the whole backstory of Vincent Price's pre-horror career, and his upbringing, his becoming a star late in his life,...all that mitigated against his ever coming out.

—**William Edward Daniel Ross**, gothic novelist (358 books, most via female pseudonyms) and former actor and acting company manager

There are levels of outing—and remember, outing is not about saying somebody straight is gay. Nor outing anyone who has no power and isn't misusing it. It's more like a secretly gay boss who discriminates and won't hire gay people—*that* person should be outed. Outing is against hypocrisy and misuse of power. It's most immediately effective against closeted, bigoted political and religious, also business, leaders. And *then* celebrities, whose images work directly or indirectly for a hetero monopoly.

The irony of outing is that it's not so urgent to out people who've never (heterosexually) married, like (Lily) Tomlin, (Stephen) Sondheim, etc....Some have feigned straight romances—with willing gays or straights—such as Jodie Foster. With most of these two types, any person who's not newt-brained can probably figure out the real story....It's the ones who marry the opposite sex and have kids, the deep-closet cases, who most need to be outed, yet they're the most protected ones; their marital and especially parental camouflage makes them less vulnerable than their more honest, less extreme counterparts who by comparison are semi-out.

—**Richard Rouilard**, former *Advocate* editor

Every gay man and lesbian woman who 'passes,' and tries to, oppresses me further and reaps the benefits of my activism while hiding the strength of our numbers from the people to whom those numbers would make a difference....Is it ethical to stay in the closet, pass for straight, assume the mantle of heterosexual privilege and enjoy its benefits while those who are openly gay suffer the oppression of their minority status?

—**Victoria Brownworth,** lesbian writer

...another reason homosexuals' so-called rights don't really matter—there's hardly any of them. It's a tiny, small group of very loud, angry people, not even a minority, even.

—loud, angry and homophobic "comic" **Sam Kinison**, who deliberately undercounted the gay population, and by whose logic whites should have more rights than non-whites, Christians more rights than Jews, and women —a statistical majority—more rights than men....

Lily Tomlin is openly feminist, anyway.

—**Brad Davis** (*Midnight Express*), who never came out as gay or bi

Look, I'll even say this on the record and have her come after me. Lily Tomlin has never officially come out and said 'I'm a lesbian.' Now I think there's a huge irony here. All the decision-makers in town know that Lily Tomlin's a lesbian. She's well established in the gay and lesbian community, yet she won't go out on a stage or before a camera and say four simple words: 'I am a lesbian.' And...as long as teenage kids are committing suicide, and as long as they're trying to deny us our rights, I think we have a certain obligation to use what we have to change things.

I think it's silly that at the Gay & Lesbian Community Center's 23-year anniversary she said, 'We've been gay and lesbian 20 years,' and then the next week we hear her publicist backtracking, '"*We*" meaning the crowd there—she didn't necessarily mean herself.' I just think you lose a measure of respect....Lily's a handy example of someone whose career is not going to be hurt by her saying that she's a lesbian. I don't see huge commercial endorsements out there that would be coming her way for not saying so.

—openly gay public relations executive **Howard Bragman**, chair and founder of Bragman, Nyman Cafarelli, Inc., in 1998

It really is an age thing.... It's also about desperation. The black actress who didn't used to care if people thought she was bi or butch. Now she always pushes her image as a lusty straight.... And the movie actor outed in that straight men's magazine who's decided he doesn't want any more people thinking he's gay. Now he says he wants marriage and love—the kind that can boost his career, he thinks. And he's straight, he's really straight, *so* straight, yeah. Just ask any of his boyfriends. Or are they all mute?

—London columnist **Hedda Lettice**, in late 1999

There are very few young actors who are out in movies. For that reason, I think Anne Heche's coming out is more significant than Ellen's. Ellen can always go to clubs or out on the concert stage on her own and earn a living, but Anne Heche always has to be employed in film.

—Sir Ian McKellen

All she said to Ellen was 'I like the show.' Of course she *hated* the show. It brings her one step closer to the day when she'll have to deal with her own problems.

—Sir Ian McKellen, on talk show host Rosie O'Donnell

The elders of the community used to say to me, 'You don't need to be so in people's faces, Howard.' And my answer was, 'Yes, I do.' I was a suicidal teenager....And I do need to be in their face. I'm sorry. I don't see anybody hiding their religion in this town. I don't see people hiding their weddings in this town. And I'll be goddamned if I'm going to be a partner to people hiding their (sexual orientation) in this town. It's not that big a deal, and the bigger deal everybody makes about it makes it a dirty little secret.

—Howard Bragman

When *My Mother, My Father And Me* was about to try out in Boston, a reporter wrote that it was having directing problems, that the director had been fired and that (playwright Lillian) Hellman was directing the play herself. Hellman phoned the paper in a rage. Without denying the story, she demanded a retraction. The writer said that if the story was true, he would not retract it. Hellman said she would see that he did.

Over the following weekend the newspaperman went to New York and visited a number of gay bars. On Monday Hellman phoned and said if he didn't print the retraction she would tell his boss where he had been the past weekend. Because the writer was open about his homosexuality, Hellman's (early 1960s) blackmail attempt fell flat.

—Hellman biographer **William Wright** (*Lillian Hellman*)

(On his coming out:) They were extremely supportive. In one second my mom went from having a tear in her eye to pinning up a picture of my boyfriend on her wall.

—Howie Klein, president of Reprise Records

I was in awe of my daughter's achievement and talent in becoming a star. And I am in awe of her achievement and courage in coming out.

—Betty DeGeneres
mother/activist/author

I felt from day one Ellen DeGeneres should have done this (come out), because I think it's a more interesting character and makes for a much funnier sitcom.

—Tim Allen

My closeted actor friends whom I've urged to come out are not so much worried that their careers will come to a full stop, because they see that hasn't happened to me. But they think, 'My God, am I going to have to talk about it as much as *he* does?' Of course not. I just happen to be a sort of bigmouth who's interested in politics and is persuaded that I can be of help. But I can assure you, I spend more time worrying about my career than I do worrying about gay activism.

—**Sir Ian McKellen**

To have a feeling that you've been (professionally) limited by who you are, as if they know anything about you or what your potential is, has always been very disturbing to me....People are complicated and capable of many, many things. All you know is that I'm gay. Or all you know is that I'm straight. You really don't know anything about me.

—openly gay TV (*Thirtysomething*), film and stage actor **David Marshall Grant**

I remember when Anthony Sher came out. He was asked by the *Times of London*, What about a film career?—which he was just beginning to have. He said, 'Look, if people don't want to work with me because I'm gay, I certainly don't want to work with them.' And that's what I feel. I don't want to work with second-rate people. In the hope of becoming very rich, I don't want to have to lie. I know English actors like Miriam Margolyes who are out at home, in London. She said to me, 'You understand that in Hollywood I'm not a dyke.' So what does her girlfriend think about that?

—**Sir Ian McKellen**

I'm 41, and my friends who are a generation older than me say, 'It's nobody's business. We don't have to talk about it.' That was sort of the accepted thing of the past. It's not the same anymore. I look at the kids coming up—18-and 16-year-old kids—saying, 'I'm gay and I'm starting a club at my high school, and I'm not going to stay in the closet.' There are people who are saying, 'I don't care if I'm a $100-million star, I'd rather be a $50 star and have my dignity.' That's the point where we're getting. So many people have chipped away this thing: Elton John and Melissa Etheridge, and Martina Navratilova in the sports world.

—**Howard Bragman**

Unfortunately, George Michael still (post-arrest) maintains that another reason he remained closeted was 'that he didn't feel like publicizing his private life.' That excuse is especially unbelievable, considering it comes from a man who once gave an interview about his testicles to the *London Daily Mirror*. In the annals of show business, such deceit might be common. But it is no more defensible for its excess. With far less money, safety, support and prestige than George Michael, queers come out every day—instead of waiting until they are 'caught.'

—columnist **Harold Fairbanks**

Agents and managers are the keepers of the closet keys. They are the ones who are continuing to promulgate the myth that stars should not come out under any circumstances. Therefore it's a little annoying to me to see these people showing up at GLAAD (Gay & Lesbian Alliance Against Defamation) functions acting as if they're doing all they can to eliminate homophobia in Hollywood, because they *aren't*. They're still hanging on to the single belief that keeps the prejudice going: that it's okay to be in the closet.

—**Armistead Maupin** (*Tales of the City*)

I realized my brother was gay, and he realized I realized it. Every so often he would introduce me to someone who was his good friend. Unfortunately, the most honest conversations did not come until he lay dying....When he became ill we talked about many things for the first time. The thing that is strongest in my mind is that he said it was more difficult to live his entire military career hiding his sexual orientation than it was to die from AIDS. That's saying a lot because he was in so much pain that if you touched his skin, he would cry out.

After his death, that stayed with me—knowing that he lived much of his life in fear. We should never ask anyone to live that way.

—**Parris Glendening**, governor of Maryland, in 1999; in memory of his brother Bruce, he lobbied for passage of a Maryland gay rights bill, which was narrowly defeated by conservative politicians

Being gay is like being a stealth bomber. It takes many years and untold millions to develop yourself, every detail of your existence is a state secret, you fly under the radar as much as you can, you pinpoint your targets with laser accuracy, and when necessary, you envelop yourself in a shield so no one will know you're around.

—**Bruce Vilanch**, head writer and center square on *The Hollywood Squares*

Although my family and friends had known for some time that I am gay, I felt compelled to speak that truth in front of the city my father loved. I wanted him to know that I could take a stand, risk myself....My father fought and eventually died for what he believed in: human rights....I risked a lot in that speech of November 24. But most of all I risked losing that life-threatening grip I've had on my heart that has for years closed me off to the possibility of love. And change.

The child in me, who died 20 years ago, is now an adult—proud, caring, and ready to fight for what he believes in if he needs to.

—associate artistic director of the Dallas Theater Center **Jonathan Moscone**, about his public coming out in 1998, on the 20-year anniversary of the murders of his father, San Francisco Mayor George Moscone, and openly gay supervisor Harvey Milk

I was so disappointed that three popular and well-known celebrity guests or honorees (at a recent AIDS fundraiser in Hollywood)—a talk show hostess, an Oscar-winning actress, and a talk show host turned producer and real estate mogul—have never gotten up the guts or seen the need to come out on a public level....Every time I see these people take the stage at any event with a large gay contingent, I always feel—yet again—that I, everyone else in the audience, and everyone else onstage is being asked to enter into the Big Conspiracy.

The Big Conspiracy works something like this: Thank you, Celebrity, for coming out tonight. To show our gratitude we'll walk on eggshells all evening, all the way around the big, fat, white elephant that sits in the middle of the stage. The big, fat, white elephant is the fact that you are gay, and everyone here knows it, and you know everyone here knows it, but we're not allowed to engage in even the most innocuous patter about your personal life or feign the intimacy that Hollywood is known for, because to do that would be to risk acknowledging the elephant. And that would make you uncomfortable. Angry, even.

And then you'd take your friends and your cachet and your money and go home, to your same-sex partners or tricks, to the gay lifestyle you enjoy—albeit with some restrictions—thanks to all those brave people who came before you and put their livelihoods and lives on the line so that someday, folks like you and me won't have to worry about losing our jobs and our lives and our children.

—*Genre* magazine editor **Peter McQuaid** (5/98)

If you don't think there's a conspiracy of silence about gay people—by nearly all heterosexuals and most homosexuals—on every level of our society—about every non-negative thing about us—then you're not using the other half of your brain.

—deputy managing editor of the *Los Angeles Times* **John Peter Brownell**, the youngest person in that paper's history to become a top newsroom executive; he died of AIDS at 33 in 1990

There is a persistent feeling among straight people that we don't really qualify as a genuine minority because we choose whether or not we wish to identify ourselves....We do nothing to help ourselves when we are asked to participate if we demur and mumble something about not wanting to be known as the Gay Guy. If we're not willing to stand up and present ourselves as integrated human beings whose sexuality is a component of a balanced and productive life, then straight people can't be expected to figure it out. They're still trying to make sense out of baseball.

—Oscar-show writer **Bruce Vilanch**, on the occasion of an "industry function" including every minority except gays, despite numerous gays and lesbians in the audience listening to the panel discuss "minority representation on network TV"

The secret of success is sincerity. Once you can fake that, you've got it made.

—playwright **Jean Giraudoux** (1882-1944)

This whole thing with Matthew Shepard happened, and it was like somebody slapped me awake. At this point it's selfish not to do whatever you can. People seem to like me. I get a warmth from them. I make them laugh. If I do this story and say I'm a gay person, it might make it easier for somebody else. So it seems stupid not to.

—**Nathan Lane**, in 1999, explaining why he decided to publicly come out

It's about what happened to Matthew Shepard. I think—as someone who has a fairly high profile and someone whom people have seen on TV for more than 20 years now—by making this simple statement, maybe people will think twice about other gay people they encounter. Hopefully they'll look at me and say, 'Well, he's succeeded, and he's got a pretty good life, and he's not out to hurt anybody.'

—E! news anchor **Steve Kmetko**, in 1999, explaining why he reiterated being openly gay in an *Advocate* cover story

Staying in the closet is a dirty job, but apparently somebody has to do it. Don't feel too sorry for all the self-loathing and nerve-wracking subterfuge the inmates must have to put up with. At least these stars' closets are surrounded by ten-bedroom homes and five acres of manicured lawns. The closet may be a cage, but it's also pure *gilt*.

—**Frank Sanello**, celebrity biographer (Tom Cruise, Sharon Stone, etc.)

Loving in Private

Gay liberation should not be a license to be a perpetual adolescent. If you deny yourself commitment then what can you do with your life?

—writer /actor **Harvey Fierstein**

The (homophobes) criticize gay people for supposedly being promiscuous, yet they also deny gay people the right to marry, and discourage them from committing themselves to one another.

—sexpert **Dr. Ruth Westheimer**

Love means never having to say you're single.

—**Rupert Everett**, *My Best Friend's Wedding*

A female lover would have to look exactly like me to really turn me on!

—**Roseanne**, who has a gay brother and a lesbian sister

No one knows what we have together, no one...I always used to be so envious of married people. Now this is it for me, for both of us, forever....Maybe it's a horrible thing to say, but Anne (Heche) and I both had the same reaction when Princess Diana died, that she had just found the man of her dreams and then he died, and how could you go on living after that without that person? If Anne goes, I want to go, that's how strongly I feel.

—**Ellen DeGeneres**

Some of them had asked me not be so open about my relationship with Ellen. I thought that was asking me to be a little less myself.... It was an education for me about how uncomfortable people (at her former agency) are with gay issues and same-sex relationships. If you're not coming from a place of truth, you won't ask the question of others....Those weren't people I wanted in my life.

—**Anne Heche**, who joined Ellen at CAA, which is under more gay-friendly management, post-Mike Ovitz

My longest relationship with anybody lasted three years—and was with a woman. The past four years, however, I've been involved with men. But I hate saying that, because I don't want to dilute the fact that a gay relationship is as valid as a straight one.

—bisexual singer **Jill Sobule** ("I Kissed A Girl")

If marriage is supposed to be for procreation, then millions of heterosexual marriages without children—like that of Bob and Elizabeth Dole—would have to be legally dissolved.

—**Harvey Fierstein**

I'm entitled to be taken seriously....In America, just about everyone can legally marry, including felons, illegal immigrants and in some states first cousins....Gay marriage would go a long way to remove the 'freak' label much of society places on us.

—"Freedom to Marry" billboard artist and CNN producer **Jill Abrams**

(There are) 1,049 federal statutes that provide benefits, rights and privileges to individuals who have the legal right to marry....Those 1,049 benefits, rights and privileges amount to *respect*....Demanding legalized gay marriage is....not about 'copying them.' It is about money and rights.

—activist and former screenwriter **Larry Kramer** (*Women In Love*, *Lost Horizon*)

The family that you acquire once you leave your own family is sometimes even more special because you really choose these people.

—**RuPaul**

Suddenly, having babies has become the latest dyke pastime.

—**Bea Arthur**, in 1998

I haven't really been successful in relationships with men *or* women. The men think I'm a big dyke, and the women think I'm a fake lesbian, so no one comes up to me except little kids with braces. And I'm like, 'Do you have parents?'

—**Jill Sobule**

There's never been a successful marriage in Hollywood.

—closeted gay star **Ramon Novarro**, in 1934, explaining why he hadn't wed (a woman)

When we do choose a spouse, partner, whatever, we do it strictly out of love. When our relationships endure, it's due to love. It's not like so many heterosexual marriages where they drag on and on, sometimes because of the kids, or what the neighbors or relatives will think, or because the wife has few financial options, or the husband doesn't know where else he'd find a housekeeper for free.

—**Graham Chapman**, *Monty Python*

I lost my virginity to an older woman. Well, let's say her name was Miss Bea Haven.

—**Liberace** (one of his male lovers later revealed that Lee lost it to a football player…)

I was much too polite to ask.

—**Gore Vidal**'s reply, when asked the gender of his first sexual partner

My first lover was a musician….He was considerably older than me, but I was from San Francisco, so I was quite sophisticated for my age.

—**Johnny Mathis**

Musical!

—**Winston Churchill**'s reply, when asked what his sole homosexual experience was like, with handsome actor-composer Ivor Novello

Is that all there is?

—**Ellen DeGeneres**, on her heterosexual experience

In suburbia they thump you for anything....People still think heteros make love and gays have sex. I want to tell them that's wrong.

—**Boy George**

I logged on (to his computer) as a lesbian once. The lesbian chat rooms are pretty fun. Until you realize that every lesbian there is really a man trying to find a lesbian.

—**Jon Lovitz**

I think there is a beauty to two women making love. It has always struck me as something natural.

—**Liza Minnelli**

The only unnatural sex is that which you cannot perform.

—**Colette**

We English have sex on the brain. *Not* the best place for it, actually.

—bisexual actor **Laurence Harvey** (*Walk On The Wild Side*)

Women love me in *My Best Friend's Wedding*. I think because women, unlike men, aren't obsessed with sex. Men tend to envy me because I'm tall and handsome. But when they find out I'm gay, most of them dislike me. Women can think on more than one level.

—**Rupert Everett**

I think that at some time in every girl's life there's another girl in school whom you cannot cease admiring. She's bright, she's funny, her socks are just right, and if she chooses to walk down the hall with you, you float. And that's a crush, and girls have crushes on other girls in school. Usually women outgrow that. Sometimes they don't.

—**Victoria Principal**, *Dallas*

It isn't that I hadn't ever considered (a lesbian relationship). I'd say, Well, would that be interesting? Would I want to? And I honestly don't think that the thought ever resolved itself.

—**Julie Andrews**, *Victor/Victoria*

My twin brother was gay and he was really my only outlet when we moved to this country (from Jamaica)....He always took me to gay bars and I loved it...people who looked much nicer and seemed to enjoy themselves more. They seemed freer. I suppose because of that...I became like a gay man.

—**Grace Jones**

I've had sex with men. Does that make me gay?

—**Rod McKuen**, poet

If you have one gay experience, does that mean you're gay? If you have one heterosexual experience, does that mean you're straight? Life doesn't work quite so cut and dried.

—tennis champ **Billie Jean King**

There are certain types of women that I'm attracted to....It's ridiculous for a woman to say that she's not attracted to other women. That's completely false....When does one decide whether it's sexual or mental?

—**Grace Jones**

My best girlfriend, Janet, taught me how to kiss...I think she wanted to go further, and I was thinking, 'Oh, that feels real good, but'...I could have definitely, definitely gotten into the feeling, the physical feeling.

—**Liza Minnelli**

If a woman came into my life who was absolutely stunning and satisfied me emotionally, intellectually and sexually, I'm not going to draw the line and say, 'I can't because you're a woman.' I find it hard enough to find someone to be with, why narrow the field?

—**Amanda Donohoe** (*L.A. Law*, *The Lair Of The White Worm*)

I wouldn't be surprised if I ended up with a woman....It seems like we're all bisexual, if you want to get kind of simple about it.

—**Lili Taylor** (*I Shot Andy Warhol*)

The only kind of gay people I find attractive are those bordering on the transvestite.

—**Donald Sutherland**

Crucifixes are sexy because there's a naked man on them.

—**Madonna**

I show sex education movies at home to our kids. It's important they not grow up in ignorance and pay the price later, or make others pay it....Yes, I show films on heterosexuality *and* homosexuality.

—**Burt Lancaster**

Particularly for a young woman in a world of AIDS, I've said (lesbianism) seems to be a safer way to explore your sexuality, rather than screwing around with a lot of boys.

—supermodel **Cindy Crawford**

Of course, who hasn't? Good God! If anyone had ever told me that he hadn't, I'd have told him he was lying. But then of course people tend to 'forget' their encounters.

—sci-fi writer (*2001*) **Arthur C. Clarke**, when asked if he'd ever had any "bisexual experience"

Fooling around today with a whole bunch of guys, seems to me you could get something terminal—like a kid.

—comedian **Henriette Mantel**, *The Brady Bunch Movie*

In California, thanks to our anti-gay Republican governor (Pete Wilson), gay and lesbian people are no longer allowed to adopt. So you have a comedienne like Paula Poundstone who has adopted and who when asked if she's lesbian, very butchly replies that she is merely pro-lesbian....So you have the pressure to deny from both show business and now from the government that is supposed to represent all citizens and taxpayers equally.

—activist **Jim Kepner**, in 1997

Paula (Poundstone) and I are very good friends. We go way back....Of course I think she's too busy to have a sex life.

—**Bea Arthur**

Having a child is a big, messy, great human process. I feel like I either will or I won't in my lifetime. I don't feel this 'I am nothing unless I have children,' like women do perhaps at a certain age. I don't think I'm nothing if I don't have kids.

—**Jodie Foster**

She is not pregnant.

—**Jodie Foster's publicist** in March, 1998, re: rumors that Foster was pregnant via an anonymous sperm donor

I am pregnant....

—**Jodie Foster** in April, 1998

I always wanted to have kids, one way or another.

—**Rosie O'Donnell**

Babies are wonderful, children are okay, and husbands are...oh, never mind.

—Dame **Flora Robson**, who never wed

The flower which is single need not envy the thorns that are numerous.

—Hindu philosopher **Rabindranath Tagore**

Joaquin Phoenix. He's that all-time dreamboat. Those flared nostrils do it for me.

—**Alexis Arquette**, on his ideal lover

I'd like to come back as Matt Dillon's knickers (briefs).

—**Boy George**, on his reincarnation preference (he was quoted several times on the same topic, occasionally switching actors)

Sleeping with George Michael would be like having sex with a groundhog.

—**Boy George**, on his more hirsute singing rival

The only person who has anything to say about what happens to my body is me and Michelle Pfeiffer.

—**Rosie O'Donnell**, at a 1992 pro-choice fundraiser, to a predominantly lesbian audience

I don't think it's right, just because someone's rich, to be able to adopt a baby easier than someone who's not rich. Though I don't doubt (Rosie O'Donnell) will be a good parent. Though that's not the issue. And she's not married, either.

—Republican Congressman **Sonny Bono**

In the old days, most actresses who were lezzies got married to guys but didn't have kids. Now it goes the other way—they have the kids but they dispense with the husbands. Which for them makes more sense, if they're determined to saddle themselves with offspring.

—Hollywood archivist **Jim Kepner**

We may have a baby together. Through Anne (Heche), that is.

—Ellen DeGeneres

Ellen and I were in Santa Barbara, walking down the street. I went to hold her hand, and she pulled away. 'What's that?' I asked, and she said (in a whisper), 'No, it makes people uncomfortable.' I said, 'Well, it makes *me* uncomfortable that you won't hold my hand. Don't discriminate against me.'

Most people think they're sympathetic to gays, but until you're on the receiving end of it you don't really understand discrimination. It's an insidious disease in this country.

—Anne Heche

I had a love affair (with actor Farley Granger). We lived together for about four years. He was under contract to Sam Goldwyn, whose attitude was very interesting. One day Francis Goldwyn, Sam's wife, invited me to tea. She said, 'You know, you're Farley's best friend. I would like to ask a favor. He takes out Miss Shelley Winters in public. We don't care about what he does in private. But Miss Winters is too old and too vulgar for him. And if he insists on taking out a girl, could he please take out Ann Blyth?'

—screenwriter **Arthur Laurents** (*The Way We Were*)

You have to think for yourself. If you buy into the propaganda, it's your own fault. Like that old concept, 'living in sin.' There's no such thing, for heterosexuals or homosexuals. It's meaningless! Stop to consider the meaning of words…and phrases. Like when they call the pope 'the holy father,' and he's neither.…Think for yourself, and *pro* yourself. The establishment isn't pro us at all, so why accept their bigotry and fictions as the truth?

—**Graham Chapman**'s advice to young gay people

A man's life is what his thoughts make of it.

—Roman emperor **Marcus Aurelius**

…a few gay men make sex their total be-all and end-all. We have so much more to our lives than just carnality. And that's why we've never had strong political organizations, why we don't have power…I want to redefine homosexuality as something more than just sex.

—**Larry Kramer**

The reason I don't want to be called 'a homosexual' is that it reduces a human being to sex—and nothing but. It leaves out the word 'love.'

—**Keith Prentice**, the "handsomest" cast member of the play and film *The Boys In The Band*

How often does somebody heterosexual get called a heterosexual? Hmm? How would they like it if that's all they ever got called…if they were *always* described as just 'a heterosexual'?

—**Leonard Frey** (*Boys In The Band*, *Fiddler On The Roof*)

I like my career so much that I'd like people to remember my music and not my personality.…The only time I actually believe in myself is when I'm singing.

—**Johnny Mathis**, who came out in 1982

If you care too much what other people think, you'll never be content or even very comfortable…if you're gay, you automatically have to divorce yourself from the opinions—or opinion—of the allegedly moral majority.

—**Sir Ian McKellen**

I was working on a movie for (producer) Carlo Ponti, Sophia Loren's husband. I went into the hospital, and that postponed the shooting. It was difficult for all of us...but I had to be with Jill (Townsend, daughter of a then-best-selling author). What made everyone angry was that I wasn't pretending Jill was just my friend. Or a friend of some boyfriend of mine. She was my girlfriend, and I didn't need to hide it...and they fired me.

—**Maria Schneider**, *Last Tango In Paris*

Montgomery Clift

I was 18 or 19 when I helped (Montgomery Clift) realize that he was homosexual, and I barely knew what I was talking about. I was a virgin when I was married and not a world expert on sexuality. But I loved Monty with all my heart and just knew that he was unhappy. I knew that he was meant to be with a man and not a woman, and I discussed it with him. I introduced him to some really nice young guys.

—**Elizabeth Taylor**

I restrict myself emotionally and sexually to a level that I can function with. I almost never have sex unless it's with a very, very close person. I go weeks, sometimes months, without having sex, because I'm on the road. I wouldn't know how to even find a sex partner!

—**Johnny Mathis**

If I were a homosexual, I'm sure I could fall in love with (director) John Waters in about half a second. Because he is one of the funniest, most charming, intelligent people that I've ever known. He's really a prime catch.

—heterosexual **Johnny Depp**

Any woman who says she never thought about lesbian sex is lying.

—**Kristy Swanson**
(*Buffy The Vampire Slayer*)

Do I like women? I like women. Do I like them sexually? Yeah, I do. Totally….It's weird. Women are so much more selective with women than they are with men.

—**Drew Barrymore**
(*Boys On The Side*)

The trouble with some women is that they get all excited about nothing, and then marry him.

—**Cher**

We (he and his wife) sleep in separate bedrooms, much like the Hays (censorship) Code. When we kiss, we both have one foot on the ground at all times. (And) we wear full protective gear.

—director **Tim Burton** (*Batman*, *Pee-Wee's Big Adventure*), who according to movie author Dr. Harry Benshoff has been labeled a "straight queer"

My sister used to go to church and fantasize about the priests. You know, when we were kids we used to play what we called Nasty Barbies, where we'd have Ken jump on Barbie and hump her. I didn't even know what it was, but it was a real turn-on. And you're turned on, and you're next to these other little girls. Does that make you a lesbian? Did you do that?

—**Madeleine Stowe** (*The Last Of The Mohicans*), to a female interviewer

With my lovers, I'm completely a woman. My body is completely a woman's body. When you get to know me, I'm a total woman. I think the male thing is just a way of surviving—outside.

—**k.d. lang**

Anyone who's homophobic is insecure about their own heterosexuality. More than that, I think it's an envy of pleasure.

—**Cybill Shepherd**

(Straight) men resent homosexuals more than women do. I think because they're more easily threatened than women, and because deep down—though they'd never admit it—they're jealous of how most gay people can have several sex partners...and have all the oral sex they want, and not have to be stuck in a loveless marriage or worry about pregnancies, abortions and kids.

—Oscar-winning composer **Paul Jabara** (*Last Dance*)

If we can take sex out of the realm of sin altogether and see it as something else to do with personal relationships and ethics, then we can finally get around to a phase...which deals with the question of sin as violence, sin as cruelty, sin as murder, war and starvation.

—novelist **Anne Rice**

The men I had sex with (for money) were *nice* to me. My memory of it is they were the only people who found me attractive, sexy and worthwhile. Girls were not nice to me! Men were. And even though I wasn't turned on by it, I don't resent these men. I have only deep love for the gay men that I was close with—all these filmmakers and artists and brilliant men I was surrounded by. How could I be homophobic about those experiences? I guess I'm not insecure in that way.

—admittedly heterosexual actor **Vincent Gallo**

I did support myself in style via prostitution before I became a successful actor. It's not at all unusual—for an actor *or* an actress—to have done that. What is extraordinarily unusual is to admit it...I'm not as pure as the driven snow, but not being a part of the Hollywood establishment, I don't pretend I am. Too much of Hollywood is like a seasoned hooker trying to pass for a knowing virgin.

—admittedly homosexual actor **Rupert Everett**

...the fastest-growing population in the world.

—**Mick Jagger**'s 1970s description of bisexuals

If you work around ordinary-looking people, you're straight or you're gay. Okay? If you work around actors, actresses, models—

male or female—you're potentially bisexual...the more attractive people are, the more tempted anyone's gonna be.

—**Joe MacDonald**, male supermodel

Fuck Helmut Newton (the photographer). Why should I take my clothes off for him? I took my clothes off for his wife.

—**Janice Dickinson**, 1970s supermodel

I saw in the *TV Guide* where some cable channel's doing a celebrity profile of Jodie Foster, like an hour, I think. I guess they're gonna run her movie credits *real slowly*....

—**Roseanne**, referring to how some stars' private lives are deliberately overlooked

Too many actresses collect husbands these days. They're trying to make men into status symbols, or things. I have too much respect for men to do that....Another reason I'm not very inclined toward marriage is that it ends too many friendships, and I value friendship highly—my friendships with ladies and with gentlemen. And *all* of my men friends are gentlemen.

—**Lillian Gish**, revealing perhaps more than she intended about her private life

One of my best friends in Hollywood was (former actress) Benita Hume....She told me how she'd been in a Tarzan movie, and how the actors were sometimes surprised by the on-camera behavior of the animals. Especially the chimp, which was a large male, passionately in love with Johnny Weissmuller.

Whenever Weissmuller came on the set, the chimp not only sat on his haunches and howled with delight, he also showed other unmistakable signs of his homosexual affection, and you couldn't shoot on him until his ardor cooled off. 'Okay,' the director would sigh, 'lights out. Everybody sit down and wait, please.'

—**Lilli Palmer**, in her memoir *Change Lobsters and Dance*

I had a queer cat...yes, a homosexual cat. I called him Thomasina, and I'm an animal lover. I talked about him to reporters...no one ever printed a word about Thomasina, oddly enough.

—screen siren **Veronica Lake**

Those anti-gay people, those fundamentalists and preachers, they say homosexuality can't be 'natural' because animals don't do it. But they're lying. Animals *do* it. Only, they don't do it together in the documentaries we grew up with from Disney, or the ones on TV even now.

—**Morgan Fairchild**, who trained to be an anthropologist

Wouldn't it be wonderful if the only way you could get AIDS was by contributing money to television evangelists?

—standup comic **Elayne Boosler**

They lie about us all the time. The truth helps us. So the homophobes don't deal in the truth.

—stand-up comic **Lea DeLaria**

(The) feminist agenda is not about equal rights for women. It is about a socialist, anti-family political movement that encourages women to leave their husbands, kill their children, practice witchcraft, destroy capitalism and become lesbians.

—evangelist/TV tycoon **Pat Robertson**'s fictitious fundraising letter for the Iowa Committee to Stop ERA (the Equal Rights Amendment)

I'm a Socialist, yes…you don't have that party here, so I'm also a Democrat.

—**Angela Lansbury**

I don't consider the Equal Rights Amendment a political issue. It is a moral issue….Where are women mentioned in the Constitution, except in the 19th Amendment giving us the right to vote? When they said all *men* were created equal, they really meant it—otherwise, why did we have to fight for the 19th Amendment?

—**Carol Burnett** in 1979

I do talk about gay rights when I can. I don't consider it controversial…it's human rights. What else could you consider it? These are people we all know.

—**Carol Burnett**

What I find a waste of time is this whole debate on is-gay-a-choice? If it was open to choosing, then most people wouldn't choose something so reviled…so discriminated against….Besides, even if it was a choice, so what? People basically choose their religions, their moral codes…whether to speak a second language…and people choose whether or not to focus on hating people different from themselves.

—**Gene Hackman** (*The Birdcage*)

I'm white and I'm blonde…I'd never been discriminated against in my life. Then, within a few days (of announcing she and Ellen DeGeneres were a couple), I all of a sudden knew what it is to be the target of hate and bigotry.

—**Anne Heche**

They should ask the straights how far they're willing to go (in pressuring gay men to wed women)? Do they want us to marry their daughters in this pretense, and use them as beards? Is it worth ruining two lives for the sake of trying in vain to change one person? They just don't think of it that way, but that's the way it works.

—**Boy George**

Their careers are real, their marriage isn't. It's *matriphony*.

—columnist **Lance Browne** of The Hollywood Kids, about a short-lived contractual marriage between a bisexual movie actor and a bisexual supermodel

Some of the most constructive and loving relationships I've seen are between men, or women. But because most gays hide their true nature, even from relatives, the world—made up of smaller worlds—doesn't realize this. Gay people need to be prouder, more defiant….And I know that's easy for *me* to say!

—heterosexual actor **Peter Finch**, *The Trials Of Oscar Wilde*; *Sunday, Bloody Sunday* (he played gay in both films)

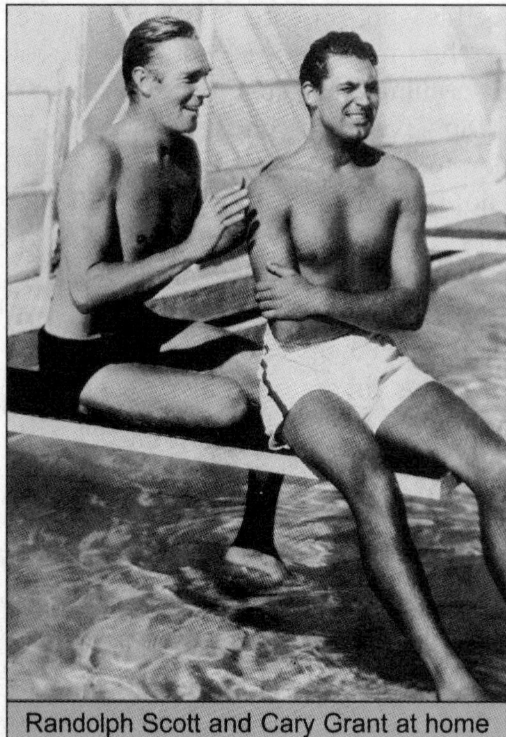
Randolph Scott and Cary Grant at home

I met Randolph Scott's last nurse. He said that Scott spoke openly and glowingly of Cary Grant as the love of his life, even in front of Mrs. Scott, who agreed with no rancor that Cary was 'a great guy.' Scott also said that all that kept him from dying when career-conscious Cary left him was a subsequent affair with Fred Astaire!

—playwright **Robert Patrick**

I didn't stay married to Donna McKechnie for long (three months), but we became the best of friends...*that* can last for decades. I don't get the expression 'just friends.' What's 'just' about friends who last a lifetime?

—closeted director-choreographer **Michael Bennett** (*A Chorus Line*, *Dreamgirls*)

If a (gay) guy marries a woman for two months, it'll be in his obituary. If he marries another guy and they're together two decades, don't count on it being in the obit. The rulers of the country and its media do *not* want you to know about gay love.

—columnist **Boyd McDonald**

Truman Capote and Jack Dunphy were a couple for some 30 years. All the publicity was on Truman's friendships with rich women, or on his feuds with rich women and Gore Vidal. Very one-sided (publicity).

—director **Robert Moore**, *Murder By Death*

My own personal in-house writer—the beautiful, the brilliant, my beloved Jane Wagner—was off writing a pilot, hopefully for me.

—**Lily Tomlin** at the 1997 Gay & Lesbian Alliance Against Defamation (GLAAD) awards show, explaining to a select audience why her personal and professional partner of over 30 years hadn't written her acceptance speech for her

It angered me (but) it didn't astonish me...nearly all the obituaries of Gianni (Versace) failed to mention Antonio (D'Amico, Versace's lifemate of 11 years)....They'd rather pretend we all hire male hookers than admit we have longtime partners.

—**Elton John** (sister Donatella Versace insists Gianni hadn't known his murderer, Andrew Cunanan)

You know that by now famous photo? Elton John at Versace's funeral, where he's crying and two people are comforting him: a man and Princess Diana....I've seen it in nine or ten papers, and the caption never identifies the man, just Elton and the princess. But the man happens to be David Furnish, who's been with Elton for several years...and they're an *open* and very devoted couple.

—actor turned literary agent **Connie Clausen**

I wasn't that surprised when the general media (in Raymond Burr's obituaries) ignored the man he lived with for 30 or 40 years. But it did come as a surprise that *Variety* left it out (while noting a much briefer marriage of Burr's to a woman).

—**George Schaefer,** producer-director

It is not my habit to write to papers after reading reviews of my books. But after coming across the one...on my novel *The Eye of the Storm*, in which she refers to me as 'living in Sydney with several dogs and a male housekeeper,' I feel I must draw your attention to an incorrect...biographical detail. The distinguished and universally respected man who has given me his friendship and moral support over a period of 34 years has never been a housekeeper....

—Nobel Prize winning author **Patrick White**, in a 1994 letter to *Time* magazine

Splendid couple—slept with both of them.

—**Sir Maurice Bowra**, at the wedding of a famous (male-female) literary couple

I didn't *sleep* with (Tyrone Power)....We didn't do it standing up. But we certainly didn't do it asleep. The end. Yes, once we did. (Asked if Power was known to be gay?) Oh, absolutely.

—writer-director **Arthur Laurents** in 1995 (by which time he'd lived with partner Tom Hatcher over 40 years)

What irritates me is the bland way people go around saying, 'Oh, our attitude has changed. We don't dislike these people any more.' But by the strangest coincidence, they haven't taken away the injustice; the laws are still on the books.

—**Christopher Isherwood**
author and screenwriter

This Administration will continue to fight for the rights and needs of lesbians and gay men in our nation. During the past four years, much progress has been made, but there is more to do.

—**Tipper Gore**, the VP's wife, in a letter to the lesbian Women's Inaugural Gala, in Washington, D.C., January 20, 1997

There is no room in American medicine or American life for discriminating against people because of their sexual orientation. Gays and lesbians are part of the American family.

—Vice President **Al Gore**, at the AIDS Action Foundation's National Leadership Awards, in 1997

My eldest son Peter is a physician, he's gay, and he and his partner have been together for 17 years....He graduated from the University of Washington Medical School in Seattle, where he now lectures and has a private practice; he is a Ph.D. in genetics; he was Phi Beta Kappa at Cornell as an undergraduate; he was a prodigy in botany, beginning to grow plants at age 6; he wrote for botanical journals at 12; and he is currently finishing a book about gay men's health...Peter is humane and intelligent, and I'm crazy about him. One of the nice things about me is that I never brag about my kids.

—*The Today Show*'s **Gene Shalit**, in 1997

What's wrong with a little matchmaking?...I believe he'd be perfect for my brother. I only want the best for him.

—**Madonna**, trying to pair Christopher Ciccone with also openly gay Rupert Everett

How many years when I was growing up did I hear guys saying that all lesbians need is a good lay? I'd tell them, 'Don't you freakin' understand? Are you fuckin' dense?'

—**Cyndi Lauper**, who shared a float with her older gay sister in Manhattan's 1994 gay pride parade

I remember Eddie Murphy doing an interview in *Cosmopolitan*, and he said how if he ever caught his son wearing his mom's high heels or making like Boy George, he'd beat the crap out of him. And I thought, 'Where's your heart, man?' And I also thought, There is some deep hypocrisy going on here, man.

—black writer **Essex Hemphill** (Murphy's interest in transvestite and transsexual hookers became public knowledge in 1997)

I have been with men. I like sex. I like beautiful people, men and women. And I'm not ashamed of it. Besides, a lot of women like that because they like to see a man...able to be with men and not embarrassed by it.

—**Andy Dick** (*NewsRadio*)

I'd done dozens of plays, I'd done film, I'd been acting for years, and all at once I become a sort of sex symbol to women, I receive more fan mail from women than ever before, and why? Precisely because I enacted a character who sometimes dresses in women's clothing! I had no idea this excites so many ladies out there.

—hetero UK actor **Denis** (sic) **Quilley**, about *Privates On Parade* (1982)

Perhaps most actors are latent homosexuals and we cover it with drink. I was once homosexual, but it didn't work.

—**Richard Burton** (né Jenkins), who changed his surname to that of his favorite instructor, Philip Burton, who at one point considered adopting him

Pigs make wonderful pets…I have a pot-bellied pig named Max. He's sort of a watchdog. But he was no help during the (1994 Los Angeles) earthquake. Not much…he woke me up, and it was happening. I was naked. I had a buddy who lived downstairs in the guest house, and he was naked but he brought his gun. Max was squealing real loud, at first no one knew what was going on. My buddy thought it was someone breaking in, rattling the windows….It was a wild scene, but not what you might think: two naked guys, a pig and a gun.

—**George Clooney**

Here lies David Diamond—underneath Tom Cruise.

—openly gay rock musician **Dave Diamond**'s reply to what he'd like his epitaph to read

You have to like someone, to love them. Unless they're relatives, but I mean people we choose….But you don't have to like someone to have sex with them. Men understand this, and I think it's why men have much more satisfactory sex lives than women.

—screenwriter **Eleanor Perry**

I don't think sex has anything to do with friendship. It's very difficult to have a sexual relationship with somebody who actually is a friend. Because there's a kind of tension and antagonism that goes on in a sexual relationship...friendship is the perfect sort of truth and belief and not lying to one another....A love-sex relationship (means) continuously lying to each other....in a friendship you do exactly the reverse.

—**Truman Capote**

If I'm making love to a woman that I love, I wouldn't necessarily be a lesbian just because she might call herself that. I feel my sexuality is as individual as my soul, and it keeps getting enriched.

—singer **Sophie B. Hawkins**, described by the Australian magazine *Lesbians On The Loose* as "at one time the gal-pal of Rosie O'Donnell"

Why should I put myself down for liking women, which is so completely natural to me?

—model, actor and mechanic **Jenny Shimizu**

Women's looks were my only books.

—Ohio-born **Natalie Barney**, for over 60 years the doyenne of Parisian lesbians

One afternoon Dutchy invited Bianca (his mother) to her cabin, offered her a glass of champagne, and showed her a book on lesbian lovemaking....'In Europe it doesn't matter if you're a man or a woman,' Marlene explained. 'We make love with anyone we find attractive.'

—producer **Budd Schulberg**, on Marlene Dietrich

I just don't want to be a homosexual. Or even an AC/DC one.

—**Buddy Ebsen** (*The Beverly Hillbillies*), on why he opposes gay rights

Most straights think we just want to 'convert' them, when they misspend so much time and effort trying to convert us. They don't seem able to realize that they can no more be converted than we can. Or that we just want to be left alone to live and love as we were meant to do.

—**Alec McCowen**
(*Travels With My Aunt*)

It's a lot easier for actors to be in the closet if they don't have loving and longtime partners. When you do have such a one in your life, then you're denying the other person and your love for them too.

—single and secretly gay UK actor **Dennis Price** (*Kind Hearts & Coronets*)

(Appearing as the subject of a UK *This Is Your Life* TV program:) They mentioned several plays and films that I'd done. But apart from my childhood, nothing was said about my life whatsoever.... (Male) director Vivian Matalon, with whom I have had a long and loving relationship, was not mentioned. Even worse, there was no mention of Geoffrey Burridge, who had been my friend for 17 years and who died of AIDS (at 35) in 1988. Not only was there no mention of him, but his mother and friends weren't asked to participate.

After the program...I was put into a limousine and sent home on my own. I don't think I have been quite so depressed in my life. I thought, What on earth am I, aged 64, covering up? What are *they* covering up? Is it such a big deal?...Would they put on Richard Burton and not mention Elizabeth Taylor?

—**Alec McCowen**, who then publicly came out and had the producers include a tribute to Geoffrey at the program's conclusion

I wouldn't use the word 'friend' or the word 'roommate' (to describe one's significant other). Those *reduce* the relationship and they don't imply love or commitment...nor would I use 'husband,' because that would imply I'm a wife.

—actor-director **Robert Drivas**
(*The Illustrated Man*)

I don't like the word 'lover,' I think it lacks dignity.

—columnist **Liz Smith**

We should get in the habit of using the word 'married.' *They* don't have a monopoly on it, and we can be as married as they are. If they can talk about a 'marriage' of two corporations or ideals, etc., we can certainly talk about a marriage between two in-love people of the same sex—who have more in common with each other than straights do anyway.

—**Frank Maya**, the first openly gay stand-up comic

If the truth be known, a hell of a lot of tinseltown marriages are *mergers*. They merge their assets and multiply their publicity by teaming up. I mean whether or not they're straight and in love or anything. The longer you act, the more often these desperate publicity hounds keep acting.

—makeup artist to the stars **Way Bandy**

Yep, I'm getting married. To the U.S. Army.

—**Elvis Presley**

Female mostly.

—**Presley**'s answer to the question "What kind of girls do you prefer?"

I'm just looking for a guy who has his own car—and doesn't live in it.

—comedian **Jason Stuart**

Newton (Arvin) was a charming person, cultivated in every way, with the most wonderfully subtle mind. He was like a lozenge that you could keep turning to the light, one way or another, and the most beautiful colors would come out.

—**Truman Capote**, explaining his attraction to his rather plain professor lover

Opposites attract. Sometimes. But similarities tend to last. You need common ground and interests to endure as a pair.

—**Dr. Joyce Brothers**

You never really know a gal till you break up with her.

—comedian **Lea DeLaria**

I decided to come out in part because I happen to be in love.

—**Dana Plato** (*Diff'rent Strokes*) in 1998

It's gay men and lesbians who have defined marriage as a bond of love, romance and mutual like, rather than—as heterosexual men historically have done—a contract involving property, chattel and male name-giving.…If heterosexual marriage is 'threatened' by gay marriage, as the Religious Right keep shrieking, then it must be a shaky or fragile institution indeed.

—poet **Allen Ginsberg**

The worst thing about the enemies of gay people's rights and of gay marriage is that they presume to pass judgment on love. They won't accept that love is love…they see nothing in common between us.…Like there's so much love in this world, they can afford to try and prevent some of it?

—director **Norman Rene**

I don't ask for your pity, but for your understanding—not even that, no. Just for your recognition of me in you, and the enemy, *time*, in us all.

—**Tennessee Williams**

Nobody knows what Anne (Heche) and I have, nobody.

—**Ellen DeGeneres**

Gore Vidal has been…with Howard Austen since about 1950. But of late he's been offering the information that they haven't had sex for years, that it's now loving but platonic.…In saying (so), he diminishes their marriage in most people's eyes. Because many, possibly most, longtime heterosexual couples haven't had sex either, not for decades or since having their kids. But they do not go around announcing the fact, and typically they'll deny it if it comes up.

—**Allen Ginsberg**

I can't imagine what possessed Carol Channing to declare that she and her husband Charles Lowe, 87, haven't had sex in over 40 years, and only once or twice before that! Let's hope this very happy and devoted couple don't go the divorce route. Charles, please say you're only kidding.

—eighty-something hetero columnist **James Bacon** in 1998 (most insiders say that Lowe married Channing's career, which he has ably managed)

I always cringe when I hear that word. I feel people will judge me as either 'She's bisexual, so she'll fuck everybody' or 'She's bisexual and fools around with women, but that's not as important to her as a male relationship.'

—singer **Jill Sobule**

We talked about people being bisexual. He said he didn't think there was any such thing. If [someone] really needed emotional support from a male, he would probably be homosexual, but if he needed the support from a woman, then he'd be more straight.

—**John Gilmore**, writing about his pal and some-time lover James Dean

Now it's chic to be 'bi.' I was ahead of my time—I was the first actress to come out as bisexual. It didn't help my career, the way it does bisexual girls' careers now.

—**Judy Carne** (*Laugh-In*), who was Burt Reynolds' first wife

It's easier for women to be bisexual, in that they don't have to be terrifically turned on to a male *or* a female partner. To get an erection, a man must either be very turned on by his partner or have a terrifically vivid imagination, kink or fantasy.

—double Oscar-winner **Emma Thompson**, who publicly discussed her attraction to Michelle Pfeiffer

(Sexual) experimentation is natural, but it can be more traumatic for the male of the species....When a woman tries another woman, she puts it down to experience. And the culture almost validates it—it's a requisite in (hetero) male porno films....Fewer men experiment, even if they're curious. For, most men feel that if once they've tried sex with another man, even active sex, they're tainted for life.

Women define themselves as heterosexual if they date or live with men. Men define themselves as *straight*—and the word's no coincidence—if they're having sex with women, and only women. Only women ever.

—**Samuel M. Steward**, writer and an assistant to sex researcher Dr. Alfred Kinsey

In the '70s, Shirley MacLaine said everyone was inherently bisexual. In the (more conservative) '80s, she seemed to take it back....In the '70s, David Bowie came out as bi, and later he denied it completely....Now, in the '90s, it's becoming more acceptable to talk about your bisexual side—if you're a girl.

—director **Emile Ardolino** (*Dirty Dancing*)

In Hollywood, the word 'bisexual' usually begins with *buy*....

—transplanted American actor **Douglas Lambert**, a.k.a. "England's Rock Hudson" because he went public about having AIDS

It never occurred to me to attend (the Academy Awards) with anyone.... but Trevor. I wouldn't think of leaving him at home...we've been together for about 17 years and we both know it's for keeps, and we each feel very privileged. Besides, my private life has never been a secret.

—**Nigel Hawthorne**, who in 1995 became the first openly gay actor to be Oscar-nominated (for Best Actor in *The Madness Of King George*)

My uncle was gay and my godfathers. I was brought up in a very gay environment (her uncle raised her)....I lived with two gay women at college, which was wonderful (and) I think that most people are really bisexual.

—**Emma Thompson** (*Howards End*)

So many young women really haven't made up their minds. The male world is so antagonistic and terrifying. I'm not surprised women turn to each other, not just for emotional but physical comfort they can't get from a man unless he is truly enlightened.

—Britisher **Amanda Donohoe**, who shared American network TV's first lesbian kiss on *L.A. Law*

(Asked about then-VP Dan Quayle's restrictive "Family values:") I don't listen to that kind of nonsense....What is family? Family is when any two people come together and make a home. A nest. There's your family values.

—**Angela Lansbury**

When two are gathered together, majorities shall not triumph.

—writer **E.M. Forster (*Maurice*)**

If you want or need that much f'ing privacy, don't become an f'ing actor!

—**Victor Mature**, former star

Relationships are all very well, but sex is wonderful!

—character blonde **Iris Adrian**

(On her short-lived marriage:) I fucked up because I succumbed. I didn't pay attention to my own heart....It was a marriage of convenience—his, that is....It was a green card situation. I realized that living a lie was not fucking worth it....He'd better run the other way if he comes into a room that I'm in.

—**Drew Barrymore** on her 1994 marriage to an L.A. bartender

She considers herself bisexual, but claims that she has never met a woman who could keep her attention for very long.

—columnist **Arlene Walsh**, on Drew Barrymore

There really are bisexual people in this town. But most of them don't let on...Some actors are seen with their girlfriend on the town. Then they go visit their boyfriends in a special apartment. It gives the (public) impression that they're normal, but that's what this business is all about.

—the late **Cesar Romero**

I think bisexual women are more sincere than the bi guys…I have to wonder about the females in a bisexual man's life—is it for real or for show, or is it from guilt?

—**Madonna**

Blondes have more funk. I think we're more honest, as well as more adventurous.

—**Madonna**

Garbo spent most of the evening (at a party) standing behind the bar flirting with me....Garbo was all over me. I nearly melted.

—**Zsa Zsa Gabor**

I love her in a way I haven't loved before.

—**Martina Navratilova**, on her relationship with model Hunter Reno, the blonde niece of ("never married" as *People* magazine puts it) Attorney General Janet Reno

Ex-model Anna Nicole Smith, who married a wealthy 89-year old man, has now been sued for sexual harassment by her child's ex-nanny. What has the busty blonde been up to?…She says she wants to be a good actress. (Perhaps she already is?)

—writer **Bob Randall**

God, she was good.

—then-hooker **Liza**, about alleged client Vanna White's oral talents, in the book *You'll Never Make Love in This Town Again*

(She has) no response, not even a 'no comment.'

—**Vanna White's spokesperson** explaining the letter-turner's loss for words over Liza's claim

With my background, it's not so awfully daring to say that yes, I have had attractions to women…there's been some bisexuality.

—blonde ex-porn star **Traci Lords**

That's what I've been repeatedly told. Not only did (bi or lesbian) Barbara Stanwyck discover Linda Evans (for her TV series *The Big Valley*), she had Linda move in with her for a time...."

—writer **Paul Rosenfield**

Gap-toothed, cross-eyed model-actress-Coaster Lauren Hutton...dancing the Texas two-step with Carrie Fisher.

—***Spy*** magazine photo caption re the 1989 birthday party for Eddie Fisher

There is a sort of lesbian mafia of bottle-blondes who run a prominent Los Angeles charity...they're very well 'covered' in that these are older gals and they definitely believe in having husbands for purposes of display and image enhancement.

—**Paul Rosenfield**

Hollywood has ingrained patterns...habits. When they did a TV movie on (late news anchor) Jessica Savitch (*Almost Golden*), they left out her Judaism, her bisexuality...and the bisexuality of her late husband. This was a supposedly non-fiction film too.

—historian **Martin Greif** (*The Gay Book of Days*)

The original ending (of *Three Of Hearts*, 1993) had Billy (Baldwin) and Sherilyn (Fenn) driving off into the sunset together. And the three of us went, 'Bullshit. In no universe would that happen except Hollywood.' We refused to support it.

—**Kelly Lynch**, on the film about two non-heterosexual women and a hetero guy (the ending was changed)

(Gay people) were banned from the movies for a quarter-century, then they included us as jokes or villains. Then we graduated to being the neighbor or friend of the straight hero. But we still had no gay friends, and to this day we don't have gay lovers or spouses. Gay love and affection and *sex*, that's the last frontier, making them admit we *do* have relationships.

—**Paul Monette**

I only knew what I'd heard and the things I'd seen (on TV and at the movies), so I thought all homosexuals lived in California or New York City. I thought we were safe, in Chicago.

—**Dorothy Hajdis**, mother of a gay sailor murdered by homophobic sailors; the eventual TV movie, *Any Mother's Child*, was declined by the major networks and cable channels

I still didn't know how babies were made when I was 20, and when I was in junior high somebody called me 'queer.' I didn't know what that meant, so I went to the (school) library....Other kids must have wondered too, because on the (dictionary) page where the word 'queer' was, it had been worn clear through! So I skipped down to 'queerer,' and all it said was 'one who queers.'

—dancer-director **Tommy Tune**

Don't ask me how, but I screwed for the first time when I was about six years old. I don't remember much about it. We were all so young.

—self-professed heterosexual **Rudy Vallee**

I swear...I never had sex with another human being until I was 28—a paratrooper in New Orleans...I didn't masturbate until I was 27.

—**Tennessee Williams**

What's better than roses on your piano? Tulips on your organ!

—**Liberace**

I love the double standard of they can stick their tongues down each other's throats in public, but if we hold hands, we're 'flaunting' it....If we mention a same-sex special someone, it's 'daring' of us, while they talk about their wives and girlfriends 20 times or more a day.

—**Truman Capote**

I think *Ellen* would still be on the air if she'd only occasionally dated (other women)...instead of having one steady, you know, relationship. But Ellen DeGeneres insisted on it being just one, and all the time, you know?

—**anonymous ABC executive**

On one of those sex-talk programs, a woman psychologist said that gay men's relationships usually last longer than lesbian ones....I always think of lesbians mating for life. Then the psychologist explained that men last longer 'cause women are more jealous. And most of my lesbian friends have borne that out.

—Andy Warhol protégé **Jed Johnson**

It's queer the way many people will still talk about gay men as 'women-haters.' Just 'cause we don't want to screw the women...when there's this, like, epidemic of straight men shooting and murdering their wives and ex's and girlfriends....Too many jealous men do something about it, instead of letting it pass.

—**Jed Johnson**, interior designer to Streisand, Saint Laurent, Gere, Jagger and others

Oh, I love everybody. A lot of women assume that I'm a lesbian, and it's kind of a cop-out to say I'm bi. I'd rather say I'm sexual. I've had relationships with women and with men. I'm comfortable with my sexuality. I love the person, not the anatomy.

My son knows that a lot of my friends love each other and are women. Love is a human feeling, not a right and wrong. I'm teaching him a nurturing, loving atmosphere. Whatever he chooses for himself, I'm supportive of. (Laughs.) And if I raise him right, he'll turn out to be gay.

—former actor **Patrice Donnelly** (*Personal Best*, 1982) in 1998

I was never really content so long as I kept thinking maybe I really did need a man in my life. A man in my life, I wouldn't mind so much, but a man in my home, that's a horse of a different color—sometimes even an ass.

—possibly heterosexual writer **Helene Hanff**, *84 Charing Cross Road*

(In gay marriages:) Neither side 'owns' or colonizes the other.

—director **Norman Rene**

I have a sexually active girlfriend who says she prefers the strong and silent type. I think she means a guy who can fix her car and doesn't sass her. My other active girlfriend says she's unhappy with the men she's known. So now she's looking for what she calls 'moody, menopausal men.' I think she means rock stars.

And my token lesbian friend is so busy with her daisy chain of girlfriends that she doesn't have time to chat and tell.

—**Helene Hanff**

I like to talk to a guy a few minutes before asking him out on a date. To find out what's upstairs…too often a Greek god turns out to be a geek god….Over the long run, education counts. You don't want someone who at 30 still thinks a thesaurus is something that died 60 million years ago.

—columnist **Boyd McDonald**

I'm too old…I can't go *out* with anyone—he'd be too young. It would look ridiculous.

—director **George Cukor** in his 70s (rather, he ordered *in*…)

I don't agree at all with the French politician Pierre Mendes France (who) said the only thing that made him feel Jewish was anti-Semitism….In Hollywood, our top three taboos are religion, politics and sex…I feel Jewish through religion, culture and survival. But I have to admit that even in my 70s, I have more frequent thoughts about being (gay) than about being Jewish. I think we identify more with what affects us on a daily—or in my case weekly—basis.

—**George Cukor**

Men aren't taught to *depend* on anyone else. How *real* that is. Most girls finally, painfully learn that there is no Prince Charming. There is no knight in shining armor on a white horse. And if there was, you'd be better off having a protected quickie with the knight and keeping the horse.

—print and TV journalist **Ruth Batchelor** (*A.M. America*)

One of the few individuals who tried to make Diana feel at home when she (joined) Buckingham Palace was Prince Charles' valet, who was gay….In April, 1987, she opened the (UK's) first ward for

People with AIDS...then she began visiting AIDS clinics and informed the press, and in that way the public, that you *can* give people with AIDS a handshake or a hug, and how they particularly need that kind of contact and warmth.

—**Graham Chapman**

People should sometimes try putting themselves in others' shoes. I get asked if it's safe to share a telephone, say, with a person with AIDS. They're afraid of getting something from us...and are unaware that it isn't airborne, it can't be casually transmitted. The virus is found in blood and body fluids....People aren't aware that *we* are at greater risk, by far, of catching something from the HIV-negative person—their germs are a danger to our impaired immune systems.

—actor **Dean Santoro**, who was also Third National Vice President of the Screen Actors Guild

Well, the royal household hadn't got involved with (the fight against AIDS)...and later, when Princess Diana tried to get her husband (Prince Charles) involved, he turned a cold shoulder, unfortunately....[This] despite his valet Stephen Barry, who had died of AIDS (in 1986).

—**Emma Thompson**

The secret of our success? Romance lingers, sex fades...we are, however, best friends. True and loyal friends.

—**Truman Capote**, on his lifelong relationship with dancer turned writer Jack Dunphy

Gianni's brilliance...is acknowledged across the world (but) his gift for friendship and loyalty was equally profound.

—supermodel **Naomi Campbell**, on late designer Gianni Versace

I'm pro-gay, but gay sex has no appeal for me. What I envy men couples or women couples, though, is that they're peers. Equals. They can be the best of friends right off the bat. They don't have to strain to be friends or to understand each other...Getting a straight man to genuinely be friends with a woman is an ongoing effort, and mostly the woman's effort!

—**Lucy Lawless**, *Xena*

Women fuck to love, and men love to fuck.

—**Carrie Fisher**, whose child's father is an openly gay CAA agent

My brother (Gianni) was not really aware of how famous he was. He was very open and friendly and trusting with people....I told him he should have security...the bodyguards. But he said he did not want to have to live that way.

—**Donatella Versace**

They made it as if Gianni was a playboy...was wild. As if he knew the murderer....It was lies. It was not the real Gianni...and he was devoted to not only his work, but his family and the man he loved, Antonio (D'Amico)....But even when they learn the truth, they don't apologize for the lies or the conclusions they jumped (to).

—**Donatella Versace**

The moment they find out someone is homosexual, they think he's oversexed, and he becomes an extension of his libido.

—**River Phoenix**, who never revealed being gay or bi

Everyone thinks Kris is so innocent. Deep down, there's trouble in that body.

—**Ina Liberace** (the pianist's niece), who sued *Family* star Kristy McNichol for palimony

...Hollywood's happiest marriage.

—**Joan Crawford**, referring to the half-century union between ex-actor Billy Haines and Jimmy Shields

No one has the right to feel that they married beneath them and stay in such a marriage...or mutual manacling.

—**Carol Matthau**, Walter's wife, a writer, and an intimate of Truman Capote

Mother was no good for anything except to create chaos and fear. She didn't like me because of my talent....And when she sang, she had a crude voice. My sisters had lousy voices too. My father had a pretty good voice, but he wasn't allowed to talk.

—**Judy Garland**, whose father was gay or bisexual

Vincente Minnelli, my second (husband), was too busy for me....(He) snored louder and longer than any man in the world. After two years of this I was going crazy. We only had one bedroom, so...one night I sat up in bed and hit him as hard as I could with my fist—the one on which I wore my heavy wedding and engagement rings. I broke the poor man's nose. He woke up yelling and holding a horribly bloody nose. I quickly took some of the blood and smeared it on his night table and convinced him he had thrown himself against it during a nightmare.

It didn't cure Vincente's snoring, but he did build another wing on the house so I could sleep in peace.

—**Judy Garland** (in the 8/67 *Ladies' Home Journal*), on her second (gay or bi) husband, a marriage fostered by their studio, MGM

Tony Perkins literally had a love-hate relationship with a lot of his (male) lovers...sadomasochism was an element of his nature. The sight of blood excited him; at least it was usually fake blood. He had all these little games, like pretend-boxers, cops and robbers, dungeon...whenever he could talk a guy into joining him. It was part of his fantasy world...but love plain and simple—love with another guy—that wasn't part of his world.

—**Brian O'Dowd**, Perkins' dresser and close friend

One day...Jimmy (Dean) asked me, 'You ever had something to do with a guy, or just fooling around?' All I'd told him at that time was that I'd gone to a Hollywood party at the Garden of Allah, and Tyrone Power, who was drunk, squeezed my hand, patted me on the head, then kissed me and said I was the most beautiful boy he had seen in a long time.

—Dean intimate **John Gilmore**, in *Live Fast—Die Young*

Sometimes just a feature can be erotic. Ty Power had the most erotic gaze you could ever see.

—**Cesar Romero**, who though widely rumored to be Power's lover, never admitted it (preferring to recall Ty as an alleged heterosexual)

Eroticism is when you use a feather, and pornography is when you use the whole chicken.

—Polish director **Roman Polanski** (*Chinatown*), exiled from the USA for having had sex with a female minor

I enjoy reading the *Lesbian News* (on whose cover she appeared)....It's one of my most common fantasies...one of the most beautiful things—two women that are lovers. I guess I just haven't found the right woman at the right time yet...I think the (lesbian-themed) movie *Bound* was really erotic. I found that to be one of the most erotic things I've ever seen. It is the hottest movie. I can't think of a sex scene that was as sexy and wonderful. Now, I couldn't handle the violence in the movie; I fast-forwarded through that on video. But the love scene—could we have more of that, please?

—**Cybill Shepherd**

Movies kind of tell you a man should have sex with a girl and have fights with other guys. If you don't want to go by the movies, that's cool...if I'm in someone else's fantasy, that's cool too. You can't control anyone's fantasies, especially if you're an actor.

—undies model turned thespian **Mark** ("Marky Mark") **Wahlberg**

I didn't even know a homosexual existed until I was 17 or 18 or something like that. Not until I went to Mexico, and there a blond Norwegian is fair game.

—**David Soul** (*Starsky & Hutch*)

Before I fully processed what was happening, (director George) Cukor was rubbing my thigh. 'I have a picture in mind,' he said. 'I'm just now doing the casting. I think you'd be perfect for it.' I did not know whether to hit him or to feel sorry for him. Then I thought, Well, this is not so bad if this is all it is. Cukor continued with his rubbing, and I pressed him for details. 'Is it a big role?' I asked. 'Oh,' he cooed, 'the biggest.'

—**Anthony Quinn**, reminiscing

I told the story about Eddie Murphy picking me up because (*The Globe*) asked. I have this annoying habit of telling the truth....It's not as though I'm into outing, but people like him are teaching younger generations homophobia. Discrediting him needs to happen. He's unhappy, and I hope he gets help.

—drag actor **Karen Dior**, in *POZ* magazine

Eddie (Murphy) has gay friends. I mean guys. Guys who don't *dress up*...and at least he's apologized (for past homophobia on the screen). He admits he was too young to know better....Mel Gibson has gay associates, very close ones. Though maybe no gay friends. But can you imagine *him* apologizing? That'll be the day.

—**Joseph Miller**, Brooklynite, original Stonewall rioter, and AIDS activist

I love Cathleen (Nesbitt, the actress), and I think it's sweet that she says she was engaged to (British poet) Rupert Brooke....But it was so long ago that I read his letters to her, and I already guessed before being told that Brooke's mother had edited out anything she didn't like in them....

—**Tallulah Bankhead** (R.B. became a symbol of Britain's World War I effort and, apart from his mother's censorship, was officially heterized. Bankhead claimed to have read, in the 1920s, some of R.B.'s love letters to another man)

Brando has admitted his bisexuality, but Wally Cox never lived to do so. It was said he was gay, anyway....Everyone says when they were roommates and friends, Wally was the one who had the last word. He was said to be quite dominant, which is funny, because he looked so frail that an ejaculation could blow him off the face of the planet!

—Montgomery Clift biographer **Robert LaGuardia**

They had no sensitivity, or at least Gadge (Kazan) had it only for his work...and in that regard, they were the most insensitive and intolerant men I worked with.

—**Monty Clift**, referring to director Elia Kazan's and costar John Wayne's homophobia

There's just certain, you know, emotions, certain body parts I don't think should ever be referred to in public. Especially not where there's ladies concerned.

—**John Wayne**

If you've got to talk about men's cocks, dahlings, then at least call them cocks. I won't have the most beautiful part of the male anatomy dismissed as a ding-dong!

—**Tallulah Bankhead**, attending the ballet, after overhearing two women discussing the semi-visibility of the male dancers' "ding-dongs"

Well, dahling, I always did want to get into Marlene's pants!

—the bisexual **Bankhead**, upon being offered a role previously accepted by (the bisexual) Dietrich

Ann Heche says she never had a lesbian experience till she met Ellen. Okay, that's possible, though not likely for someone who'd done as many movies as she had. But Heche also says she never had a lesbian or even AC/DC thought or fantasy till she met Ellen. Right, yes. And I believe in the tooth fairy! I don't mean to sound mean, but it just doesn't add up!

—**Dana Plato**, *Diff'rent Strokes*, who at the time of her death in 1999 was engaged to a man (however, *TV Guide*, in a biased article about a male child-star survivor, erroneously linked Plato's death from drugs with her lesbian-roommates experience)

People used to think of Hollywood people as being at the forefront of sophistication and daring. Times have changed...celebrities are, understandably, among the last to leave the closet....These are individuals, individualistic yet highly conformist, constantly seeking an audience, and an audience's approval. Some seek to shock, but only slightly. And the ultimate shock remains homosexuality, or any part of it.

—UK author **Anthony Burgess** (*A Clockwork Orange*)

One difference is, back then (1969) we were clear that most non-gays hated us. Now many lesbigay people delude themselves into thinking they are safe and accepted, until there's another horrific murder or another anti-gay proposition (on the ballot) to remind us just how very fragile our gains have been....(We) seek legal recognition from a system that was not created to protect us....Another (difference) is that after Stonewall we...told straight people that if they didn't like us, they should just get out of our way.

—professor and author **Karla Jay** (*Tales of the Lavender Menace: A Memoir of Liberation*)

In a nutshell, liberals want rights, or liberties, for themselves and for others. While conservatives only want rights for people like themselves—they want to conserve, or maintain, the existing social order, injustices and all....Some minorities can no longer be held down...(but) gays can, and because most gays are in the closet and won't speak for themselves, conservatives can keep demonizing non-heterosexuals and can drive tremendous fundraising and votes this way. Don't show them as our relatives, don't show them as loving people with relationships, just show them as sex maniacs, and pretend they're a huge menace—predators and civilization-destroyers—rather than the victims and culture-makers that they tend to be.

—hetero musician **Frank Zappa**

The queen we would rather see on our postage stamps is not stripped to the waist and wearing spray-on red trousers.

—*Daily Mail* columnist **Simon Heffer**, trying to speak for all Britons after the issuance of a postage stamp honoring the memory of Queen frontman Freddie Mercury in 1999 (other bigots complained about commemorating a man who was gay and had died of AIDS)

As with (Jean-Paul) Sartre's explanation of anti-Semitism, gay-hating is less a feeling about particular people than a profound attachment to maintaining the existing social order....The creation of the 'homosexual menace,' not unlike the fantasy of a worldwide Jewish conspiracy, transforms the average man into a valiant defender of the 'normal'—a process that celebrates and reinforces the sexual status quo....Just as the mythology of anti-Semitism magnifies the power of the Jew, gay-hating recasts the homosexual as sexually and socially dangerous.

—**Michael Bronski**, author of *The Pleasure Principle*

There will be no decent apartment available (in Marseilles, France in 1941) until we have kicked out all these ignoble Yids who are burdening us.

—31-year-old oceanographer **Jacques Cousteau**, using the ignoble tactic of blaming a minority for the majority's problems, in a letter published for the first time in 1999, in the newspaper *Le Monde*

It might interest you to know that I have just reopened a classic old movie theater here in Decatur, IL—the Avon—and this weekend we are (belatedly) showing *Gods & Monsters* as a first-run in this town! Furthermore, I have been threatened by local Christian groups for the audacity of screening a 'gay movie' (sic), and local Jerry Falwell types threaten to picket my theater! It's getting awfully difficult to be a straight, heterosexual (sic) male, and be the target of all these threatened homophobes!

—ASCAP composer and publisher **Skip Huston**, in a mid-1999 letter to *Scarlet Street* magazine

The kindly, charitable image of Christianity has again been torn asunder by more recent reactions like the Holocaust and the indifference and contempt of most churches to gays suffering through AIDS, not to mention the myriad of active malcontents like the sons of anti-gay preachers following in their fathers' harmful footsteps for the money and attention, and the straight Christian fundamentalist pickets at Matthew Shepard's funeral with signs that read that this young man so monstrously tortured to death by their evil sons was now 'burning in hell.'

—Cincinnati AIDS activist **Russell John Hartzell II**

It really doesn't matter who you love, it matters that you love.

—Roseanne

In this era of political and religious attacks on the gay and lesbian community, their lives are an excellent, a perfect example of true, genuine family values. Love is love, it's a constant, it's the speed of light, cannot be changed, cannot be slowed down.

—Tom Hanks

I was 17 and I kissed a girl for the first time. And the earth moved and the heavens opened up and I looked around and I felt like I was the most alone person on this earth—as far as I knew there were no other girls who had ever kissed any other girl ever. And the thought that I would be isolated and rejected for the rest of my life was a very, very real one. Then one day I (found) a little pamphlet on homosexuality and it had this little pencil drawing of two girls holding hands, and my heart leapt. I was not alone. So someone somewhere had seen two girls holding hands.

I didn't care if the pamphlet said we were sick or whatever. All I cared about was that image, the feeling of hope. And if the power of one small drawing was so great to me, imagine what the work all of us are doing means to young gays everywhere today.

—Melissa Etheridge, at a Gay & Lesbian Alliance Against Defamation (GLAAD) Media Awards show (still not televised, despite the superstars in attendance—gay, hetero, bi, and closeted)

I really started going to those lesbian pride meetings to meet other women.

—k.d. lang

One reason I became an actor was because I heard you could meet queers in the theatre.

—Sir Ian McKellen

You know, Monica, I had a sex dream about you.

—**k.d. lang**, to Monica Lewinsky at *Vanity Fair*'s 1999 Oscar party, as reported by Liz Smith

If you are sexually adventurous, then I don't think heterosexuality would preclude you from trying whatever's out there.

—**Hugh Hefner**, founder of *Playboy*

A reporter asked me when I first knew I was gay. I said to him, 'About the same time you knew you were straight.'

—**Sir Ian McKellen**

In the '50s, people were blackmailed for being homosexual. It was worse in the States than in England because people were afraid to talk about it here. That was the atmosphere when Stephen (Sondheim) was growing up. And I think it was especially important to him that his parents not know. Bear in mind his mother has only recently died (in 1992, at 95 years). And it's only recently he'd begun to publicly identify himself as a homosexual. I really think it had a lot to do with his mother.

—Sondheim biographer **Meryle Secrest**

I wanted (daughter Chastity) to grow up, get married, have a child, get divorced, and live happily ever after.

—**Cher**, now a member of P-FLAG (Parents & Friends of Lesbians And Gays)

At 26, that lie (being in the closet) was like a prison I'd been in all my life. I knew this huge lie would continue to eat me up inside....I said 'I'm gay,' and then saw my mother's expression change to one that said 'You are no longer my son.' Suddenly she was ice-cold and wouldn't look at me...I moved to California (but) my father got together an army of 'prayer warriors' and they began sending me letters and making telephone calls, insisting I either repent or die.

And death is a constant theme in these letters, as if death were a better option than living this life, because they believe being gay is 'a sin unto death.' Even my 11-year-old sister wrote that God can change you or kill you....Then I realized I could help other people by sharing my story.

—**Stuart Miller**, 33, author of *Prayer Warriors* (Miller grew up near Nashville among fundamentalist Christians; his father founded the Believers' Chapel)

Isn't it a violation of the so-called sodomy law for lawmakers and preachers in those states to have their heads up their asses?

—singer **Michael Callen**

Religious fundamentalists talk about 'the devil' so much, it's an obsession. Yet the devil, or devils, are among us—the people who spread so much hate, and so needlessly....Always, they talk about hell, and they're the very ones who create a hell here on earth.

—author **Paul Monette**

Pat Robertson talks about 'darkness.' He says that in countries where gay people have more rights, 'darkness' is falling. He seems to forget—conveniently, as a professional Christian—that the Dark Ages were what followed Greece and Rome when the Church took over, when the Church became law—a religious dictatorship—and it went unchallenged until the Renaissance, which was a body of gay male artists looking back to pre-Christian times, to Greece and Rome, when homosexuality was accepted, for inspiration and for justification.

—**Stanley Shapiro**, Oscar-winning screenwriter (*Pillow Talk* starring Rock Hudson, and the Cary Grant vehicles *Operation Petticoat* and *That Touch Of Mink*)

It occurs to me that the 'gay agenda' is just this—to be able to introduce your mom to your friends, especially at Christmas.

—gay writer **John Weir**

People have to look beyond themselves—their own group. I called up this gay catalogue in Texas, and it was December, and they said, 'Merry Christmas....' I said, 'Thanks, and Happy Hanukkah,' and the male operator said, 'Oh, I'm not *that*'—maybe he didn't know the word 'Jewish.' But I wrote the company a letter explaining—because every time, it was 'Merry Christmas'—that they're treating non-Christians the same way that heterosexuals treat homosexuals. The very same: as if everyone is, or should be, a member of that majority group.

—**Michael Callen**

It's just true: a lot of gays need to re-examine whether and why they're racist or anti-Semitic or anti-feminist and so forth. Yes, heteros need to examine and deal with their homophobia, but they're not the only group that needs to delve inward and come up with some more loving alternatives to the usual mind-frame.

—**Dana Plato**, *Diff'rent Strokes*

This may sound shitty, but any lesbian who has done well or has been in the public eye is always turned down by other lesbians.

—model/actress/mechanic **Jenny Shimizu**

A lot of people have accused Scully of being gay. She's single, she's a strong, independent, suit-wearing female who chooses not to shack up with (a male) whom some people consider the sexiest male on TV. And all I have to say to this is: Thank you!

—**Gillian Anderson** (*The X-Files*), at a gala fundraiser for the L.A. Gay & Lesbian Center

It was my first time kissing another girl, and you know, girls can be so judgmental. I care much more about what women think than men, so I really wanted to impress her.

—**Selma Blair**, on smooching Sarah Michelle Gellar for the film *Cruel Intentions*

I've been interested in women since I was 12 years old. I think I could definitely fall in love with a woman, but I've always been more into men.

—**Ione Skye**

I've thought about it, when relationships don't work out with guys, and you think, God, this woman friend is so wonderful, it would be so much easier. But really, it's going to be the same damn problems.

—**Lucy Liu** (*Ally McBeal*)

I think any relationship is tough, period. Though they're more tough for people who always want to get their way and aren't lucky enough to find someone to give in to them—like husbands usually find with wives....I like that with gays, it's more based on equality, two peers—two men or two women. The roles aren't defined, and the romance doesn't end because a baby, planned or unplanned, is born....Also, the woman doesn't have to change her last name and identity and all.

—**Helene Hanff** (women don't legally have to change their surnames upon contractual marriage)

Relationships are the brakes on sex....You can't have sex all the time. That would make it routine and dull, like overeating. But we most of us tend to think, or act, on the short run. Instead of the long run. Instead of waiting for Mr. Right, we usually go for Mr. Right Away.

—**Jed Johnson**, director of *Andy Warhol's 'Bad'*

Gay people have the same right to lose half their stuff as everyone else.

—openly hetero comic **Richard Jeni**, on same-sex marriage

Do I have to have a stance? I'm for it. I'm all for it! I'm not big on marriage—I'm commitmentphobic myself—but if a couple of other (gay) people want to do that, I think it's terrific.

—finally openly gay **Nathan Lane**

I'm as married as most any ordinary guy, and that includes the occasional strayings that the male libido is subject to....I am married...it's the bigotry of church and state that prevents my married state being clear to everyone else. Even though we reportedly don't live in a religious state....

—**Truman Capote**

They used to say that if men had sex together, 'What will happen to the baby population?' Well, take a look. There's plenty of come to go around, thank you very much.

—**Gore Vidal**

The other side—the side's far right, which is never far from wrong—says that with gay civil rights and 'special rights' like the right not to be fired for being gay or the right to the same economic benefits as straight marrieds—we're trying to 'homosexualize' America. Bull! Never mind that they're always trying, and unsuccessfully, to heterosexualize us....All we do demand is equality, an acceptance of people's differences and the right to love and be left in peace.

—**Pedro Zamora** (*The Real World*)

It's true that laws can't make people like you. But they can make people desist against you....Other minorities may not be universally loved or accepted, but the laws can protect them. If straights don't want to give us the same protective laws, then why should we pay taxes—same as they do, or even more, and *more* now, thanks to the Republicans' Contract on America that gives an *additional* tax break of $500 to the parents of every kid under 18!...We pay and pay, we do our duty, have the same responsibilities, but *none* of the legal privileges and protections!

—**Forman Brown**, of L.A.'s Turnabout Theatre, which the non-pro-gay *Time* once called "Hollywood's toniest vaudeville show"

You want hypocrisy and perversion of public morality? Nevada has long recognized (legally) the perhaps necessary evil of heterosexual prostitution. However not until the late '90s did it legalize homosexuality—gay sex between two consenting adults, belatedly overturning a decades old law that could be, and was, used to invade the home of male couples. That's patriarchy for you: law that caters to straight men wanting to buy sex, and that degrades women and all gay men and criminalizes their relationships.

—**Steve Smith**, president of L.A.'s Gay Men's Chorus

I always wanted to be kept—but no one would keep me more than a week.

—Truman Capote

The real clue to your sexual orientation lies in your romantic feelings, rather than in your sexual feelings. If you are really gay, you are able to fall in love with a man, not just enjoy having sex with him.

—novelist/screenwriter
Christopher Isherwood

I'd be quite prepared if I was living with another man to put that in front of everything else in my life. It's not the sex that I miss. It's the sunsets.

—Sir Ian McKellen

I am prepared to believe that the sense of romance in those of our brothers and sisters who incline towards love of their own sex is heightened to a more blazing pitch than in those who think of themselves as 'normal.'

—Laurence Olivier, as quoted by Tommy Tune in his memoir *Footnotes*

I consider myself bisexual. It wasn't that I was sexually attracted to men *per se*, but you know, if you do something for a while you can acquire a taste for it.

—Andy Warhol "superstar" **Joe Dallesandro**

A lot of woman have had bisexual husbands. But as far as I'm concerned, that means he's gay and trying to pass for straight. And marriages like that don't last. Well, they can—if the wife is frigid!

—Joan Collins

Who cares if a women who once loved men now loves women? Who cares if someone's love fluctuates between women and men? What's the big fucking deal? Let's stop being so judgmental of everyone who doesn't fit into our boxed-in perception of what is love.

—Gillian Anderson, *The X-Files*

The point is, sex is just part of it. That's why 'homosexual' is as lousy a descriptive word as 'heterosexual' would be if it was used as endlessly, as maliciously. Sex. Yes, wonderful. But it's a *part* of the picture. Admittedly a bigger part for most men, gay or straight, than for women. But the greater part of the picture is love, crush, affection, relationship, courting, requiting, bonding, breaking up, regaining hope, starting again.

—**Graham Chapman**, Monty Python

Any love is natural and beautiful that lies within a person's nature; only hypocrites would hold a man responsible for what he loves—emotional illiterates and those of righteous envy who, in their agitated concern, mistake so frequently the arrow pointing to heaven for the one that leads to hell.

—**Truman Capote**

She's a loving, feeling girl.

—**Cissy Houston**'s response to rumors that daughter Whitney was lesbian (in other words, mama said no way)

First, the Christian Right ran those vile 'conversion' ads in papers, masking their hateful bigotry with concern and compassion. Now it's television...ads with a mother saying her son didn't know he could just walk away from being homosexual by praying to their harsh, intolerant version of Mr. God....There are always bigots like this, but what's disgusting is America's tolerance of intolerance...and that there are always newspapers and TV stations willing to run these filthy lies.

—actor **Charles Pierce** (*Designing Women*)

You read about it time and again. In gay papers only. How a major urban daily (newspaper) will turn down a paid ad for gay rights, then turn around and take a paid ad by some hate-vending group against gays...newspapers that are supposed to be fair! Impartial?! Can you imagine any other minority group putting up with such treatment?

—attorney and frequent CNN guest **Tom Stoddard**

It's now reached the point (in the U.S.) where half of all new AIDS cases are black people. Yet the radical right is still using the lie that AIDS is 'gay.' They still use it in their fundraising literature and their anti-gay commercials and what-not. They *know* it's not so. They don't care. Most people will swallow anything, especially if they *want* it to be so.

—**Paul Schmidt**, gay poet and translator

If the Christian Coalition followed its own logic, they'd be running ads urging straight women to change and become lesbians in order to avoid AIDS.

—**AIDS Action "Hotwire"** on CC ads exhorting gays to "become" heterosexual to avoid contracting AIDS (August 14, 1998)

If you are going to love someone of your same sex, then do it. Do it responsibly, do it beautifully, do it with commitment, do it deeply. Promiscuity, both homosexually and heterosexually, is dangerous, and if you're going to be doing that, you really have to protect yourself.

—singer **Gloria Estefan**

I used to think 'promiscuity' meant when you said 'I promise' a lot.

—gay comic **Frank Maya**

Every time I say a kind word about gays I hear from people, and some are damn mad. People throw Leviticus, Deuteronomy and other parts of the Bible at me. But it doesn't bother me. I've always been compassionate toward gay people. People are shocked by some of the things I discuss in my column, but that's their ignorance. You can't help that.

—pro-gay *Dear Abby* columnist **Abigail Van Buren** (unlike her twin sister Ann Landers)

It's...how do you describe it? Funny? Pathetic? Sad? All these books, from both extremes, trying to explain what it says in the

Bible about homosexuality. Why explain?—it's right in the Bible. It is *not* a gay-friendly book. Period. Neither is the Koran, the Torah, or most other 'holy' books. Get over it! So what? Do you know how long ago those books were written? And by what kind of tunnel-vision men? Get over it, and get on with your love and your life!

—composer **Lionel Bart** (*Oliver!*)

Do you know *I Left My Heart In San Francisco* was written by a gay man to his lover? That is *so* romantic, but I wonder if everyone probably thinks it's a regular love song from before when San Francisco became a ...gay symbol.

—**William Como**, *Dance* magazine editor

They were pushing me as, in a way, an American David Bowie. It worked for him, but I guess that's over there (in Britain). After I came out and said I was gay, the radio people...everyone dropped me...and it's not like I'm supposed to be some romantic leading man. This is rock, glam rock, it's not love ballads or something!

—singer **Jobriath**, who in 1973 became the first openly gay rock performer if not star

The powers that be hate that (homosexuality) isn't invisible or mute anymore. But the thing they're most dead-set against is making or admitting there's any connection between it and romance. Romance, you see, is a potent marketing tool.

—pro-gay **Elizabeth Montgomery** (1933-1995) of *Bewitched*

People forget that 50 years and more ago, most heterosexual couples did not necessarily get legally married. In 19th-century England, most were not....One of the biggest reasons, apart from straight propaganda, that nearly every Hollywood movie ended with a new, about-to-marry girl and boy was to encourage all heteros to marry—to join the system. A controlling system.

—film historian **Carlos Clarens**

Marriage is the only contract between two human beings that they cannot by their own mutual consent terminate. They have to apply to the government for its dissolution. Which is no coincidence. Government is a self-feeding, ever-growing organism.

—feminist author **Kate Millett**

Marriage may or may not breed children. It usually does breed hypocrisy.

—Dame Peggy Ashcroft (*A Passage To India*)

Vivian Vance (*I Love Lucy*'s Ethel Mertz) married a younger man who was gay, an editor named John Dodds. She was happy to snag a younger man important in his field, and one who wouldn't beat her (like prior husband Phil Ober)....He was happy with her limelight, with her crowd and the Hollywood connection—Hollywood just dazzles and seduces people, you know—and probably with his new rep. But it was a shame, and they each lost lots of friends because of it. Plus I suppose many a night's sleep—you know what I mean.

—Paul Rosenfield, Joyce Haber's former legman

People are talking about you and Lucy, you ought to be careful about the hugging and kissing you do on the show. You behave like a couple of dykes in heat.

—Vivian Vance's jealous actor husband, Phil Ober

When Cary Grant was married to the fabulously wealthy Barbara Hutton, she paid all the household bills and servants' wages. She had a mania for soft drinks, couldn't live without her cola, and let her servants drink all they wanted. Or they could have, if not for Cary. He rationed them behind her back—one cola a day. ...True, he was her only husband who didn't take any alimony, but not because he wasn't a skinflint. Besides, Barbara knew a secret or two about Cary Grant, and he didn't want her to talk. She was like her uncle, E.F. Hutton: when she talked, everybody listened.

—*L.A. Times* columist **Joyce Haber** (a 1999 American Movie Classics *Great Romances* program ficti-romanticized the Hutton-Grant marriage)

Everybody wants to be Cary Grant. Even I want to be Cary Grant.

—actor **Cary Grant**

If Rock Hudson married Gomer Pyle, would his name be Rock Pyle?

—**1960s joke** (Pyle was played by Hudson's friend, at least, Jim Nabors)

There was this (TV) program, it was titled *Animals Are People Too*, and it had two dogs getting married, which ordinarily I might find cute or amusing. But the segment showed a minister wedding the two dogs, and it appalled me, because here are people oohing and ahing over the supposed marriage of a female dog and a male dog, and the minister lending his dubious presence, and at the same time most people are angry and self-righteous over the idea that two *people* of the same gender might love each other and want to commit for life and have their own wedding.

—theatre director **Ron Link**

For the first time in White House history, an openly gay couple was invited by President Clinton to a state dinner…honoring Colombian president Andres Pastrano. *Rolling Stone*'s publisher brought along Matt Nye, the handsome fashion designer responsible for the end of Jann Wenner's long marriage to Jane Wenner.

—November 1998, issue of *Fab!* Magazine

It's all about what you're used to…Time was, there were no black people in (TV) commercials…I remember Virginia Woolf quoting a male chauvinist in her book *A Room of One's Own* (1928); he said, 'A woman composing music is like a dog walking on his hind legs—it's not done well, but you are surprised that it's done at all.' And Mozart had a sister—but being female, with centuries of male-dominated tradition behind her, she was sadly never encouraged to explore her own musical genius by her family or her culture.…In other words, same-sex couples and same-sex marriages only seem odd or weird to most of us now because of centuries of repression...because we're never given a chance to *see* them.

Someday people will look back, and it'll seem weird that it ever seemed weird.

—**Howard Ashman**, Oscar-winning producer and lyricist of *The Little Mermaid*

Too many people can't visualize what they haven't had presented before their eyes. That's the case with gay weddings, now that more and more gays and lesbians are doing the ceremony. All most straights see is two grooms, two brides, you know, two gowns or tuxedoes...they see what the clothes *look* like—*different*—instead of seeing the individuals and the love involved.

—choreographer **Joe Layton**, who did the all-hetero musical numbers for gay producer Ross Hunter's *Thoroughly Modern Millie*, starring Julie Andrews

There's marriage and there's marriage, and there should be (legal) gay marriage. Get this: in July, 1995, a Cincinnati judge ordered a man to marry the woman he'd gotten pregnant, and beaten by his own admission. So there you have *marriage* as a *sentence*, and it struck me how unbelievable that the law gives preference to a marriage where one partner physically abuses the other than a marriage in which both halves of the same gender merely love each other. Sick, sick, sick!

—Cincinnati AIDS activist **Russell John Hartzell II**

There are a number of oddities with those politicians who quote the Bible when it suits them. For example, both House Majority leader Dick Armey and House Speaker Newt Gingrich are divorced and remarried, which means they are living in sin by their own rules, which I guess they mean for everybody else to follow except themselves.

—columnist **Mark Haile** (also literary events coordinator for gay A Different Light bookstore)

Well, my present relationship with Jonathan (Thomas) is going on 28 years. I tend to have long-term relationships.

—playwright **Edward Albee** (*Who's Afraid Of Virginia Woolf?*)

I'm the longest married woman in my family.

—lesbian writer **Dorothy Allison** (*Bastard Out of Carolina*)

I saw this TV movie, I guess, and I happened onto a scene where black and white people were helping a black family remove some racist graffiti on the wall of their home. That's great. But if the 'n' word was the 'f' word, would the others be there helping? Would such a scene even get filmed? The truth of it is that white people don't always have ethnic-minority friends or neighbors, yet everybody—whites, blacks, etc.—has gay or lesbian relatives, or both....We don't see media images, or hardly ever do, of straight solidarity with gay relatives, friends, neighbors, etc. That's unfair, and it's one-sided, very much so.

—actor and gay rights activist **Brian Hurley**

The media have shown that they can affect a lot of people's attitudes and help diminish prejudice....They've done it with black characters and interracial themes. Leaving out lesbians and gays, of course. But also leaving out most every other minority, hetero *or* homo....What I'd love to see is a gay Asian character! Even any East Asian character! Hollywood, and the media, are so narrow and narrowly focused—wake up! America has more than *one* minority! And every minority includes *us*—gays are *everywhere*.

—**Ryan Nakagawa**, Chief Ethics Officer of the Los Angeles Metropolitan Transportation Commission

When somebody tells me, 'You're going to lose your career,' I say, 'I don't believe God works that way.' You fall in love, you're happier than you've ever been—and now you're going to suffer for it?

—**Anne Heche**

But love I never liked. *Love* is a four-letter word I never use—and one that is never used on me. If anyone was ever in love with me, it must have been a well-kept secret, because I never heard of it. Love is a mistake.

—curmudgeon **Quentin Crisp**

When one is in love one begins by deceiving oneself. And one ends by deceiving others. That is what the world calls a romance.

—cynic **Oscar Wilde**

Where's the man could ease a heart/Like a satin gown?

—**Dorothy Parker**

I was wondering lately what chance women have for happiness when you consider that two-thirds of the word *happiness* is *penis*?

—feminist comedian **Elayne Boosler**

The difference between dogs and men is that you know where dogs sleep at night.

—gay former diving champ **Greg Louganis**

Boy George with drummer Jon Moss.

The downside of (George Michael's arrest) is that everybody points the finger and says, 'See, look at gay people. They're just really sad. They go to toilets and wank, and they don't have relationships, and they don't love each other.' And I hate that. That annoys me because I am not that kind of person. I'm romantic.

—**Boy George**

The proliferation of gay characters on TV has antigays upset because these shows carry the message they least want to hear. Gay people can be nice, normal, everyday folks. Demanding that gays live in closets ultimately diminishes the family and society rather than preserve them.

—**William C. Stosine**, in a *TV Guide* letter re article "In With the Out Crowd" in May 1, 1999, issue

Richard Deacon

I don't care if a young friend prefers Ethel Merman to Greta Garbo. But if he hasn't heard of either one, then he's way too young, forget it.

—**Richard Deacon** (*The Dick Van Dyke Show*)

We were together five years (but) she's young. She still had to have some experiences in life.

—**Sandra Bernhard**, on former partner and *Sports Illustrated* swimsuit model Patricia Velasquez

I was pleasantly surprised to learn that Rita (Mae Brown) wrote *Rubyfruit Jungle* partly to woo—is that the word?—Alexis Smith. Now *that*'s an attractive older woman.... I always heard she was one of us. But being a movie star, I guess she figures silence is golden.

—lesbian writer **Audre Lord**

As for looks, you do the best you can. We all know we'll be old, once enough time passes. And by that time, all the expensive things you bought won't console you for a life that hasn't had love, curiosity and pleasure.

—**Gianni Versace**

John Phillip Law and Jane Fonda, *Barbarella*.

Back in the '60s, I got a raging crush on John Phillip Law after I saw him in *The Sergeant* where Rod Steiger kissed him and in *Barbarella* as that gorgeous blind angel....I don't know if he is or he isn't, but I'm kind of like the housewife in Des Moines on the topic of, say, Rock Hudson's or Cary Grant's sexuality: I'd rather not know. At certain moments, ignorance can be bliss.

—**Howard Brookner**, director-producer-cowriter of *Bloodhounds Of Broadway*

I'd already come out (to gay readers), in France and then in *Christopher Street* (magazine). But then I was on National Public Radio and I was asked if I was traveling with my wife (friend and associate), Mary Woronov? Not for the first time…(so) I declared, 'We're not married. I'm gay and Mary's a painter.'

—actor-director **Paul Bartel** (*Eating Raoul*)

Nobody hardly recalls who Mr. Melnitz was, yet when they renamed the Melnitz Theater (at UCLA), there was an outcry in some quarters. Due to it now being called the James Bridges Theater, after the Hollywood director, because a very significant sum was donated in Mr. Bridges' memory by his significant other, the actor Jack Larson….People don't want to know; it's a civilian form of don't-ask-don't-tell.

—actress **Susan Strasberg** (Larson played Jimmy Olson on TV's *Superman* and Bridges helmed *The China Syndrome*, among other hits)

Clint (Eastwood) talked openly about his own early years and how desperate he'd been to work and how he'd become very close, a protégé actually, with his first mentor, a director, a Mr. Lubin, who Clint said was gay. 'We spent a lot of time together, traveled together. He liked me a lot; got me into the talent program at Universal, gave me a lot of breaks. Bought me some nice clothes too. That's when people started wondering about us!' Clint laughed.

'So come on, Clint. You can tell us the truth.'

Clint glanced up sheepishly and said, 'I'll never tell.'

—**Sondra Locke**, Eastwood's longtime girlfriend and costar, in her memoirs (Arthur Lubin created TV's *Mr. Ed*)

In most ways it was a damn good picture. But if we remade *Midnight Cowboy* today, the whole relationship between Buck and Ratso would have to be sexualized or at least made, you know, like in love… to be sexually or erotically honest. And if John Schlesinger directed it again, I'm sure he'd insist on it!

—**Jon Voight** (now openly gay Schlesinger won an Oscar for *MC*)

If the Republicans who control (Congress) think that who I sleep with or who I love makes me unfit to be an ambassador, then their grip on reality, past or present, is very shaky.

—philanthropist **James Hormel** (of the meat-packing company), whose nomination by Pres. Clinton as ambassador to Luxembourg in 1997 was repeatedly stalled by Senate conservatives; in mid-1999, Clinton used a constitutional provision that allows a president to bypass the usual confirmation process during a congressional recess and named Hormel 'interim ambassador,' serving until the end of 2000—Hormel thus became the U.S.'s first openly gay ambassador

Yes, I have (played gay roles)....Particularly if one has worked in films or plays set in the past, there are bound to be king's and...other leaders, and generals....Of course it does depend on the willingness of the filmmakers to present the truth, if such characters are the focus of a particular work.

—UK actor and former James Bond **Timothy Dalton**, whose gay portrayals include French King Philip II, the lover of England's Richard the Lion-Hearted

Corydon (by gay French writer Andre Gide) dovetailed with Freud's ideas in recognizing homosexuality as a manifestation of the spirit and not simply the genitals.

—author **Robert Drake**, *The Gay Canon*

When we say someone's gay, we're talking about sexual orientation, not their sexual activity. It's not our fault that every time someone says 'gay,' people think 'sex.' That's *their* twisted problem.

—writer **Vito Russo**

What has to be changed, and will be changed, and we will no longer put up with—though it'll take time—is all of us contributing to a society that however blesses the heterosexual union while making outlaws of both the homosexual union and the homosexual single.

—gay artist **David Wojnarowicz**

I remember in junior high school, we were practicing football tackling, and the coach got upset that I wasn't knocking the other guy down and vice versa. The coach yelled, real loud and sarcastic, 'Hey! Fight each other—don't *love* each other!' It was meant to embarrass us, but I know that for me it suddenly made me aware of how perverted the adults' value system is and what a backward establishment we all have to live under.

—**Warren Casey**, author-lyricist (*Grease*)

The only way (to combat homophobia) is to reach kids and stop the hate.

—**Anne Heche**, who with Ellen speaks to lesbian and gay teens across the country

It is in the brain…that the great sins of the world take place.

—**Oscar Wilde** (*The Picture of Dorian Gray*)

Keeping your sex life out of the public eye isn't a bad idea—more heterosexuals should try it—but having to hide the one you love, or the fact that you love, that is a burden too heavy and hurtful to request…worse, when it is *demanded* of us.

—gay German director-writer-actor **Rainer Werner Fassbinder** (*The Marriage Of Maria Braun*)

Lizabeth Scott

I'm in love with a wonderful life, a life of living alone.

—former (never contractually wed) movie star **Lizabeth Scott**, whose career was hurt by a 1950s outing

My life right now is very happy, um, living in a gay relationship. I'm very happy with that.

—**George Michael**, in 1998, supposedly a former heterosexual

No. I thought I was (in love with a woman). I thought I had [fallen in love] a couple of times.

—**George Michael**, explaining in 1999 that the first time he fell in love was in the early '90s, with a male

It's just as much work for an attractive person not to have sex as it is for an unattractive one to have sex.

—supposedly asexual but gay **Andy Warhol**, who once described love as what happens "when some of the chemicals inside you go bad"

As more than a casual pastime, (sex) is too heart-scalding and costly, however you interpret the latter adjective.

—**Truman Capote**

I sometimes feel that Americans feel it's almost a duty to have a good sex life. You know, 'These are my rights, and I'm going to make love to as many men as I can, and I'll feel guilty if I don't.'

—British actor-writer **Simon Callow** (*A Room With A View*)

Renato (Ugo Tognazzi) and Albin (Michel Serrault).

Once, I asked a priest friend if he were homosexual, as I was rather sure that he was. He ended the subject by telling me, 'I am a celibate, as you must realize.' But still I wondered, 'All right, but when you have fantasies or dreams, it is *men*, isn't it?'

—French actor **Michel Serrault** (*La Cage Aux Folles*)

I don't make music in order to pick fights with the Catholic Church. Besides, the church's stands on homosexuality and women make the pope look far more ridiculous than any pop song could....The *Post* headline was much better than winning any Grammy.

—sapphic singer **Joan Osborne**, referring to a *New York Post* headline ("Furor Over Grammy Star!") the day of the Grammy's, occasioned by her song "*One Of Us,*" whose interpretation of God didn't match the Church's

It must be a crazy person who chooses to be gay in such a homophobic world.

—South Africa's Archbishop **Desmond Tutu**, who's also allegedly anti-Semitic

After I starred in *The Cardinal*, you wouldn't believe how many priests propositioned me. Among them some renowned for their denunciations—no pun intended—of lesbians, bisexuals and particularly gay men.

—actor turned author **Tom Tryon**

Well, another reason I'm against (homosexuality) is that opposites are supposed to attract. It's only natural.

—actor turned politician **Ronald Reagan**

Opposites attract in fiction, mostly.

—screenwriter **Anita Loos**

With so many (hetero) married couples, they sit at the table in a restaurant and they don't talk...but gay couples do tend to talk to each other. Because after the sexual passion is over, a pair of men, or lesbians, they're still best friends and have plenty in common.

—**Ben Bagley**, producer of hit off-Broadway revues *Cole Porter*

I don't know why some people are surprised to find I've been happily married. They may confuse me with the love-lorn character I played (in *Our Miss Brooks*)....Others remember me from the old movies, where I often had to wear glasses. It was in the script. They used glasses for a number of reasons, none of them very flattering. Particularly for women. A female wearing glasses often gave rise to all *sorts* of rumors!

—**Eve Arden**, TV star and film supporting actress (*Mildred Pierce*)

You look at the pictures back then, and if a guy wore glasses, it was code. Something was 'wrong' with him. He was 'too smart' or he was queer, or both—it usually went together....Now they don't dare to do that—too many guys wearing glasses.

—**Gene Kelly**, actor-director

Like, a Rudy Galindo gets flack from some quarters for being 'too soft.' What does that really mean? What do they really want? Rudy is graceful, mild, he's pleasant...would they prefer some caveman who might rape their daughters? Why don't people think before they speak?

—singer, dancer and theatrical designer **Howard Crabtree**

Homosexuals make the best friends because they care about you as a woman and are not jealous. They love you but don't try to screw up your head.

—**Bianca Jagger**

What an expression: 'women-haters.' Men *and* women will throw it at us, just because we don't want to pork women...yet it's the husbands, ex-husbands, boyfriends, jealous ex-boyfriends, ad nauseum, the ones who bash their women—the women they think they own—or even murder....that I'd call the *real* women-haters.

—attorney and businessman **Sheldon Andelson**

I probably would have gone bankrupt without all my gay fans. They're not just fair-weather friends. Because if you guys like someone, you kind of stick with them.

—**Cher**, accepting a gay-rights award

Oh, yes. Gay audiences and British audiences, it must be said, are kinder to older women. Because they are still interested…I know that some actresses who might be otherwise washed up have had their careers extended thanks to their gayest (sic) fans.

—**Bette Davis**

Myths take a very long time to die; it's either a case of numbers proving them wrong or shouting them down. Like women drivers—endless jokes, and some desperate stand-up comics still do women-driver jokes. Despite the fact, for how many decades, that women are generally and statistically better drivers than men! That's an almost-dead myth….Or the one, very much alive, that if a man loves or lusts after men, he must be feminine because quote-unquote *women love men.* No exceptions, right? Well, honey, it takes more of a man to seduce another man than to seduce a woman.

—singer **Carmen McRae**

Here's a myth and a half!…When a straight guy meets a gay guy, right away he thinks to himself that the gay guy wants to suck his dick. I say, 'Doll, don't flatter yourself.'

—**Scott Valentine** (*Family Ties*)

They don't puzzle it out…put themselves in your place. I had a straight friend, friend of the family, and after he learned I was gay he asked me confidentially if that meant I'd be coming on to him. Politely, I shook my head. Actually, the guy was way too old, too heavy, too fat, too wrinkled. What was he *thinking*?! Is *he* attracted to every female human being on earth? Wake up and smell the reality!

—novelist and columnist **David Feinberg**

Love is love. We're told little boys should love little girls and little girls should love little boys. We know it's not so.

—**Julie Harris**, theatre, film and TV star (*Knots Landing*)

My mother was engaged to a man, and I had been sleeping with that man's son. My mother said, 'Oh, I'm going to get married to this man,' and I said, 'Oh, good! It can be a double wedding!'

—writer **Edmund White**

I was drunk, and it just felt right.

—**Robert Downey Jr.**, on kissing his male best friend

God forbid a straight person should acknowledge that there are pleasures associated with his anus.

—**Phil Hartman** (*NewsRadio*)

My father was very cool about my coming out. He said, 'Son, if it makes you feel any better, I've sucked a cock before.'

—**Alexis Arquette**

I told them because of my role in *My So-Called Life*. I knew I was going to be open about it to the public and so I had a talk to them first. When I told my mom she cried for two hours and then she was fine. I told my dad on Christmas Eve and he threw beer cans at me. Then he kicked me out of the house. I lived on the streets for about three months before the show started. It was the lowest point in my life. But I was fortunate in that I could see the light at the end of the tunnel. So many gay kids on the street see no end in sight.

—**Wilson Cruz**

I want to kill myself.

—**Wilson Cruz**, revealing the most frequent thing young gay fans write to him

Gay Youth 3.41 Times More Likely to Attempt Suicide

—**headline** in June, 1999, issue of *4-Front* magazine, re a new study published by the American Medical Association's Archives of Pediatric & Adolescent Medicine (it had been thought the figure was "only" 3.0)

These statistics underscore that anti-gay prejudice is a life-threatening problem. Suicides and violence against gay people will continue as long as extreme right-wing groups continue to dehumanize gay Americans and anti-gay harassment flourishes unchecked in our nation's schools.

—**Human Rights Campaign**'s reaction to the above

It's incomprehensible the way some parents treat their gay sons and daughters—unbelievable to me.

—supermom and author **Betty DeGeneres**

If you would have told me I would have been at the march on Washington standing before a million people and being seen all over the world, I would have told you you were nuts.

—**Dorothy Hajdys-Holman**, who has marched, spoken and lobbied since the 1992 murder by two shipmates of her sailor son Allen Schindler, 22

It's just hard to understand how anybody could go against a hate-crimes bill that includes everybody: race, creed, gender, sexual orientation—any reason for a hate-crime act.

—**Betty DeGeneres**, on the failure of Wyoming's state legislature to pass a law against hate crimes in the wake of Matthew Shepard's torture-murder

I was brought up to believe that we weren't to lie, yet it seems like just because somebody is gay that (others) want them to live a lie, or...they end up dead. That's why Allen ended up being dead, because he was tired of living a lie.

—**Dorothy Hajdys-Holman**; her son's murderer is eligible for parole in 2002, and his accomplice served only 78 days in a military prison....

They have to convert our agenda into something aggressive. Two guys wanting to be happy together are invading *their* marriages. Helping a kid who's getting beaten up in school is promoting homosexuality....Equal rights they call *special* rights....Yes, the right-wing in our country has such great respect for the truth that they use it only in emergencies.

—Congressman **Barney Frank**

'Homo' Carved Into Student For Liking Rock Band Queen—

headline in June, 1999, *Edge* magazine, re two Massachusetts prep school students who carved the word into a 17-year-old's back in letters four inches high because he liked what one assailant deemed "a gay band" (the local police chief deemed the incident "apparently a disagreement over the style of music (the victim) liked")

When any of you say, 'This is not about you, Ms. Kuehl. We like you, Ms. Kuehl,' I want to tell you something. This is very much about me. This is about me being kicked out of my sorority at UCLA, about me losing my series, *The Dobie Gillis Show*, because of my sexual orientation.

—actor turned California Assemblywoman **Sheila James Kuehl**, after the defeat in Sacramento of her "Dignity For All Students" Bill AB 222, which would have barred discrimination against and harassment of gay students in the state

Our self-appointed enemies try to act concerned and kindly though stern. They'll say that we're 'trapped in a gay lifestyle.' What we're trapped in is the anti-gay climate of insults, harassment and violence that they've created....Homosexuality is not the problem—the problem is homophobia.

—**Peter Malatesta**, restaurateur and Bob Hope's gay nephew (who later died of AIDS)

Right-wing extremists can live their lives the way they want to, but it's unfortunate that they want to impose their values on other people.

—**Dean Trantalis**, gay rights advocate who helped pass a new domestic partners law in Broward County,

Florida, that gives gay or hetero unwed couples the right to be treated as immediate family regarding hospital visits and the designation of health care surrogates; it also offers health benefits to partners of unwed county employees and gives companies which do the same a bidding advantage for county business

Unlike black people who are born to black parents, Jewish people who are born into the Jewish religion, Hispanics born to Hispanics, homosexuals are the only minority born into the enemy camp. So we have to hide. Homosexuals, male or female, have it particularly hard. I think that heightens our isolation, our loneliness, and our unique sensibility as camouflage.

—author **John Rechy** (*City of Night*), who is half Hispanic

Average high school students hear anti-gay epithets 25 times a day....When teachers hear these comments, they fail to respond 97% of the time....80% of gay youth report having been verbally abused....Gay youth are more than five times as likely as their straight classmates to skip school because they feel unsafe.

—according to the **Gay, Lesbian & Straight Education Network**

Being a teen and being in school, that was the worst part of my life. Kids are far more aggressive, even violent, than most adults, but with all of the adults' prejudices.

—*Oliver!* composer **Lionel Bart**

When religion becomes a money making enterprise, it always needs an enemy to keep the followers' interest...and Jerry Falwell has a magazine which he always tries to keep at fever pitch by attacking some new target, from Ellen DeGeneres to Tinky Winky, women's music fairs,...now his latest hate claim is that the two Columbine High School murderers are gay! And they're *not*. These people are dangerous because they'll say anything, the more hateful the better.

—L.A. theatre director **Ron Link**

The wonder is that with all they go through, gay students do not erupt in violence....Gays tend to repress their reactions, and the fact that they are inevitably victims and almost never aggressors isn't exactly something to brag about....Call a queer a 'fag' and he'll shrug it off, being used to it... (but) call a straight boy a 'fag' one time too many and he might explode in your face.

—**Pedro Zamora** (*The Real World*)

Reading, writing and revenge.

—the new "three r's," as noted in an **Asahi Shimbun** article about post-Columbine U.S. high schools

...(hetero) kids so petrified they might be what society hates that they act out violently to prove they're not. Perhaps you've acted out to protect your secret shame, or perhaps, like me, you've turned the hatred inward

But despite public jawboning about 'safe schools' and how children must be taught tolerance early on, inoculation against hatred still doesn't include sexual orientation. Our kids' blood-letting through suicides, gay-bashing and gut-wrenching silence is acceptable to adults who prefer the comfort of denial and benign neglect. Only after America faces up to its hate addiction and admits to its deadly dysfunctional attitudes towards sex and sexual orientation will we all truly be equally able to enjoy life, liberty and the pursuit of happiness.

—award-winning lesbian journalist **Karen Ocamb**, in 7/99 *Genre* magazine

It (growing up gay) might be different now, at least there's more (role) models now. It was *literally* unspeakable. It's hard to remember how shame-based it all was, but it was the worst thing that could happen.

—writer-director **Don Roos** (*The Opposite Of Sex*)

The thing with the hate groups who the media makes so respectable, like they're just the 'other' side of the issued where gays are concerned, is that they value an unborn fetus over the life of a gay grownup, an adult human being, or a gay or lesbian teen...and I'll go out on a limb and say that I imagine the most fanatically anti-choice types—the ones who approve of the bombings of (abortion) clinics and the murder of doctors—are the ones who most deeply instill in their kids the age-old values of hating gays and people they think are gay.

—producer **Ben Bagley**, who helped discover such talents as Bea Arthur, Chita Rivera and Tammy Grimes

You can't prove you're not gay. What can you do, *not* blow a guy?

—TV star **Norm MacDonald**, who was gay-bashed but is still, reportedly, far from pro-gay

Prosecutors Say Youths Killed Man Who Complimented Their Looks

—June, 1998, **headline** in *Frontiers* magazine, re two youths who beat a gay man to death in West Palm Beach, Florida

They're not brave, the gay-bashers. They're bullies and they're cowards. They look for the easy fights. Typically two against one...sometimes a whole gang against two gay men....They'll characterize gays as 'pansies,' as non-fighters, however they themselves never pick an even fight.

—**Jacques Rosas**, full-time campaigner for Greenpeace who was gay-bashed by six males with a baseball bat in West Hollywood in 1991

It's like being gay-bashed all over again.

—composer and soap star (*As The World Turns*, *Loving*) **Keith Pruitt**, who in 1993 was viciously gay-bashed along with boyfriend Jacques Rosas in Greenwich Village by three New Jersey youths; a year later, when Pruitt was well enough to audition for roles, he found that the knowledge that he was gay prevented Hollywood from offering him contract roles as before, meaning a reduction in status to a mere recurring role

I know of no other oppressed group without a physical safety zone. I don't see Klansmen burning crosses in black housing projects. (But) I see freaks deliberately going into gay areas to practice violence.

—hetero author **Andrew Vachss** (*Choice of Evil*)

Being black makes me very aware of the homophobia in my community...I am actually more likely to die from homophobic assault than from AIDS. AIDS prevention *is* in my control.

—transsexual activist **Cei Bell**, in the *Philadelphia Daily News*

White folks is always being surprised...like every minority in this country is one big, united coalition all together. But you take a poll, you'll see blacks are even more down on gays than whites. (It's) just that most of the famous anti-gay loudmouths are white—and plenty rich!

—**Howard Rollins** (*In The Heat Of The Night*); a 1997 *San Jose Mercury News* poll found that 58% of blacks labeled homosexuality "wrong," vs. 36% of whites

I don't know what people want of gays and lesbians in this country. If it's a 'choice,' how many people want to make that choice? Gay people are supposed to have sex 50 times in the afternoon. 'Okay.' I want *one* lover and I want to be monogamous and have the right to marry. 'No, you can't!' So they don't know what to do about it. They just don't like us. *They just don't like us.*

—leading Hollywood publicist **Howard Bragman**

It is a great shock at the age of five or six to find that in a world of Gary Coopers you are the Indian.

—author and screenwriter **James Baldwin**, on realizing he was gay

I remember one time I scratched this girl's back in the middle of the night—I was, you know, nine, and she was 12, and she asked me to scratch her back. A nun ran over, ripped me off her back, threw me against the lockers, beat the shit out of me, and called me a lesbian. I didn't know what a lesbian was.

—singer **Cyndi Lauper**, whose older sister is openly gay

Extreme heterosexuality is a perversion.

—anthropologist **Dr. Margaret Meade**

I wish that homosexuals were born with a little horn in the middle of their forehead so we couldn't hide so easily. At least if you can't hide, you have to stand up and fight.

—**Harvey Fierstein**

The Killing Fields

—**title** of a *Vanity Fair* article about the exceptionally high murder rate against gay men in Texas

My idea of gambling was walking through Central Park, whistling a show tune.

—Texas-born **Tommy Tune**

I think a big, big part of it is jealousy. Straights don't see all the shit they put us through. They just see, or think they do, that we're having a ball, balling. Without families to support...and we have better clothes, look better...our homes are nicer, and we seem to have high-profile or creatively fulfilling jobs. So they hate us, and their sons beat us up.

—ICM agent **Eric Shepard**

The first half of our lives is ruined by our parents; the second half by our children.

—one heterosexual view, from legendary attorney **Clarence Darrow**

Love is an agreement between two people to overestimate each other. I grew up in a broken marriage; my mother and father proved every day that marriage doesn't work.

—a view of heterosexual marriage from musician **Artie Shaw**, whose wives included Ava Gardner and Lana Turner

Yes, I did write that if they ever stopped laughing, they might get married. What I meant was, I think laughter is as far as their relationship goes.

—columnist **Herb Caen**, on Merv Griffin and Eva Gabor

I've been with women for 14 years, and I've been with a man for two. I'm still a dyke. The homosexual part of me never goes away.

—Maria Maggenti

I've always wanted male friends that I could be real intimate with and talk about important things with and be as affectionate with...as I would be with a girl…I thought I was gay for a while…but I'm just more sexually attracted to women. But I'm really glad that I found a few gay friends because it totally saved me from becoming a monk or something.

—Kurt Cobain

My introduction to the gay world did two things. One, saved me from life in prison for murder, which is probably where I would have wound up. How? Because the gay world showed me that you didn't have to beat up every man you saw or hurt people to make a point. It gave me a whole other attitude, a calmer attitude. Two, it taught me never to be homophobic, even before there was such a term. I think because I grew up in a period, especially later on, when the people I looked up to were like Dave Bowie and Mick Jagger…those characters were my heroes….That's what I liked about the period, that a man could say he liked both, that he appreciated both the look of a man and the look of a woman without being stereotyped.

—Joe Dallesandro, Andy Warhol "superstar" of the '60s and '70s

I'd never seen men hold each other. I thought the only thing they were allowed to do was shake hands or fight.

—writer **Rita Mae Brown**

Shall I compare thee to a summer's day?

—from a **Shakespearean love sonnet**, written to another male

I am homosexual. All of my lovers have been men. Some of them think they are straight, but that's my problem.

—author and filmmaker **Kenneth Anger** (*Hollywood Babylon*)

With me, it's not a matter of (gender). I fell in love with (Boy) George and he happened to be a man. When I stopped going out with George, I went out with women, but it doesn't mean I wasn't homosexual when I was with George.

—**Jon Moss**, Culture Club's drummer, in the late '90s

No, son, daddy wasn't a transsexual, daddy was a transvestite. If I was a transsexual, you wouldn't be here.

—**Dee Snider**, on VH1, answering his son's questions about his days with the shock-rock band *Twisted Sister*

There is much more acceptance now....My children—the way my children were raised in my house—they were allowed to say 'fuck' but they were not allowed to say 'fag.'

—singer **Helen Reddy**

Vulgarity is simply the conduct of other people.

—**Oscar Wilde**

Nobody is ever shocked now-a-days except the clergy and the middle classes. It is the profession of the one and the punishment of the other.

—**Oscar Wilde**, whose 1895 sentence to two years at hard labor for "homosexual acts" effectively broke his health and led to his death a few years later

Anyone who finds a penis obscene is forgetting where he came from.

—activist **Stan Griffith**'s sign, in the 1971 Hollywood Gay Pride Parade

We have to redefine what obscene is. We're so shocked by nudity or, say, two men holding hands in public, but not two straight kids making out in public, en route to yet another teenage pregnancy. ...What is obscene is a judge in Florida....giving custody of a little girl to her father, who admittedly killed a woman, than to her mother, because the mom is a lesbian...I'd say our justice system is pretty obscene.

—**Roseanne**

Good parenting has nothing to do with sexual orientation...and 'moral fitness' should take into account a child having to live in an abusive situation.

—ACLU attorney and associate director **Michael Adams**, after a Mississippi Supreme Court gave custody of a boy to the child's stepfather—a convicted felon, drinker, drug-taker and wife-beater—instead of the child's father, a gay man living with his male partner, in 1999

Male violence is too easily dismissed, and even expected, in our society....In regards to (the "homosexual panic" defense for attacking or even murdering gay men), if women reacted violently every time a man made an unwanted or unwarranted proposition, we would have a male population that was maimed or significantly smaller.

—**Gloria Allred**,
"attorney to the stars"

Every time there is an anti-gay measure the ballot, and this has been proven, anti-gay violence escalates. The anti-gay climate, or the measure, gives the gay-bashers just the excuse they need....In 1997 the conservative Right organized against the gay community as never before, with over 120 anti-gay measures in states across the land, and about one-fourth of those became law. And violence against gays and lesbians increased proportionately.

—producer **Ben Bagley**

Man Who Fought Against Gay Adoption Molests Child

—**headline** in 7/99 *Fab!*, about an anti-gay activist in Indiana who has been charged with molesting a nine-year old girl

If they're gonna worry about gay teachers supposedly molesting the boys in schools, how come no one's worried about the straight (male) teachers molesting the little girls?

—**Roseanne**

I love these TV shows that *tell* us what to like, how to behave....I mean, a show (on the E! cable channel) about 'Sexy Men.' Fine, cool. But the full title is 'Sexy Men: What Women Want.' They still feel the need to *instruct*—like without all the thou-must-be-straight rules and conditioning on TV, everyone would otherwise grow up to be gay!

—theatre director **Ron Link**

There's always a large lesbian contingent on the crews in New Zealand, (so) we started playing up to [it] on the set. We'd drop a few jokes into the scenes here and there. They weren't in the script, just impromptu lesbian high jinks on the day of filming. But we've moved on. I mean, how long can you keep that going?

—**Lucy Lawless**, *Xena* star; the answer is, as long as one can keep heterosexual subtext or high jinks going

She did support it (Ellen's coming out in real life and in her series). But then (Barbara Walters) asked where our show could possibly go after that, what kind of plots it could possibly have? That just amazed me. Where do the straight shows *go*? It seems like the plot of every episode of every sitcom is centered on a heterosexual date or a heterosexual affair or a marriage. It's not like we don't have private lives too—romance, dates, the works.

—**Ellen DeGeneres**

Cydney Bernhard (sic) with three-month-old baby Charles (Foster) takes a walk on Malibu beach with Jodie Foster. The pair wear matching rings; Cydney was the first person—after her mum—to hold the baby, and they take their dog to the vet together. But apart from that, they're just, um, longtime companions.

—**caption** from 12/98 issue of Australian *Lesbians On The Loose* magazine

Jodie Foster and her close friend Cindy Bernhard (sic) were a happy family the other day when they were shopping on Rodeo Drive with Jodie's son Charles, now seven months old. The two of them admit they are raising him. Cindy met Jodie on the set of *Sommersby* six years ago where Cindy was the production coordinator. Since then, the girls have been very close. No one knows for sure the nature of their relationship, but the story goes that they are wearing matching rings. And Jodie trusts Cindy as a surrogate mother when she can't be around. And how Charles was conceived and who the father (sic) is, is another secret.

—columnist **Arlene Walsh**, 4/99 (with a fraction of this information, a male-female couple would be "known" to be lovers; as for the "father," it's an *open* secret...)

When I was growing up, my parents didn't have the *words* to talk about me being gay. So they didn't talk about it...but now there *are* words that can be used (non-negatively)...I also think it's up to us to push those words—like, it's sort of insulting when a gay couple has been together longer than a straight one for somebody else to ask one gay guy about his 'friend.' I'd reply, 'My partner—or my lifemate—is fine. How is your *friend*—er, wife, that is?' It's up to us to get them used to it...and if we're uncomfortable or embarrassed about it, for sure they will be too.

—**Keith Christopher** (*Another World*, *Guiding Light*)

Here we were in the '60s, marching and singing 'We Shall Overcome,' feeling liberal and proud, and this gay world was opening up to me. I began to question what it must mean to live a life in the closet. To live life as a lie. To have to endure the humiliation of the YMCA arrests and things of that nature. Meanwhile, the Catholic Church was saying, 'Love the sinner, hate the sin.' The Church was legitimizing homophobia while *it* is one of the world's largest institutional closets. So I began to see that gayness is not a moral issue, and that we all had to do something about homophobia.

—pioneering talk show host **Phil Donahue**

I've become a champion of (gay rights)...because I sit in group therapy and watch tortured intellectuals who've struggled all their lives with their homosexuality. When I see what pious clergymen and fearful heterosexuals impose on them, I *do* want to speak out on their behalf.

—director **Blake Edwards** (*Breakfast At Tiffany's, Victor/Victoria*)

Where is it written, and even if it is, so what, that the majority is somehow better than those less common? I think most people believe that, but not from rhyme, reason or logic. Deep down, I always felt proud of Judaism—what we've contributed, have endured, and the fact that we worship God, with no middle man....With straights, just because there are more of them, how would that make them better? The violence and overpopulation and poverty come from them...and I think that heterosexual sex acts, including oral and anal ones, are not any more graceful, moral or somehow 'acceptable' than gay ones.

—novelist **David Feinberg**

You hear how straights hate to think about gay sex. I think it's fear of the unknown. Or revulsion at the unknown, the same way many of us are kind of repulsed by things or words like 'vulva' or 'vagina,' etc. The difference is, we don't sermonize about our distaste...and I can never help thinking that mixed with *their* distaste is more than a smidgeon of jealousy, as well as curiosity.

—UK skater **John Curry**, aka "Nureyev on ice"

I think gay people are like blondes: there are fewer of them, but they have more fun.

—gay writer **Rita Mae Brown**

I think everybody's curious....The fact is, up until this point, I haven't been drawn to having a gay relationship, and it doesn't seem as though I'm gay. But who knows? I mean, life is a series of surprises.

—Kenneth Branagh,
UK actor-director

Not that I know of.

—singer **Willie Nelson**, when asked "Have you ever made love to a man in this lifetime?" (Nelson recorded a song titled "Cowboys Are Frequently Secretly Fond Of Each Other")

Once or twice when I was younger. Yes (laughs). I mean…no… not exactly… directly (laughs). But you know how those things are.

—**Bruce Springsteen**, when asked if a man had ever made a pass at him

Oh, God! Can you please just write 'Oliver laughed'? I can't tell you that. I'll be in deep shit. I won't deny it….That's all I'm going to say on this subject.

—director **Oliver Stone**, when asked if he'd ever had "a homosexual experience"

I'd rather hang out with straight guys and not get any sex than hang out with gay guys and get sex. Sometimes, every now and then, I score.

—gay director **Gus Van Sant**, whose occasional screen homophobia has been noted, e.g., the gay shrinks in *Good Will Hunting*

(Pier Paolo) Pasolini struck me as being very compartmentalized. He apparently had a very considerable member himself. I've heard that he'd go to those very rough districts and say, 'I bet that my dick's bigger than yours,' and that was the way he got guys to show off to him.

—actor **Terence Stamp** (*Teorema*; *Priscilla, Queen Of The Desert*); gay but not gay-positive director Pasolini was eventually killed by a hetero hustler

There is nobody in the world that you can't get if you really concentrate on it, if you really want them. You've got to want it to the exclusion of everything else. That's how I got novelist Jack Dunphy. Everybody said I could never get him; he was married to a terrific girl, Joan McCracken. I liked her too, very much. I was just determined. I concentrated on it to the exclusion of everything else. It turned out it was a good thing on all fronts.

—**Truman Capote**

I think gays who go after straights give us all a bad name and have something the matter with their psyche or self-esteem...not that everyone doesn't have a little bit of bisexual in them.

—director **Norman Rene** (*Prelude To A Kiss*)

Not everyone gay is into anal sex. That's one huge stereotype. Not everyone....For me, sex is often quite funny. You know what's a good definition of trust? Two cannibals who agree to give each other oral sex.

—**David Bertugli**, editor in chief of the Italian-American *Daily Express* in Rome

I've never been an anonymous-sex kind of person. I need to know who they are, where they come from, and how many brothers and sisters they have.

—diving champion **Greg Louganis**

It seems the Beverly Hills police department has little better to do than try and catch or entrap celebrities in johns, like Robert Clary (*Hogan's Heroes*) and George Michael, thus sending the message that all those guys do is cruise toilets, which represents a smaller percentage of homosexual men than the percentage of straights who pick up female prostitutes...notice how the heterosexual men who solicit the girls usually get off the hook, while it's the prostitutes who get their names in the papers and get arrested and fined....It's still mostly a government by and for straight men.

—actor **Mart Dayne McChesny** (*The Guiding Light*)

They don't send Karl Malden in there. We're not talking Columbo with his dick out.

—**George Michael**, describing in Britain, the young, attractive undercover cop who busted him in Beverly Hills

We need to let the bigots know we have always been here…always will be. You see, we reproduce from *your* bodies!

—UK lesbian activist **Gwyneth Davies**

If you can't raise consciousness, at least raise hell.

—Rita Mae Brown

The last refuge of intolerance is in not tolerating the intolerant.

—George Eliot, in an 1857 letter

I have gay members of my family, my best friend is gay, and in the last ten years the reason I've upped my advocacy for gay and lesbian rights is because I think AIDS is a direct result of the homophobia we have in this country, and as long as people hate fags they're not going to care about AIDS.

—Kathy Najimy

When I was Matthew Shepard's age, my greatest fear was AIDS, because I had no idea then how the virus was spread. Now, 16 years later, there is still no cure for AIDS, but there is prevention. We can instruct a Matthew Shepard in how to protect himself against infection by HIV. But could we instruct him in how to protect himself against hatred?

—writer **David Leavitt**

In the brutal con game to which Matthew Shepard fell prey, what was exploited was nothing less than a young man's trust and hope and eager longing, if not for love, then at least for friendship, for camaraderie. In this game, kindness can be held out as bait; sex can be used as a lure. The payoff may be death, as it was for Matthew Shepard, or it may be robbery or gay-bashing or merely unkind, ignorant words. But few of us walk away unscarred, if we are lucky enough to walk away at all.

—David Leavitt

Dishing in Public

I told her, 'If I switched, I would switch for you.'

—**Barbara Walters**, to *USA Today*, on what she whispered to k.d. lang on Walters' show *The View*

I don't buy it. Anne Heche says she wasn't gay till she saw Ellen DeGeneres across a crowded room. Now, Ellen's okay-looking. But not great-looking. Brad Pitt, *he's* great-looking. Still, I don't think if I saw him at a party, I'd suddenly turn gay. Do you? Don't answer that!

—**Rodney Dangerfield**

There's something about her that I don't like: she's mean...I remember her coming around to my house, and she was just so rude to everybody....She acts like a spoiled brat all the time...I understand wanting to make something out of yourself and working really hard....But she's just too rude. For me to like Madonna, she'd have to be nicer.

—**Cher**

Now we're being asked to be extremely sympathetic to Ronald Reagan because he has Alzheimer's. Where was his sympathy for anybody who had AIDS—a man who for years wouldn't even *speak* the word, when he was supposed to be the leader of our country?

—comedian turned San Francisco politician **Tom Ammiano**

She's had very bad luck with men, so why not move a female lover into Kensington Palace? Di would have lipstick lesbians lining up to woo her.

—**Jackie Collins**, to Australia's *New Weekly* magazine, which noted that adding 'ke' to her name (Di) would have 'maximum tabloid effect,' in an article titled "Princess Bi" in 1996

Fuck you, and fuck your father!

—**Harvey Fierstein**, on a 1997 *Politically Incorrect* (censored) to Michael "son of Ronald" Reagan, when the former First Adopted Son opined that gay people "deserve" AIDS

I hate (John Updike). Everything about him bores me. He's like a piece of mercury, you put a drop in your hand and you try to hold onto it....I just think (Billy Graham) is a complete, total phony. I'd like to see *his* Swiss bank account....I despise (Steve Allen). I think he's so insensitive...you sometimes pop your ears because you can't believe what he just said (and) I wouldn't read his books or watch his TV programs....I think the present pope (John Paul II) is an excellent woman in drag. And I kid you not!

—**Truman** "the tiny terror" **Capote**

Ever since they found out that Lassie was a boy, the public has believed the worst about Hollywood.

—**Groucho Marx**

How come RuPaul always has white people's (blond) hair? To me, it's that majority thing—he wants to be another race, maybe another gender, I dunno....Somehow it looks more natural on him than when those Oriental ladies tint their hair red or blonde.

—**Howard Rollins**

I used to get mistaken for Mary Martin, which is hard on a performer's ego. There may be a superficial resemblance, but I do *not* sing, and I *do* like men.

—actress **Jean Parker**

I don't know, but to me he seems gay. He claims he's not, but I've never seen, like, a guy who's not gay seem so gay....What can I say?

—**Norm MacDonald**, on Chris Kattan (also of *Saturday Night Live*)

Larry (Olivier) had a marvelous effeminacy about him....

—**Sir John Gielgud**

We never became lovers, but we could have—like *that*!

—**Sal Mineo**, on costar James Dean (*Giant, Rebel Without A Cause*)

...the drugs (today). Even John Barrymore, a chronic alcoholic, would be shocked. Not just Drew (Barrymore)—and so young!—but so many others. Just *kids*, and all this cocaine. Very young actresses...in the old days, actresses used to powder their noses from the *outside*.

—**Cesar Romero**

Kathleen Turner and Jack Nicholson in John Huston's 1985 success *Prizzi's Honor.*

Homosexuality is so much in fashion it no longer makes news. Like a large number of men, I too have had homosexual experiences, and I am not ashamed...I have never paid much attention to what people think about me. But if there is someone who is convinced that (costar) Jack Nicholson and I are lovers, may they continue to do so. I find it amusing.

—**Marlon Brando**, in Paris in 1976

I was very disappointed to hear that. Of course Ivan tried to retract everything he had said, and that made it a little hard for me to trust him....As nervous as it made him to hire a gay woman to play a heterosexual, after working with me I know Ivan is gonna sing a different tune from now on.

—**Anne Heche** in 1998, on director Ivan Reitman's public "nervousness" over casting her opposite Harrison Ford in *Six Days/Seven Nights*

Tom (Selleck) is so big...he could, you know, just grab me. I was like Vivien Leigh to his Clark Gable.

—**Kevin Kline**, on *In And Out*

I remember there was one time I went to kiss Kevin, and I missed his mouth. I said to myself, Why did you do that? It's not so hard.

—**Tom Selleck**, whose kissing scene with Kline was shot "about 30 times"

I don't watch this show because I'm watching RuPaul while you're on.

—guest **John Tesh**, to homophobic host Craig Kilborn (*The Daily Show*)

One of those tabloids ran this story that Jane Fonda and I had an affair. I couldn't believe it! I called Jane and asked her if she thought we should sue, but she said it was sort of a status thing now that everyone's coming out of the closet. Besides, she said, who'd believe she ever slept with me?

—**Shelley Winters**

I'm the only straight actor that I know of who has played this role.

—*Seinfeld*'s **Jason Alexander**, who did the Nathan Lane role in the film version of *Love! Valour! Compassion!*

It's sad how Pee-Wee Herman (actor Paul Reubens) gets caught once with his pants down or whatever, and that not only pretty much sinks his career, but the guy practically becomes a dirty joke forever more.

—UK star **Benny Hill** (one prior arrest for the same victimless "crime" had preceded Rueben's 1991 arrest)

I was so disappointed in Will Smith, doing that gay part (in *Six Degrees Of Separation*) and then saying no at the last minute to the kissing scene. That's some message to send, about being unprofessional and insecure....Now it's come out that Smith went to Denzel Washington for advice, and Washington said not to do it....Gay black people have *no* role models, and that is a crying shame.

—**Michael Peters**, choreographer of Michael Jackson's "Thriller" video

At least they haven't made this Michael Jackson into a movie star. That surprises me, now that there's no level they won't sink to (in Hollywood)....This is a guy who sells photos of his baby to the *National Enquirer*...greedy and insecure to the max. He should also apologize for calling himself the king of pop, which no one else calls him and which he never was! And while he's at it, he should apologize to people of every race and gender for that face, one of the worst of his tasteless adventures.

—director **Samuel Fuller**

It's not so courageous for me to be out...I'm a fashion designer. Though look at these big names in America, and *they* are mostly in the closet! Why?...The one I admire is Elton (John). So many of the big singers, they become weird or lost and addicted by the time they are older. But Elton turned it all around. He is better than ever, and healthier...and honest about himself. He's happier, for now he shares his life with a man he chose for himself, not like when he married a lady for his (hetero) fans.

—Gianni Versace

What happened to (the murdered) Versace is a lesson to everyone, in different ways. But everyone must be more cautious. Safe living—safer living. More so for people who have the wealth and the fame that the media makes everyone envy.

—also openly gay fashion designer **Giorgio Armani**

I do want to play a gay James Bond...but time will tell if this project is possible in Hollywood....Where the straight James Bond has the Bond girls, you know, Ursula Andress or...Grace Jones, I could, uh, rendezvous with Dennis Rodman, for instance.

—Rupert Everett

Ingrid (Casares, openly lesbian former model and nightclub owner) and I are still good friends. She really knows who she is...I think lasting friends should have a strong sense of identity.

—**Madonna** in 1998; her friendship with reluctantly "bi" Sandra Bernhard did not last

Cindy has been calling a lot, but I'm taken and I don't stray.

—**Ellen DeGeneres**, jokingly, on reports that Cindy Crawford had wanted to be on her show (she appeared in the final episode)

Years and years ago, when I first heard that rumor about Julie Christie and Lauren Hutton (allegedly a couple), my temporary ambition was to be a lesbian in a ménage-à-trois!

—UK comic **Frankie Howerd** (sic)

I wouldn't have been interested, and if I had, it would still have been a ménage-à-blah.

—**Elsa Lanchester**, on Janet Gaynor and Mary Martin

Very, very pretty in a gothic painting sort of way.

—**Neil Patrick Harris** (formerly *Dougie Howser, M.D.*), on Johnathon (sic) Schaech

Excellent actor, very attractive, very charismatic. I don't mind losing parts to Matt.

—**Harris**, on Matt Damon

Barry Manilow did a TV movie. Did you see it? He played a heterosexual—it was like science fiction.

—comic/politician **Tom Ammiano**

Ellen DeGeneres' film debut and performance (as a heterosexual) must be seen to be believed, or not to be believed.

—writer **Jim Kepner**, on *Mr. Wrong*

She isn't one, but Bette Davis could enact a lesbian beautifully, I'm certain of it.

—**Beryl Reid** (*The Killing Of Sister George*)

I've seen (Rosie O'Donnell) in three or four movies now, and she has generally had the same effect on me as fingernails on a blackboard. She's harsh and abrupt and staccato and doesn't seem to be having any fun. She looks mean.

—critic **Roger Ebert** in 1994

It's hard to say if the Gabors play dumb or are that dumb, but once at a taping, in front of a sizable audience, Eva Gabor was there. So was a well known closeted gay man—no, not the former talk show host. And he came on wearing a very summery seersucker suit—he looked good in it. So Eva, in one of those whispers that half the audience can hear, said to him, 'Dahling, I adore your cocksucker suit!'

—author **Paul Rosenfield**
(*The Club Rules*)

This story may be apocryphal, but it's revealing. It got told a few times, but it never got into print....On the set of *The Pride And The Passion*, Frank Sinatra used to call (his costar) Cary Grant 'Mother Cary,' as in a once-famous story, 'Mother Carey's Chickens.'...The point is, supposedly there was a difficult scene, there were retakes, and still the director wasn't satisfied. When the director walked off, supposedly Cary Grant mumbled about the end of the picture, 'I'll be glad to see the back of him.'

That's when Sinatra said to his cronies, 'I'll bet Cary says that about all the boys.'

—film critic and historian **Parker Tyler**

I once told a story to my dear friend and protégé Marilyn Monroe, and afterwards I added that it was probably apocryphal. She said to me, 'Oh, Sidney! You mean you can't tell if it's properly punctuated?'

—columnist **Sidney Skolsky**

Baggy pants are for baggy people. Young guys have no business wearing them...I remember Tom Jones. He'd go up on stage, and his pants were so tight, you could tell his religion.

—Broadway director-choreographer **Joe Layton**

Shakespeare Eats Bacon.

—1960s graffito, referring to the possibly gay or bi William and the definitely homosexual Sir Francis

He (the Duke of Windsor) pretends not to hate me, but he does, and it's because I'm queer, and he's queer but unlike him I don't pretend not to be.

—Sir Noel Coward, to Truman Capote, according to Coward biographer Clive Fisher

I read that the American polls said (former California governor) Jerry Brown (elected mayor of Oakland in 1998) couldn't get elected as senator because he was unmarried....Yet *we've* had a Jewish head of state (Disraeli) and a female one (Thatcher), and you've had neither. ...Your last apparently gay president (Buchanan) was in the 19th century and couldn't get elected today because he never married.

We've had a gay prime minister—I have to be cautious here, though I'm sure he'd never sue—in my lifetime. I can't say what party he belonged to or whether he married—everyone in Britain knows whom I have reference to—but he was one of the ones before Thatcher, though not quite so butch—but no one is.

—**Graham Chapman**
(*The Life Of Brian*)

Sonny Bono never had any talent himself. He was ambitious, he was a businessman, he's a manipulator. He found Cher, groomed her, then used their association to acquire fame and fortune....As a politician (then mayor of Palm Springs), he's using people's fears and prejudices to acquire further fame and power. Don't think this man, amiable and goofy though he appears, isn't dangerous.

—**Dack Rambo**, on the homophobic politico

Pat Paulsen (and his fake presidential campaign). He knew it was a joke: what unlikely, inapt (sic) guy *wouldn't* run for public office? Alas, now it's a reality, with characters like Dan Quayle and a slew of has-been actors from Reagan to Sonny Bono running for office. And worse, and appallingly, winning.

—**Dick Sargent**, *Bewitched*

I hear that Hillary Clinton did have affair in college with one of us, but don't worry. She didn't inhale.

—lesbian comic **Robin Tyler**

Nancy Reagan was known to have dated many men. However by the time she was engaged to Ronald, the studio had even restored her virginity. An effort was made to give the impression that she had been working so hard on her career that she had had no time for men until Ronald Reagan came along.

—author **Patricia Seaton Lawford**

The Reagans were the most outspokenly anti-gay First Couple we ever had. Having their son marry and give up being a ballet dancer was just part of it....And part of their hypocrisy was that when Ron and Nancy wed, back in the oh-so-puritanical '50s, she was already some months pregnant with their first child....

—**Tom Ammiano**

I think Madonna is mostly a bad influence on (young people). I think she's too willful...I liked (Debbie Harry of) Blondie better. She just sang. She never opened her mouth. Well, you know what I mean.

—late politician and former singer **Sonny Bono**

Just think, if Madonna did a country-western album, she could bill herself as Mae Donna. She says she needs to keep reinventing herself....She could redo standards like 'Stand By Your Boy-Toy' and 'P-A-L-I-M-O-N-Y' or adapt some of her own hits like... 'Like A Virgo' or 'Justify My Trailer Home.'

—singer **Michael Callen**, on the future big-screen *Evita* (*Don't Cry For Me, West Covina?*)

He's okay....You know how they say some personalities are too little for the movies, so they wind up in TV? His was too little for TV. So he's doing the political thing...he's already gone a pretty long way on very little—and mostly on Cher's back.

—**Divine**, on costar Sonny Bono (*Hairspray*)

Man, if I could ever get people to talk about me the way they talk about Liberace, I would really have it made.

—**Elvis Presley** in the 1950s, at the Eagles Nest nightclub

I'd like to have the ability of James Dean...but I'd never compare myself to James Dean.

—**Elvis Presley**

I was disgusted by (James) Dean's 'hep cat' attitude and insolent manner. I hate that kind of person—what Dean represents. I hate this kind of New York school of acting—this 'dirty shirt' school of acting, as it's called. It should be outlawed, along with this rock-and-roll recording business. I'm trying to have the whole episode shelved. Nothing would please me more [than if we can] have it burned.

—**Ronald Reagan**, who hosted TV's *General Electric Theatre* and tried unsuccessfully to ban a G.E.T. episode Dean had appeared in

I want to go to Hollywood and become the next James Dean.

—**Elvis Presley**

I loved Jimmy Dean. I even had a crush on him. We all did.

—bisexual **Sammy Davis Jr.**

Jamie (Dean) and I were very close friends....It was always platonic between us.

—**Eartha Kitt**

James Dean was fine, so far as he went: three motion pictures. But I don't think his vulnerable-little-bad-boy act would have taken him far for much longer....Some of us have to build up a mystique or reputation by working in picture after picture, decade after decade—versus dying suddenly and instantly achieving that mystique and cult icon status.

—**Robert Mitchum**

I never met Jimmy Dean, but how I wish I had.

—**Elvis Presley**

Jimmy would never, ever have come out of the closet, no. He was far too ambitious...he was always seeking attention and approval, although he'd be the first to deny it...I don't believe he'd have lived much past 30, definitely not 40. If it hadn't been that car crash and his racing, it would have been something else. That boy absolutely had a death wish; he spoke about death and 'flirting with death' to almost anyone who would listen.

—**Jim Backus** (*Gilligan's Island*), who played Dean's dad in *Rebel Without A Cause*

Sal Mineo

One of Dean's deep dark secrets was his upper bridge—he had three false teeth. He also tried to hide his middle name, Byron. His mother had given him that after the (bisexual) poet, and Jimmy used to love poetry as a child, but his father would call him a sissy. Jimmy was an only child, and he was lonely. Then his mother died, and he was just a boy, and his father never did let up on him or befriend him. His mother's death was the central fact of Jimmy's life—of that he made no secret.

—**Sal Mineo** (*Rebel Without A Cause*, *Giant*)

Jimmy rarely socialized with other actors, especially members of the *Rebel* cast—not even Natalie Wood and director Nick Ray. He was not friendly with other Warner contract players like Sal Mineo or Dennis Hopper. In time, Sal would be one of the few to publicly state his distance from Jimmy, while desiring to have been closer in any way possible. Following Jimmy's death, others like Hopper and Nick Adams would not be able to resist fabricating personal friendships that had little to do with real life.

—**John Gilmore**, ex-actor and Dean intimate and biographer (Gore Vidal later wrote of an affair between Dean and Nicholas Ray)

(Dean) was up for a (posthumous) Oscar for *Giant*, his last movie. But he didn't win, partly because Jack Warner didn't push him in an Oscar campaign. He only wanted to promote living actors who could keep bringing in profits for him.

—**Geraldine Page**

I knew Leonard Spigelgass, who wrote so many wonderful plays and movies....He said that when James Dean was new to Hollywood, he came to see him, to see what Leonard could do for him. Well, Leonard saw right through him...Dean tried playing the hick, yet he was very sharp and extremely ambitious. He wanted to seem helpless and grateful for any consideration, yet he was ruthless and a user.

Leonard said he was known for appealing to homosexual men, using them as connections, then dropping them. And (though) Leonard wasn't a homosexual, he said to me that he felt tempted to lead Dean on, just for the eventual pleasure of dropping him first.

—**Ida Lupino**

An hour with a dentist without Novocain was like a minute with (novelist) Carson McCullers.

—**Gore Vidal**

Gore Vidal...a boy with...a funny, rather attractive face—sometimes he reminds me of a teddy bear, sometimes of a duck....His conversation is all about love, which he doesn't believe in....He's a pretty shrewd operator—or would like to be. He wanted advice on 'how to manage my career.' He is very jealous of Truman (Capote).

—**Christopher Isherwood**, in his diary

Oh, God knows, (Marlon) Brando thinks he's intelligent. He looks at you with his oh-poor-you eyes, as if he knows something you don't know. But the truth is, you know something he doesn't know—he's not very intelligent.

Acting couldn't be a very fulfilling occupation for an intelligent person. Writing is obviously more fulfilling.

—**Truman Capote**

Soon after the suicide of the esteemed Japanese writer Yukio Mishima, whom I knew well, a biography about him was published...to my dismay, the author quotes him as saying, 'Oh, yes, I think of suicide a great deal. And I know a number of people I'm certain will kill themselves. Truman Capote, for instance.' I couldn't imagine what had brought him to this conclusion.

—**Truman Capote**, who died at 59 via alcohol and drugs

(Writers) Dorothy Parker and Clare Boothe Luce weren't the best of friends....There's the story of the two of them entering somewhere at the same time—Luce gave in and let Parker go first but said out loud, 'Age before beauty,' and Dorothy retorted, 'Pearls before swine.' There's also the time Dorothy uttered one of her many memorable quotes and Clare grudgingly noted, 'I wish I'd said that,' and Dorothy replied, 'You will, Mrs. Luce, you will.' They didn't call her Luce Lips for nothing!

—**Truman Capote**

Why any writer should still be in the closet is beyond me...Of course Patrick Dennis (a pseudonym), who wrote *Auntie Mame* and other high-camp novels, was gay. But he had a wife and kids, so that kept his reality under wraps...eventually he left them, stopped being a writer and became a valet in Palm Beach—said being a valet was the best time he'd had in his life! Takes all kinds.

—**Bob Randall**, novelist (*The Fan*)

You (Americans) had Liberace, and we (British) have John Inman (of the TV sitcom *Are You Being Served?*). The gay stereotype, who insists that he himself can't necessarily be sexually categorized, and even that his character (Mr. Humphreys)—who makes Liberace look somewhat butch—isn't necessarily gay! Talk about self-deception....

—**Alan Napier** (the butler in TV's *Batman*), who in later life admitted, "I discovered that my first wife was a lesbian. That sort of thing has a very discouraging effect on a young man"

(Truman Capote) told me this story about a great friend of his who was a friend of Errol Flynn's. This guy and Flynn were drinking in a bar and Flynn passed out early, and the guy brought him back and threw him on the bed—completely nude. He went back to the bar and realized he could make some cash off this. He said, 'Anybody who wants to see Errol Flynn in the nude for ten dollars, come see me.' He gathered quite an entourage and escorted them all up—maybe 50 or 60 people—and brought them through the room where Flynn was passed out.

—**Peter Beard**, in George Plimpton's 1997 *Truman Capote*

Yes, we have seen each other nude...we did live together.

—**Amanda Bearse** (*Married With Children*), on her two-and-a-half year love relationship with Sandra Bernhard

Being European, I'm very at ease with my body out of clothes. And I never gave a second thought to doing such a scene.

—supermodel **Claudia Schiffer**, on her sexy love scene with French actress Beatrice Dalle in Schiffer's 1997 screen debut, *Black Out*

It helps to dislike your costar in a love scene, and Cary (Elwes) and I didn't care for each other much. He's rather a pompous Hollywood blond sort, and he's since gone very Hollywood—I hear he's even acquired an American accent there....But no one had any complaints about our love scene in *Another Country*, except that it was too brief.

—**Rupert Everett**

I don't know what it is that makes the American male so prudishly shy....Madonna shows everything, tells about her sexual slumber parties when she was a girl...by contrast, Brad Pitt is genuinely upset about those nude photos of him in *Playgirl*, and he's suing. But if you've seen them, you know it's no big deal. Literally. Not many big stars are, well, *big*.

—**Stephen Fry**, *Wilde*

I think he thinks he's better than other people. And in particular, other gay people. And that's why he's never been able to say he's gay, because if he says he's gay, he has to align himself with people like me and Jimmy Somerville and the drag queens. And he thinks he's a different type of homosexual. George actually thinks he's too good for the gay community.

—**Boy George**, on George Michael, who essentially came out as bisexual after his arrest

The first day we were on the set shooting (*Philadelphia*), Antonio (Banderas) was in those tight pants and was wearing that cute leather jacket, and I just thought, I'd flip over this guy. I'd be nuts about him.

—Tom Hanks

It wasn't that bad. It was like kissing a dog, you know? You know this is unnatural and incorrect, but somehow it doesn't bother you that much.

—the politically incorrect **Jerry Seinfeld**, on his small-screen kiss with costar Michael Richards on *Seinfeld*

I said to him, 'So was it as good for you as it was for me?'

—openly gay mogul **David Geffen**, on meeting Keanu Reeves after the rumor that the two had gotten married

Doesn't 'Keanu' mean 'I like it up the ass' in Hawaiian?

—Pauly Shore, during his standup comedy act

We'd all heard (Janis Joplin) was AC/DC...I thought she'd be easygoing and open-minded....After we worked together, she said to me in a tone of relief, 'I'd expected you to be a fag!'

—photographer **Francesco Scavullo**, now openly gay

I don't know whether or not Vincent Price was gay. I worked with him professionally once and got the impression that he and his wife, (actress) Coral Browne, were probably bi and had worked out a nice arrangement between themselves.

—horror author **David Skal**

There's one guarantee about Jodie Foster's baby: he/she will be a smart one. After months of background checks on potential sperm donors, Jodie reportedly settled on a scientist with an IQ of 160.

—columnist **Romeo San Vicente**

(Gore Vidal) is infected with that awful competitive spirit and seems to be continually haunted over the successes or achievements of other writers, such as Truman Capote. He is positively obsessed with poor little Truman Capote. You would think they were running neck and neck for some fabulous gold prize.

—**Tennessee Williams**

I think these homophobic, virulent Pats (Robertson and Buchanan) are troubled, insecure, angry men. Men who wish they had a butcher name than *Pat.*

—columnist **Boyd McDonald**

And now Pat Robertson, who uses tax-free money to pursue anti-gay initiatives (in various states) is warning Orlando, Florida, that it can expect hurricanes, earthquakes 'and possibly a meteor,' all because they finally allowed the rainbow flag to be displayed there. What century or millennium is this guy living in?

—**Harvey Fierstein**

Character actors, to coin a Hollywood phrase, are more interesting. ...A unique specimen was our own Vladek Sheybal (*Dr. No, Women In Love*). ...One of Vladek's quirks was a very personal one: he told a few people that when he masturbated, he did it with gloves on. The reason he gave was that he didn't want to risk giving himself AIDS.

—British actor **Harry Andrews**

He's got a pin-up image, which he hates. The only trouble is, whenever they ask him to take his trousers off, he does,

—**Michael Caine**, on costar
Richard Gere

If Hollywood has turned into a banquet for fools, Quentin Tarantino is surely at the head of the idiot table. *Jackie Brown*...is unthinkable, unwatchable and unfit for lepers. Pam Grier...looks like 45 miles of bad tarmac...like Lady Chablis, the ugly drag queen in *Midnight In The Garden Of Good And Evil*....The point of the movie is simple: $16,000 a year and (a stewardess') health benefits are no longer enough to keep an old broad in tequila sunrises.

—critic **Rex Reed**

One hears about Eddie Murphy and those transvestite hookers. Then one remembers all his homophobic movies. It's like the flowered bedspread calling the checkered drapes gaudy!

—**Elton John**

One of (Michael) Jackson's former cleaners described how she once found a small jar filled with a clear chemical in a cupboard. Floating inside was part of a human nostril, and the label on the outside gave a date of January, 1980, and a reference to his very first nose-job.

—**Jean-Paul Bourré**, author of the Jackson bio *The Making of a Monster*

I went to Mr. Blackwell's house for his annual worst-dressed list proclamation, and he made his entrance down the grand staircase. He waved his hand and informed all us journalists, 'There's nothing here that isn't 19th-century.' I couldn't resist asking, 'With all your money, couldn't you afford new stuff?'

—L.A. radio host **Gregg Hunter**

I've refused to be on television because the people were boring. ...I never would be on Merv Griffin's program.

—Truman Capote

They're (fellow writers) all jealous, I'm sure. Norman Mailer used his own money to star in three films, but I'm getting paid. And Jimmy Jones and Irwin Shaw told me they were jealous. And Gore Vidal must be *dying*. But then I always said that Gore was the only person who could possibly have played Myra Breckingridge.

—**Truman Capote**, who costarred in the film *Murder By Death*

I do remember (Andy Warhol) sitting in my living room the first time I saw him, and him telling me about his mother and how he lived with his mother downtown and they had 28 cats, and he seemed a very shy, pale person, rather like he is today. Only much shyer. That's my first memory of him. I can see him in the room sitting on this pink couch, but I don't remember how he got there!

—**Truman Capote**, on whom Warhol had a crush when Andy was new to New York

I'd been bopping along with Jimmy (Dean) toward the Warner Brothers commissary and Sal Mineo was up ahead of us. Jimmy sneaked up behind him and pinched him on the right cheek of his ass. Sal jumped, startled, his big brown eyes wide as cake plates.

His face flushed red when he saw it was Jimmy, and then he giggled, which started Jimmy laughing. Sal's face beamed with admiration and awe.

—former actor and Dean intimate **John Gilmore**

I don't like jokes about AIDS. That ticks me off. Anybody telling jokes about Rock Hudson should be slapped on the wrist or have his face ripped off, depending on the tastelessness of the joke.

—football star turned actor **John Matuszak**

Greg Kinnear is that vaguely handsome but exceedingly bland guy who hosted *Talk Soup* on one of those cable channels....He's trying movies—very trying. And his latest role is a gay one, in *Old Friends* (re-titled *As Good As It Gets*). Which is a kind of progress, you could say: gays too are now officially boring.

—Allen Ginsberg

Looks like the guy in my prison-rape fantasy.

—**Marilyn Manson**, on Antonio Sabato Jr.

I'm not homosexual or anything, but you're gorgeous! You should get (chest) implants, John, then I'd be with you. We'd finally be together.

—**Howard Stern**, to guest John Stamos

I'm mad at Andrew Dice Clay, because he's bigoted and homophobic and all that, and he's Jewish but he pretends he isn't. I met him, and I reminded him that he's Jewish.

—**Roseanne**, on the alleged comic born Andrew Silverstein

Paul Lynde

The only gay person that I knew (growing up) was Truman Capote, and I had to leave the room if he was on Dick Cavett's (TV) talk show. 'Cause it was so embarrassing. I felt so dirty and so exposed. I grew up in a very conservative family....And Paul Lynde. Those were the only gay images we had.

—screenwriter-director **Don Roos** (*The Opposite Of Sex*)

Being Puerto Rican, my role mode, one of them, when I was growing up, was Chita Rivera...also Harvey Fierstein. He used his art to create something beautiful and moving and that helped so many people at the same time. I still think *Torch Song Trilogy* is a brilliant piece.

—Wilson Cruz

Most of the gay people, honestly gay people, I knew about as a kid were writers. Entertainers were never openly gay, though you could guess about some, like Liberace...I admired Tennessee Williams, and when the big-time magazines kept attacking him, you just knew it was due to his homosexuality, and how he insinuated gay nuances into his plays. But when I saw the movie from his *Night Of The Iguana* I was so disappointed how anti-lesbian it was, 'cause that's homophobia too...Years later, I read how Tennessee said that (director John) Huston had added the lesbophobia to the movie's script. So I went back and I read the play. True, it wasn't as bad as the movie, but it was homophobic too...and I guess the biggest let-down is always when somebody gay is anti-gay.

—soap actor **Keith Christopher**, *Another World*

I published (his first) novel, *Other Voices, Other Rooms*, in 1948, when anything gay was way ahead of its time....You get used to the hateful swipes from homophobes and closet queens like Hemingway...some people nicknamed my novel 'Other Vices, Other Rooms.'...What's rather pathetic is the way Gore (Vidal) has become obsessed with me...and he tries to discredit me by attempting to make fun of how I look and sound. He, of all people! And he isn't beneath trying to spread rumors that I'm dying from cancer, which I most certainly am not.

—Truman Capote

What can you say about Liberace that everyone hasn't already thought? Except that he made an art of lying—a minor art....He had a small role in *The Loved One*, and now he's taken to stating in public that I offered him the lead, which I never did, but he wanted it...Mr. Joyboy (played by Rod Steiger) is supposed to be a heterosexual—what could I tell Lee? At some point I did say he didn't have a movie star face, a phrase I'd heard in Hollywood. He said, 'My face is fine.' To myself, I said, 'It's fine for you—you're behind it.'

—director-producer **Tony Richardson**, father of actresses Natasha and Joely (Vanessa Redgrave's daughters), who denied he had AIDS but died of it in 1991

I have been independent since 15, when I began supporting myself after leaving school. I sold drawings. Then I did modeling and met actors and directors. At 17 I met my father (actor Daniel Gelin). But he was an egotist who wanted only to talk about himself—typical of most actors....My father being famous in France never helped me—*he* never helped me. As with so many fathers, it only means he is the man who got your mother pregnant, to put it delicately. My *mother* was my parents (plural).

—openly bi **Maria Schneider**

I don't discuss my family, but I miss him very much.

—**Johnny Carson**, on his gay stepson Tim Holland, who died of AIDS at 32 in 1994 (Holland was the only child of ex-wife Joanne Carson, in whose L.A. home Truman Capote died)

My advice is, if at all possible, don't have an actor for a father or a mother. Or both, as I did....Sometimes I'm bitter, sometimes not. But an actor parent does tend, especially a father, to be, at times, little more than a witness to your growing up...or a much older sibling. Because most actors have never really grown up.

—gay playwright **James Kirkwood**, who was the son of Lila Lee and James Kirkwood Sr.

The English are like the Americans. They think someone else's sexuality reflects on them...but sexuality is so very individual....When I was doing *The Private Life Of Sherlock Holmes* (1970), it was a series of confrontations with the son of Conan Doyle (who created Holmes), and he was opposed to our version of a possibly homosexual Holmes...despite the ambiguities in the character as written to begin with....He kept invoking his father's name, and I kept thinking, So much fuss over the presentation of a character who never existed!

—director-producer **Billy Wilder** (*Sunset Boulevard*)

It's their hypocrisy that gives the lie to conservative 'family values.' The far-right needs a rallying target, and we're it...instead of embracing their lesbian and gay relatives, they victimize us....Some anti-gay politicians and preachers will say the line, 'I love my gay son or daughter, but I don't condone his or her lifestyle.' To get their true meaning, substitute the word 'life' for 'lifestyle'....

—author-activist **Candace Gingrich**, half-sister of Newt

Some of the entertainment figures most opposed to outing are the ones with relatives they prefer to keep *in*...Tyne Daly (*Cagney & Lacey*, *Wings*) won't admit that her father, actor James Daly (*Medical Center*), was gay and had a male lover whom she and her sisters evicted from (the men's) apartment after James Daly died. That now wouldn't be politically correct to admit, and today most celebrities—the female ones more so—don't want to alienate their gay fans.

—**Howard Ashman**, producer and Oscar-winning lyricist (*The Little Mermaid*)

You know, an image used to be something carved and usually made out of wood or stone. But in show biz, it's created by publicists and the press and made out of exaggerations or lies. Look at Cary Grant, one of the better illustrations of the truth that if a lie is repeated often and loudly enough, it becomes universally credible, even cherished and defended.

—**Dick Sargent** (*Bewitched*), who had small roles in Grant's films *Operation Petticoat* and *That Touch Of Mink*

It's no secret that my grandmother was gay.

—**Eric Preminger**, son of director Otto Preminger and Gypsy Rose Lee, whose mother Mama Rose was immortalized in *Gypsy*

Jackie Kennedy Onassis' father was a handsome fellow—Jack Bouvier. Of course everyone knows he went to school with Cole (Porter), and Coley did more than Jack to hide the knowledge of their sex affair…there was other evidence that Jack went both ways. But to his credit, he never denied his once close friendship with Cole.

—**Truman Capote**

The thing I find offensive is when a gay or bi man has a kid and the kid goes wrong, and then media analysts—and not just the tacky tabloids either—try to deduce how the father influenced the son…Christian Brando's mother went tabloid with her homophobia, saying Marlon being bi was why Christian shot his sister's boyfriend, and that he was even named after some (alleged) French actor lover (Christian Marquand) of Brando's.

But now it's even worse, with O.J. Simpson and the tabloids trying to make out like O.J. became a wife-beater and (alleged) murderer all because his father was gay and a transvestite and lived in San Francisco!…Even though the guy walked out on O.J. and the mother early on….The most offensive thing is that such homophobia and crackpot psychologizing sells.

—**Keith Christopher**, *Guiding Light*

I'm a survivor…I been through a lot. But since the cops stopped me and Eddie (Murphy), I've gotten threats. I been told to keep my mouth shut….

—self-described "tranny hooker emeritus" **Atison Seiuli**, who a year after the Murphy episode died under questionable circumstances in 1998; according to the *L.A. Weekly*, the LAPD is not investigating the death

Ty (Power) used to tell this story he'd heard on some movie set about these two little fairies who were part of a crew…nobody knew exactly what they did, but everyone had his suspicions....One day, at the end of shooting, somebody yells out, 'Kill the blowers!' And the one fairy boy wails to his friend, 'But we're too young to die!'

—**Cesar Romero**, repeating some typical redneck Hollywood humor

I think (producer) Dawn Steel (former head of Columbia Pictures) astonished some people....I agree that it's not something which should still be going on. Today it's gay characters, in the 1960s it was black characters...who will it be in the future? I also think such test marketing is anything but perfected, and as proof I offer the fact that her film, with the excision, still failed to draw audiences.

—ex-publicist **Richard Condon**, on Steel's mid-'90s decision to edit out a character's homosexuality after teenage audiences professed dislike for him; the flop movie was aimed at teens (non-gay teens...)

I had not a great relationship with (director) Herb Ross....Whoopi Goldberg had a (female) lover (in the script)...but that was gone (from the movie)....After I directed, I realized it's better to direct your own stuff, (though) scripts change for a lot of reasons, and it's not always the director being malicious or not getting it.

—screenwriter **Don Roos**, on *Boys On The Side*

Isn't he homosexual?

—**Jackie Onassis**, to a Karen Lerner (who replied, "Well, I never heard he wasn't!") at the third wedding of her younger sister Lee Radziwill, to Herb Ross, as reported in the bio *In Her Sister's Shadow*

We're both bisexual...and it's beautiful.

—French actor **Maria Schneider** in 1973, about herself and costar Marlon Brando

Maria (Schneider) is never false. She doesn't know falsity.

—director **Bernardo Bertolucci**, on his *Last Tango In Paris* star

I never felt any sexual attraction to Brando. He's almost 50, and he is only beautiful to (the neck). He was very uptight about his weight; he kept pulling curtains whenever he changed his clothes.

—**Maria Schneider** in 1973; she also outed Bertolucci as bisexual

Ingmar Bergman has criticized Bertolucci, as I do, for his lack of honesty in *Last Tango*...it was meant to be a man and a youth, and the famous scene of anal sex with Maria Schneider should have been of Brando and a young man.

—French actor-director **Cyril Collard**, whose bi-themed *Les Nuits Fauves* won Best Picture in 1993

I don't care. I am not a symbol of anything. I am just me, I am just Maria....A friend said that in a book, Lily Tomlin said how angry she was for me, I think because I said I am bisexual and I have had probably 50 men and 20 women. I think because more men than women.

—**Maria Schneider**

I've worked the same bookstore circuit as Lily Tomlin. She has as many homosexuals standing in line at her book signings as I do. But God help you if you ask her why....

—**Armistead Maupin** in 1989; in 1996 he again declared his disappointment in Tomlin

Neither Nicole (Brown Simpson) nor I were or ever could be gay.

—author **Faye Resnick**, after claiming an affair with her late friend

For the record, I'm straight as an arrow. I like women.

—model/porn star **Paul Barresi**, upon revealing his alleged "two-year affair" with John Travolta in 1990

(Asked at what age he realized he was gay:) Does fetus count? I guess I've always known. I can remember as a kid watching television, that Scott Baio totally did it for me.

—**Wilson Cruz**

He's both shy and snotty, a difficult combination.

—former producer **Julia Phillips**, on George Michael

Charles Lowe once took me aside and confessed that he had a crush on Carol Channing's career....Some men do marry the actress whose career they're managing, the better to legally control her career and its source. Whether the man loves the woman is entirely beside the point, in show biz terms.

—Broadway director-choreographer **Joe Layton**, on Channing's manager-husband

More than Garbo herself, I did relish the notion of becoming Garbo's husband.

—secretly gay **Sir Cecil Beaton**, who wooed the lesbian or bisexual Swede in vain

I had this real attraction to Lukas (Haas). I think he's the most beautiful, perfect boy. He's meek and handsome and likable in a very special way....He told me he played (guitar)...so we played for 40 minutes. It was so good I called my A&R guy and told him, 'Lukas Haas is in Bunny.'

—actor-musician **Vincent Gallo**, on how his band Bunny acquired its second member

It's not cheating if it's with a movie star. Most anyone would be flattered, even honored, to do it with a movie star. Plus, they mostly are very good-looking....If Rita Hayworth, who was heterosexual by the way, asked another woman or a gay man, who would say no? These are charming, gorgeous world figures whose attention is most flattering, believe me. And most men, if a Tyrone Power, a Rock Hudson or one of the newer hunky star actors made the offer, would be hard-pressed to refuse.

—choreographer **Hermes Pan**, who was a close platonic friend of Hayworth

If he hadn't been Errol Flynn, I wouldn't remember. We were both drunk—it was the first time I ever had a hangover—and it took him the longest time to have an orgasm. I never did.

—**Truman Capote**, who had a Flynn fling while visiting California

I missed my chance with Jimmy Dean, but I was jail bait anyway. ...When I met Elvis Presley, I knew I'd try everything to get him between the sheets. Or to get him—anywhere, any way....And he was *my* fan, which blew my mind....But nothing happened. I think Elvis, whatever curiosity he might have had, would never try sex with another guy for no better reason than he'd always heard you shouldn't.

—**Sal Mineo**

I don't regret it (filming Elvis on his TV show only from the waist up while he performed). Young people have too many distractions and bad influences. Elvis is a fine boy, but what he did (with his hips), he did without really thinking what it could mean to some people.

—conservative columnist turned talent host **Ed Sullivan**

When people found out I was the Marlboro Man (in the 1960s), it definitely acted as an aphrodisiac for lots of them. They suddenly lit up—sexually—in front of me—I had sex with one well known California politician that I later found out was very anti-gay in his voting—see, I was never the least political till I owned a (Palm Springs) gay bar and suffered the discrimination head-on...I once got the chance to meet Robert Taylor, and he said to me how he loved westerns and the Marlboro image...he made it clear he was interested. But in his case, I'd been forewarned—this guy didn't have two faces, he had four, and I wasn't interested in star-fucking for the sake of it. Truth is, I always found most of those Hollywood types phony as hell and lousy lays.

—**Christian Haren**

I used to think Lillian Hellman had such a sense of fairness and integrity. Until I found out about her play, *The Children's Hour*, and its (1961) movie version that almost caused a friend of mine to contemplate suicide; later I found out she was lesbian, which came as a complete surprise...Hellman had taken a true story from 19th century Scotland that had a neutral ending. To make it more acceptable, she made it a homophobic ending—the real lesbian kills herself from fear and self-hatred. It's an ending that I'm sure has haunted many female and some male homosexuals ever since. So much for the integrity of the now much-praised Ms. Hellman.

—film historian **Carlos Clarens** (Hellman was secretly bisexual)

Joan Rivers, who admires her, says Nancy Reagan is not anti-gay; in spite of Nancy Reagan's anti-gay public statements. Why does Joan Rivers say this? Because, she says, Nancy Reagan does have some gay friends. Yes, but. Those friends are anti-gay. Uncle Toms and Republican closet cases. There are gays and there are gays....

—author **Randy Shilts** (*And the Band Played On*)

(Charlton Heston) goes about positioning himself as an Anita Bryant for the new century...from righteous to self-righteous....He figured...he might as well come out of the closet as a full-blown extremist....For years after playing Michelangelo in *The Agony And The Ecstasy*, he has maintained that the painter wasn't gay, or he wouldn't have accepted the role. Michelangelo just got a bad rap because he spent a lot of time on his back.

Just as we are beginning to celebrate a season of Gay Pride (in summer, 1998), along comes another Anita Bryant, another Donna Summer, to make us realize there will always be one more battle to be fought and that the war is far from over.

—columnist **Harold Fairbanks**, after NRA president Heston's most controversial speech yet

(Charlton) Heston is an example of Hollywood's coin-fed casting process via looks or height rather than talent. In *Khartoum* he played, uninterestingly, a very interesting historical character, General Gordon, who was (secretly) gay. *I* played a *more* interesting, also gay, historical character, Lord Kitchener, who was an even greater military figure....A Hollywood spectacular which went on to lose millions of pounds, *Khartoum* focused entirely on the less interesting character, played by the less able actor...*Khartoum* was one of the bloated productions that helped, back in 1966, to kill off costume pictures altogether.

—**Peter Arne** (who also noted Heston's non-English accent as the Englishman)

There was a time when Americans believed Englishmen to have a monopoly on homosexuality. Ms. Shirley MacLaine, the actress, once called me a 'fag' on the strength of my accent. The fact is that many New York homosexuals affect an English accent, probably for purposes of tribal identification as well as distinction from the Lee Marvin-tongued meat-and-potatoes beer-from-a-can men whose notion of sexuality is a Saturday night urge fulfilled in five minutes.

—author **Anthony Burgess** (*A Clockwork Orange*)

Brad Davis had a small role in (*Chariots Of Fire*) ....I'd known he was bisexual, and thought him attractive. But I was rather shocked when he came on to me on the set. That's rather unprofessional. *Off* the set, that's different...Americans tend to be aggressive about all their wants, it seems.

—Ian Charleson

(At a 1970s ERA (Equal Rights Amendment) party at Marlo Thomas' Beverly Hills home:) Shirley MacLaine held court, ignoring anyone she didn't think important enough...she spoke mostly to Gloria Steinem and (Congresswoman) Bella Abzug. When Gloria introduced me to her, Shirley pointedly turned away. At that point in her life, Shirley apparently didn't shake hands with lesbians...if there were photographers in evidence. Gloria, looking embarrassed, then introduced me to Marlo Thomas, who, having a set of brass ovaries, couldn't have cared less...But MacLaine shocked me because she's from Virginia. Did she leave voluntarily or did the matrons drive her out due to bad manners?

Kate Jackson, from Birmingham, did shake my hand when we were introduced but quickly moved on. It could have been that she...also didn't want anyone to take a photograph of us together, or it could have been that she was so hot at the time, thanks to *Charlie's Angels*, that everyone wanted her attention. At least she didn't pretend I wasn't there. I gave her a lot of credit for being there in the first place...I was hardly the only lesbian or bisexual in the crowd. I was the only one honest about it.

—Southern writer **Rita Mae Brown** (*Rubyfruit Jungle*)

They'll never get married.

—columnist **Sue Cameron**, on Oprah Winfrey and longtime beau Stedman Graham, in 1995

Lisa spends more time with her ex-husband Danny. This marriage is a total crock.

—**Sue Cameron** in 1995, on Michael Jackson and Lisa Marie Presley, who reportedly arrived and left in separate cars the night of Diane Sawyer's puff interview

Who're they kidding?

—an **anonymous agent**, quoted by Sue Cameron in *Beverly Hills (213)* in 1995

When Princess Diana's brother had a night out at a gay club, the tabloids had a field day, even though photographers weren't allowed inside—Diana was there...protocol being what it is, no one asked *why*....But it was daring of everyone (there), and I prefer to think most of the British reading public were above the level of speculation as to whether Diana's son, the heir to the throne, might 'turn gay' because his uncle attended and danced at a gay club.

—actor **Donald Pleasence** (*Halloween*)

We were in this little town on the edge of the Sahara, and there was nothing to do at night except go to this disco. But it was all men dancing with men because women weren't allowed out at night. So we're standing at the bar, watching all these guys dancing, when Sean (Connery) leans over and says to me, 'Do you mind if I dance with your driver? Mine's too ugly.'

—**Michael Caine**, on the filming of *The Man Who Would Be King*

What kids don't know is that in the '50s and '60s, here in California, it was illegal for homosexuals to be served a drink or to gather in public places or to dance or even touch—an accidental touch could land you in jail, never mind a grope or a slow dance....You had a few movie stars from that period, fellas like Rock Hudson or Dan Dailey, who had the guts to be seen in a gay bar. But these fellas seldom could let themselves go and just dance—the terror of all they'd read and heard stayed with them, even after the laws were changed.

—**Christian Haren,**
former Marlboro Man

The first great love of Truman Capote's life was a college professor (Newton Arvin) who had a horror of not being known as, shall we say, discreet....Like many homosexual men, he had a collection of sexually stimulating erotica—primarily photographs and short stories. This, in the early 1960s, was illegal, and he was raided and arrested...given a one-year suspended jail sentence. He wasn't allowed to teach again, and he only avoided jail by naming over a dozen other men who had similar so-called pornography in their homes, including two colleagues.

I declare this for two reasons. Truman won't, due to affection for his late lover. And because the profusion of witch-hunt books now appearing almost inevitably ignore the witch-hunts of political but homosexual men in this nation which continued after the Hollywood variety had officially ended.

—Capote's some-time friend,
Tennessee Williams

I've been told that most blond actors don't make it big in the movies. If they're not angry or arrogant, like Alan Ladd was or Robert Redford, then movie insiders think of them as being gay...or 'soft,' like Tab Hunter or Troy Donahue...though Donahue's rumored to be straight and Ladd (to have been) AC/DC....This is my first big break, and it may be my last lead in a motion picture, because starring in a film about a deadly disease is a stigma that I doubt will ever be overcome by a would-be commercial actor.

—**Geoffrey Edholm**, who died at 33 in 1989 and starred in the first commercial movie about AIDS, Arthur Bressan's *Buddies*

Hollywood tradition is that the leading man be aggressive, even obnoxious, in strong preference to mildness....There are film stills of Johnny Mack Brown opposite Joan Crawford in *Laughing Sinners* (1931). But he was replaced by Clark Gable, and the reason was that Brown just came across as too nice. Unlike Gable.... In Hollywood, nice guys do not finish first.

—author **Carlos Clarens**

John Schlesinger, director of *Day of the Locust.*

I haven't worked with many actors, being a music man. But I do know that there's a whole category of actors who, if they communicate with you at all, the first thing they want you to know is: they're actors but they're not gay. And don't you *dare* think they are! And these can be straight actors or gay ones, and a few claiming to be formerly gay...this whole town is about illusions, honey.

The worst and the most unpleasant actor I ever worked with is someone named William Atherton. I'll say no more....Is he still working? I know he's not still starring. There *is* a God.

—**Paul Jabara**, who appeared in John Schlesinger's *Day Of The Locust*, costarring Atherton

George (Tobias) never married. But we didn't get that close, and

I can't say if he was (gay).

—**Dick Sargent**, on the actor who played the husband of Mrs. Kravitz, super-snoop, on *Bewitched*

The public only hears the denials (when celebrities are outed). They don't hear the reports that many outed celebs won't confirm or deny...often forced not to admit it because of their network or producers...It's odd with *Frasier*, with the (openly) gay (Dan Butler) playing the butch sports guy, and then (David Hyde Pierce), playing the beyond-prissy brother (Niles). He's on the show every week; the sports guy isn't, and that may be the key....(Pierce) has been outed time and again, but he never denies it. They say he lives in Silverlake, a gay community in L.A., with his (male) partner....It just seems behind the times to erect this wall of silence, when so many TV people are saying yes, markedly so in comedy.

—actor **William Hickey** (*Prizzi's Honor*)

As a gay Jew, or a Jewish gay, I feel alienated in rural areas. Because there are almost no Jews there, and while there are gay people everywhere, in the country they're as silent as a stuffed closet....Of course in show biz you have silent Jews too...the Dinah Shores, the non-stereotypes like Tina Louise (*Gilligan's Island*)...even fashion types like Ralph Lauren....It's not a real melting pot if the only ones who have to hide or melt are the ones who are different.

—novelist **David Feinberg**

Poor Giorgio (Armani)...he is a friend, and he makes me laugh. I hear him give an interview, he says it is terrible, he has a beautiful house on a Mediterranean island. But it is so big and he is so busy, he has the problem to find the time to fill it with beautiful things! He makes me laugh, but it is true, the problems: when you are not rich, there is not enough space. When you are, it is too much space and not enough time to shop.

—**Gianni Versace**

I think I have made my friend Steven Seagal stop being homophobic. I hope so!...I think these men are like that only at first, because they only know what they have heard, they don't know real people who are gay....I think he gets too much criticisms (sic), but he is trying to be a better person and more spiritual, and he meditates a lot now.

—**Gianni Versace**

We were like brothers. He taught me about art, and I taught him about music. You never left him without being stimulated about some aspect of fashion or art or life. There was no fear with Gianni.

—**Elton John**, on Versace

This business about Madonna mourning over Gianni Versace, who she used to make fun of, and now she's writing his eulogy in *Time* magazine. I love it!

—**Sandra Bernhard**,
former Madonna pal

Sandra Bernhard's pregnant. I wonder if she's following in Madonna's maternal footsteps? But she's doing it the Jodie Foster way, not the Madonna way, if you catch my meaning....

—**Scott Thompson** (*The Larry Sanders Show*)

I have a friend who likes to say she can't keep Ellen DeGeneres and Jodie Foster straight....But beside being blondes and, uh, you know, there's little common ground. Ellen always wears pants and she's a big comedy talent. Jodie is much more comfortable with her body but has no humor whatsoever....Ellen seems huggable; Jodie seems like she might condescend, on a good day, to give you a cold handshake.

—**Eric Shepard** of ICM, one of the first openly gay agents

Princess Diana is, I think, the only member of that entire (Windsor) family who has true movie-star appeal. It truly stands out, and even more when she is with some of them.

—**Gianni Versace**

It was over an AIDS event to promote Gianni's (Versace) work, but she pulled out at the last minute because of pressure from the palace. I wrote her a stiff letter, and she wrote me a very stiff letter back. I just wanted her to let me *know* she was going to (pull out), instead of reading it in the paper....We both sulked for three months. It was when Gianni was killed that we (next) talked to each other.

—**Elton John** (who has his own AIDS foundation), on his temporary estrangement from Princess Diana

Andrew Cunanan (Versace's murderer) didn't even have HIV, yet the media—from Tom Brokaw to the *New York Times*—presented him as an HIV predator...an AIDS monster.

—**Sean Strub**, founder of *POZ*, the magazine by and for people with HIV

Howard Stern got flack when he criticized Filipino people, but of course never a ripple when he says gays are immature and can change if they click their heels three times or whatever....I was disgusted by how all the press was linking Cunanan's homosexuality to his being a serial killer. I mean, gays are typically the victims of violence, not its perpetrators! If anything, we're renowned and ridiculed for *not* fighting or pushing back....They kept labeling (Cunanan) a 'gay murderer'...they wouldn't think of calling him a 'Filipino murderer,' yet that culture, from which he came, is very (religiously) fanatical and intensely homophobic. Cunanan was a self-hating homophobe, a vengeful choirboy cum gigolo who wanted fame and fortune—or at least fame, any way he had to achieve it.

—producer **Ben Bagley**

One good thing: he finally killed someone who deserved it.

—**Jay Leno**, on Andrew Cunanan's suicide (and countering those columnists and commentators who felt Cunanan's victims "had it coming" for being gay)

I think Ellen's (DeGeneres) movie (*Mr. Wrong*) is entertaining, but I wonder what short-sighted jerk decided to feature Amy Grant on the (musical) soundtrack? Grant is an uncaring, unrepentant homophobe, and this is Ellen's movie all the way. I think she'll come out eventually—she's already giving clues—and I *know* I won't be buying the (musical) CD, because I don't help enrich those who hate me and deny my civil rights.

—**Jed Johnson**, Andy Warhol acolyte turned interior designer to the stars

John Wayne once said the only homosexuals he ever heard of in Hollywood were all hairdressers. Well, apart from his being hard of hearing, I don't mind, because Hollywood is full of gays, and if I'm the best hairdresser in town, then I must be incredibly good.

—**George Masters**, hairdresser to Marilyn Monroe and other stars

I have actually seen Mel Gibson described as 'a complex man.' Rather, he is very simple, and a man of many complexes—dislike of homosexuals and small families among them.

—**Patrick White**, Australia's only Nobel Prize-winning writer

Most actors go to Hollywood to try and become someone else. Unfortunately, Charlton Heston didn't succeed.

—TV talk host **Ricki Lake**

(To renew his American visa as an Australian "alien" to attend business meetings in Los Angeles:) Stephan (Elliott) found that the U.S. government has a section on 'inadmissible classes.' These include 'aliens who are mentally retarded, insane, or have suffered one or more attacks of insanity; aliens afflicted with psychopathic personality, sexual deviation, mental defect, narcotic drug addiction, chronic alcoholism or any contagious disease; aliens who are paupers, professional beggars or vagrants; aliens who are polygamists or advocate polygamy' and so on.

What's so funny is, that sounds like a list of half the inhabitants of L.A.!

—producer **Al Clark** (Elliott, the writer-director of *The Adventures Of Priscilla, Queen Of The Desert*, is now openly gay)

We export our more ambitious women who are bi or lezzies, mostly to the States…that feminist singer who was a big hit in the '70s, the blonde one who was a bigger hit and married a gay boy, and that rather stiff actress who went to Hollywood and married a bigger (male) star who's also gay or bi, but they legally defy anyone to say so....I don't mind. I think it makes Australia a more honest place and keeps Hollywood down to its usual standard.

—Sydney columnist **Paul Petersen**

When I was a kid, we had some neighbors from Australia, and the husband used to joke that Aussie men had wide shoulders and Aussie women were quite manly....When I was making *Christopher Strong* with Katharine Hepburn, I used to joke with a friend that Katie was quite the Australian. Which of course also went for our director.

—leading man **David Manners** (*Dracula*, *The Mummy*); *Strong*, Hepburn's first starring vehicle, was helmed by lesbian Dorothy Arzner

Hedda Hopper once asked me why I left Adelaide (Australia). I don't recall what I said to her, but I wanted to go out into the world and as an actress play big, powerful, fascinating characters. I had no desire to spend the rest of my life shuttling between a cottage and a garden, wearing a little gingham dress.

—Dame Judith Anderson

A reporter from New Zealand once said...to Charles (Laughton) that he was big Down Under. Of course I refrained from saying I'd heard the same thing before, from one of Charles' boyfriends.

—Elsa Lanchester, Laughton's contractual wife

American television loves such gay spokespeople as Camille Paglia and Andrew Sullivan. They're on TV frequently because each is an aspiring male heterosexual—the way they think, talk and argue....Television likes a diversity of faces, but not diverse points of view.

—Australian professor and author **Dennis Altman**

The term 'post-gay' is the complete absence of style, wit and humor, and it is best illustrated by the works of Andrew Sullivan and others who promote participation in a miserably stupid attempt at being accepted by society through looking and acting like everyone else.

—author **Michael Thomas Ford** (*Alec Baldwin Doesn't Love Me*)

I would like to see drag queens take (homophobic) senators Trent Lott and Jesse Helms, bind them with used nylons and stuff panties in their mouths, and teach them the pleasures of prostate stimulation using Jeff Stryker dildos and thermoses from Teletubby lunch boxes.

—Michael Thomas Ford

Me, Cindy Crawford and Elvis Presley.

—Yasmine Bleeth's idea of the perfect threesome

Yes, I have fantasized about having sex with Tom Cruise and his wife Nicole Kidman.

—Tori Spelling

Like everyone else, I want to sleep with Leonardo DiCaprio. But I guess I'd want to marry Tom Cruise because he's much more reliable.

—Jon Stewart, host of *The Daily Show*

Alec (Baldwin) *does* love me. I even have the letter from him to prove it, which is framed and hanging over my bed. But Billy (Baldwin) hasn't spoken to me since I called him 'too bony,' so I think there's no hope there.

—author **Michael Thomas Ford**

On *Politically Incorrect*, John Schneider—remember him from *The Dukes Of Hazzard*?—was quite stirring in expressing his belief that there should be separate public bathrooms for gay and straight men. He rationalized that mixing of the sexual preferences could lead to some sort of harassment. John, dear, if you can't control yourself, use the ladies room!

—*Fab!* Columnist
Romeo San Vicente

Rupert Everett seemed horrified when I asked him if he's a top or a bottom. (Maybe he's versatile.)

—columnist **Michael Musto**

The white boys (in America) and the English boys can come out. Why should I come out? Alex Haley didn't come out. Where would it have gotten him? With the white guys, they can get some mileage out of it. So forget it.

—**Howard Rollins** (TV's *In The Heat Of The Night*)

Dahling, I've had my share of merry (gay) leading men. I've even been called one myself! But it is definitely disconcerting when my leading man *and* my director keep making googoo eyes at each other and think I'm too self-absorbed to notice! Good God, dahling, I can spot an erection at half-mast half a theatre away!

—**Tallulah Bankhead**, directed by Tony Richardson in Tennessee Williams' play *The Milk Train Doesn't Stop Here Any More*, costarring Tab Hunter

Roddy McDowall and Sir John Gielgud

I basically played Tallulah Bankhead (in the murder mystery film *Evil Under The Sun*). My character, Rex, is a gossip columnist, but I mimicked Tallulah's voice and mannerisms....No, I never worry myself about all that, no...no, stereotypes and—what?—homophobia in the movies? No, I just don't concern myself with all that.

—**Roddy McDowall,** stereotypical actor

I wanted, after I did Gene Krupa (on the screen), to play Elvis Presley. I thought I could do it....I also wanted to play with Elvis Presley, though I didn't think I could do that. Be allowed to, I mean.

—**Sal Mineo**

I just love The Supremes. They remind me of me.

—**Little Richard**

I think Little Richard's the nelliest singer that's still in the closet....He thinks religion is his cloak of invisibility—you know, like in the old fairy tale.

—**Johnnie Ray**

Liberace talked publicly about his mom and brother George. But not about his niece and nephew. The tabloids brought out that she and Kristy McNichol were a hot item. The only one Uncle 'Lee' should have been ashamed of was the nephew, after what he did to his own sister.

—**Michael Callen** of The Flirtations; in 1988 Lester Lee Liberace, 33, was ordered into a state mental hospital for seven years after stabbing Ina Liberace, 28, in the stomach with an eight-inch kitchen knife

Would that be...because...they were...homophobic?

—talk host **Tom Snyder**, after actor Michael Jeter explained he'd been attacked by bat-wielding males in New York who thought he was gay

I was remembering Monty Clift. People who aren't fit to open the door for him sneer at his homosexuality. What do they know about it? Labels—people love putting labels on each other. Then they feel safe. People tried to make me into a lesbian. I laughed. No sex is wrong if there's love in it.

—**Marilyn Monroe**, to journalist W.J. Weatherby

Gore Vidal is a favorite novelist of mine. But he's lost points with me because he won't forgive the late, lamented Truman Capote for having been the better, more imaginative writer....One way he's doing it is by remembering Capote as some odd-looking, odd-sounding kind of fruitcake oddball! Which I find rather pathetic and sad.

—actor **Gary Merrill** (Bette Davis' final husband), who dedicated his memoirs to Vidal

I asked Marlon (Brando) (if he'd been to bed with a mutual friend) and he admitted it. He said he went to bed with lots of other men, too, but that he didn't consider himself a homosexual. He said they were all so attracted to him. 'I just thought that I was doing them a favor,' he said.

—**Truman Capote**

Truman Capote had a limited imagination. That's why he wrote so few novels...and even his most famous title wasn't his. It later came out that Truman had heard about a man who'd had a Marine spend the night with him one Saturday. The man was so sexually delighted that the next morning he offered his guest breakfast anywhere he wanted in Manhattan, no matter how expensive. Well, the Marine was from the sticks and had only heard of one expensive place in New York, so he suggested how about breakfast at Tiffany's?

—gay novelist **James Leo Herlihy** (*Midnight Cowboy*)

Errol Flynn had no taste, really...so his career went down the drain. Because he let his little head rule his big head, if you know what I mean.

—**Truman Capote**

It's like a bad soap opera. If I had written it, I would probably have Monica Lewinsky pull off her wig and turn out to be a man.

—**Gore Vidal**, on the Clinton sex scandal

Better oral sex than Oral Roberts.

—**Gore Vidal**

You know what I found absolutely inexcusable about Truman Capote and Gore Vidal? I found out neither one ever voted—or so they've said. They don't vote in elections. What horrible examples, and they even bragged about not voting! Gay men *have* to vote, we *have* to get into office the legislators who are willing to help us...achieve equal rights, to recognize us as citizens and taxpayers, not some religion-fueled 'controversy' or 'issue.'

—attorney/activist **Tom Stoddard**

There's a lot of leftover self-hate in older gay men, even when they're *out*....(Gore) Vidal says he doesn't write about happy gay men, he writes about 'reality.' It must mean he's unhappy himself....Mart Crowley, when he wrote *The Boys In The Band*, said ("I hope there are happy homosexuals. They just don't happen to be in this play."). He was justifying his selling out. But Vidal's statement, God! Today, in 1998? What an old sourpuss!

—**Mart Dayne McChesney**

He is purple—the gay-pride color—and his antenna is shaped like a triangle—the gay-pride symbol....As a Christian, I feel that role-modeling the gay lifestyle is damaging to the moral lives of children.

—preacher **Jerry Falwell**, trying to out cartoon character Tinky Winky of the Teletubbies

Substitute the word 'Christian' with 'bigot,' and you'll get where my cousin is coming from....This whole thing set me off. It's like, hello, Jerry, the same blood that runs through your veins runs through mine. There is a connection. So what do you have to say to that?

—Falwell's 37-year-old relative **Brett Beasley**, a computer sales executive, who came out as gay after Falwell's Tinky Winky episode

My father keeps in touch with Jerry regularly, although the subject of my sexuality has never come up. My family has totally accepted me. They're Lutherans. Jerry, whose mother is a Beasley, is a conservative Baptist. I've never liked him, because of his views on gays and other issues. But we've said hello at lots of family gatherings and at restaurants (in Lynchburg, Virginia)....His reaction just proves that, in his case, bigotry is thicker than blood.

—**Brett Beasley**, after Falwell publicly claimed not to know who he was

When the movie version of *Funny Girl* came out, I pleaded with my dad to drive me into Manhattan, where it was exclusively playing at a fancy movie theatre, and amazingly, Dad agreed—though I'm sure he would have rather seen *The Green Berets*. My heart was racing in anticipation of seeing Streisand turn her off-center qualities into beauty through sheer persistence and talent. Alas, my parade was rained on when we got there and found that the admission price was three times the usual one. Dad, who's straight, didn't think it was worth it, so we got right back into the car and rode home in stunned silence—all mine.

—columnist **Michael Musto**

I remember when I did *Lust For Life*...John Wayne was rather upset. He said, 'Kirk, what the hell are you doing, a guy like you, you shouldn't be playing parts like that.' He was upset that I should play [painter Vincent Van Gogh], who had a homosexual problem with Gauguin. He said, 'What are you trying to do?'

—**Kirk Douglas**, who helped break the blacklist which Wayne endorsed, by hiring blacklisted writer Dalton Trumbo to write *Spartacus*

Lou Sheldon is an idiot. Everything that he said is a lie and is just wrong.

—actor turned California Assemblywoman **Sheila Kuehl**, responding in 1999 to preacher and Traditional Values Coalition leader Sheldon's comment that Kuehl's proposed bill banning discrimination against gay students, AB222, should be biblically renamed AB666

People immediately think of Siegfried and Roy. They just assume if someone is involved in magic that maybe they're gay.

—model **Claudia Schiffer**, who had-been engaged to rumor-object and magician David Copperfield for ages

It was the first time that I realized that I wanted to fuck a man.

—**Peter Townshend** of The Who, about watching Mick Jagger prancing about in the early '60s

The trouble with Tony Curtis is that he's interested only in tight pants and wide billing.

—director **Billy Wilder**, in the 1960s

Kevin is my homosexual crush. If I were gay, the first guy I would sleep with is Kevin Smith (of *Chasing Amy*). The second one would be Leonardo DiCaprio—but only for the long hair he had in *The Man In The Iron Mask*.

—**Ben Affleck** (*Good Will Hunting*)

If there is such a thing as reincarnation, I would like to come back as James Dean.

—**Mercedes McCambridge**, who appeared in *Giant* and played male in *Touch Of Evil*

At a restaurant the other night. Next table, there's RuPaul, the big drag queen. Waiter asks him about his salad, what kind of dressing would he like? Guy answers, 'Cross.'

—**Rodney Dangerfield**

Oh, it was *very* different then. One wasn't always sure what to judge on. But if a woman wore pants a lot, we suspected....I worked with Charlie Farrell, and I never guessed he was reputed to be...gay. Of course he *would* flirt with any ladies on the set, it was expected and normal....The one we suspected was his wife (Virginia Valli). And it was because she wore pants quite often and she just adored golf!

—**Bette Davis**

Zsa Zsa Gabor has all these Stone Age ideas about lesbians in prison. She ought to open a book once in a while, instead of her mouth...and all that plastic surgery! One more face-lift and she'll have pubic hair on her chin.

—former talk host **Virginia Graham**

Cher is of a certain age and is very careful about her lighting and all those things. She does take a long time to pull herself together before she'll face the camera. She's marching into cronedom and she's not happy about it....(Plastic surgery-wise) She views herself as a work-in-progress.

—gay writer and Hollywood Square **Bruce Vilanch**

Divine

Troy Donahue—you know, his hair was the 8th wonder of the world....Now he says his (1960s) movie career suffered from his being confused with another blond star who was gay (Tab Hunter). Not quite. Troy's hair got thinner, and the rest of him got fatter. He ate his way out of a career. I'm lucky—I was no beauty, but I ate my way into a career!

—**Divine**

I hate Calvin Klein. I hate all those people who've taken what was once one of the most beautiful and luscious things I've ever seen—the male torso—and turned it into just another torso, any old torso, a bland, plastic, identical torso just like everyone else's.

—**Michael Jeter**

Truman (Capote) was so boyish for so long, looked so young. Then at some point, the pudginess began. I guess he got lazy or stopped caring. I once asked him if he took any sort of exercise, and he said yes, indeed. What kind? I asked. 'Massage,' he drawled.

—gay writer **Glenway Wescott**

In many instances, the dumbest (actors) are the most gifted. Sir John Gielgud, the kindest man alive, an incomparable technician, brilliant voice; but, alas, all his brains are in his voice. Marlon Brando: no actor of my generation possesses greater natural gifts; but none other has transported intellectual falsity to higher levels of hilarious pretension.

—**Truman Capote**

Tennessee (Williams) has made a fixed association between me and (Stanley) Kowalski (in *A Streetcar Named Desire*). I mean, we're friends and he knows that as a person I am just the opposite of Kowalski, who was everything I'm against—totally insensitive, crude, cruel. But still, Tennessee's image of me is confused with the fact that I played that part. So I don't know if he could write for me in a different color range.

—**Marlon Brando**

I admired Jane Fonda until she got into the exercise kick. She was brave to oppose an immoral war (in Vietnam). But why did an Oscar-winning actress turn to cranking out one exercise video after another?...That Hollywood influence, it's pernicious. Like, the L.A. approach to natural remedies is to have laser plastic surgery instead of using the knife.

—**Frank Maya**, the first openly gay stand-up comic

Elton John hasn't only sworn off of drugs....He says that nowadays the only foreign fluid he'll introduce into his body is a *latte*.

—British actor **Christopher Gable** (*The Boyfriend*)

(At Elaine's restaurant in Manhattan:) Tommy Smothers was tongue-kissing Phyllis (Diller) and so I said, 'If you can tongue-kiss her, you can tongue-kiss me.' So he gave me a quarter of a tongue-kiss and said he'd give the rest when he knew me better.

—**Andy Warhol**, in his published diaries

Andy Warhol and I used to do 'cum' facials, using our own, of course, not each other's. He'd heard Mae West used to do it too. Of course, she couldn't use her own. She used what the musclemen in her club act produced for her. I wonder if it works better if it's somebody else's?

—**Tommy Tune**, in his memoirs

Jeff Stryker wants to somehow transcend being a porno star. That's ridiculous. He keeps saying how far he's come—that people used to think he just had a big dick and no brain. Could be. Maybe now they think he just has a big dick and a little brain.

—porn star **Leo Ford**

A closet intellectual.

—columnist **Liz Smith**, on Carol Channing

Their *cause* is gay teens? That's really funny. My cause is getting a gay teen.

—California comic **Sandra Bernhard**, on activists Ellen DeGeneres and Anne Heche

Brilliant career move.

—**Danny Bonaduce** (*The Partidge Family*), when asked to comment on fellow former child star Rusty Hamer (*Make Room For Daddy*) blowing his brains out. Arrested for assaulting a transvestite hooker who declined to provide him with sex, Bonaduce later quipped, "I grew up in Hollywood, where half the girls I knew had dicks."

Now, I realize it's not easy being an instant superstar, Leo, but frankly your act already is getting a little old....(Teenage fans) are a notoriously fickle lot, favoring bland, blond androgyny (theeeeere's Leo!) one moment, then suddenly demanding steroidal masculinity the next.

—*Variety* editor **Peter Bart**, in a 1998 open letter to Leonardo DiCaprio

Hush-Hush: What closeted pop sensation makes the rounds with the guys in South Beach even though he is known to be a sex symbol? Some of the editors know the scoop but have decided to keep it hush-hush and let him have his day.

—**Arlene Walsh**'s June 9, 1999, column (note the use of "even though"; all editors—except one tabloid which asked whether the Hispanic hunk is gay—routinely keep "hush-hush" the fact that most any star is gay...)

My old friend Bill Piper Jr. of the famous aircraft family told me his roommate at Harvard was Katharine Hepburn's brother. 'He was effeminate,' said Bill. My comment was, 'That's something that could never be said of Kate.'

—octogenarian columnist **James Bacon** (both men indirectly acknowledging the long-standing rumor that at least one member of the Hepburn household is homo- or bisexual...)

Though some critics doubted that the movie-going public would buy Anne Heche as Harrison Ford's love interest in *Six Days/Seven Nights*, the film opened a solid #2 at the box office....If we bought Kate Hepburn's simpering at Bogey in *The African Queen*, we shouldn't blink twice at Heche and Harrison....Get a clue. It's called acting. Every gay who's ever been in the closet does it *very* well.

—*Lesbian News* reviewer **Katharine Russell**

Katharine Hepburn may or may not have had sexual affairs with Spencer Tracy, who was basically alcoholic and impotent, or Howard Hughes, who was bisexual and bizarre, or her agent Leland Hayward, who was straight and married another client, Margaret Sullavan. But she did have other, enduring affairs that *nobody* talks about. Or rather, that nobody writes about.

—author **Paul Rosenfield**, who was working on a Hepburn bio at the time of his death

Howard Hughes did have an affair with Cary Grant, whom he influenced into becoming a Republican. They were close for decades, presumably long after the sex was through....When Hughes was flying his plane to the Malibu location filming of *Sylvia Scarlett* (1935), the gossip columnists covered up the fact that he was always visiting Grant by writing that he was wooing Grant's costar, Kate Hepburn.

—**Carlos Clarens**, biographer of George Cukor, who helmed *Sylvia Scarlett*, Kate's cross-dressing vehicle that was ahead of its time and bombed badly

I didn't get a chance to become a movie star because the deal, for a wonderful movie tailored especially for me, fell through. On account of a mean-spirited critic who confused me with a tall black drag queen at a Josephine Baker concert. The way he wrote it, naming me in the same paragraph, gave the impression that I was the flamboyant drag queen and gay fan of Baker. Which was the beginning of the end for the Hollywood big boys, where I was concerned. The producing team called me up and warned, 'They kept it quiet about Cary Grant, but he wasn't out dancing around in drag onstage with Josephine Baker!' Never mind that I had *never* done drag. The movie was never made, and I never became a movie star, and I think it would have been a big hit.

—dancer/actor **Tommy Tune**, who came out in 1997

Tony Perkins, to my knowledge, never dragged himself up. No, he recoiled from things like that. He was afraid of being associated with that. Understandably, most gay men are. Because most don't do it, yet there's that media association of gay equals drag. Look at J. Edgar Hoover. He *once* dressed up (in a dress). So they've taken that one documented fact and *voilà*, now he's known and ridiculed as a cross-dresser.

—screenwriter **Paul Monette**

Straights put down Hoover as a drag queen, and some gays put him down because he looked like a bulldog. The man (head of the FBI for decades) should be disliked for something far more substantial—and not that he was in the closet, back when everyone else was too. He should be villainized because he was an ultra right-wing nut who abused his position and had no respect whatever for democracy or justice. And yes, he hated his fellow homosexuals, except for his one steady boyfriend. That was perhaps Hoover's one good point: instead of being promiscuous, he was devoted to (Clyde) Tolson for most of his adult life. Then again, you have to question Tolson allying himself with a man who was such a despot and who hated his own kind.

—gay author and professor **John Boswell**

I was one of those who initially found (lesbian writer) Camille Paglia amusing...despite entreaties from friends and colleagues who warned that Paglia was really only about promoting Camille. Dear Everyone: I'm sorry. Sometimes one is so wrong, those two words are about all you can say—except perhaps to add emphasis: I'm sorry I was so absolutely wrong. And to the critics of this newspaper who warned me about giving Paglia a platform: You were right. What an utter (homophobic) screwball Paglia has turned out to be.

—**Jeff Epperly**, editor of Boston's gay paper *Bay Windows*, in a 1998 editorial

What I most disliked about Tony Perkins was his two faces. After he married a woman , he felt free to be publicly anti-gay (in interviews). At the same time, he was engaging in homo sex every chance he had, and he had countless chances! Nothing worse than a homophobic homosexual——unlike heteros, they don't have the excuse of ignorance.

——Hollywood host **Samson DeBrier**

Tony's hobby was boxes. And I don't mean squares or rectangles.

—Dack Rambo

...the new Anthony Perkins film, *Box Lunch*.

—producer **Ben Bagley**

They've done a musical on Peter Allen in Australia (in 1998), and they're thinking of taking it to London or Broadway. The thing that tees me off is, in 1975 when I toured Australia, I took Peter down as my opening act. It was sort of a welcome home for both of us. The press was so vicious to him, I can't tell you. I mean, they called him a poofter, they were merciless. I saw Peter in tears from how cruel they were to him. Now he's dead and they're all, 'Our Peter, our boy.' Couldn't they have said one nice thing while he was alive?

—Helen Reddy

Tyrone Power was in England...this was some time in the '50s. And he saw some recruiting poster for the British Navy. It said, 'There's an opening for you in the Navy!' And he said, he joked, he wanted to join up right away, wink, wink. But one reason I remember it is that about the same time, the usual demented gossip columnists were pairing him with Eva Gabor. Or was it Zsa Zsa? No, I think Eva—she later had the for-show relationship with that closeted (TV personality).

—gay UK actor **Peter Arne**

Four or five years ago, I was invited to someone's birthday party, and George (Michael) was there. And he was talking to me about his boyfriends and lovers, you know...I said to him loads of times, 'Why don't you just come out, because everyone knows you're queer.' I've been the bane of his existence, let me tell you.

—**Boy George**, in 1998 (he began outing Michael in the 1980s)

I knew George (Michael) before he got famous, before *Wham!* He was our friend. He used to hang out with us at gay clubs. I guess I resented George because when he got successful, he became very stuck-up....I think he thinks he's better than other people. In particular, he thinks he's better than other gay people....If he says he's gay, he has to align himself with people like me and Jimmy Somerville and the drag queens, and he thinks he's a different type of homosexual. George actually thinks he's too good for the gay community.

—**Boy George**

The institutional tendency to closet people who are admired is that much greater when they are big moneymakers for someone. Look at Shakespeare, who has become an industry. The man from Stratford-Upon-Avon almost certainly did not write those plays. The two aristocrats who are the most likely authors—at a time when publishing was strictly for the lower class—are each bisexual...but the town of Stratford, which is a tourist magnet, and the whole Shakespearean academic community aren't likely to try and dig the truth out. They have no incentive to do so, and every incentive to deny the truth if anyone else does so.

—writer **Glenway Wescott**

I am haunted by the conviction that the divine William (Shakespeare) is the biggest and most successful fraud ever practiced on a patient world.

—19th-century author **Henry James**

No, I do not believe that the man from Stratford wrote what we call Shakespeare's plays. And I am far from alone in this belief.

—Shakespearean actor/director **Sir John Gielgud** (Freud and Mark Twain were two others)

Is Jeremy Irons gay? I used to think so. Not just because of *Brideshead Revisited*. But I doubt he is. It's just that he seems so totally English.

—theatre director **Ron Link**

Elton (John) is now queen of the entire world....He works mourning better than anyone on this earth.

—columnist **Michael Musto**, after Gianni Versace's and Princess Diana's funerals

I moved to England to escape theatrical stereotypes....Personally, I've enjoyed the change. It's a cultural thing. Here, people don't think Rimbaud is a Sylvester Stallone character, or that matricide is when you kill yourself in bed...and I got tired of a culture where a John Travolta can be considered a real actor, never mind some kind of a hetero sex symbol! England to me is more real.

—actor **Kenneth Nelson**, of the play and film *The Boys In The Band*

(On why the British are "superior" to Americans:) One, they speak English. Two, when they host a world championship, they invite other countries. Three, visitors to the office of the head of state are only expected to go down on *one* knee.

—**John Cleese** (*Fawlty Towers*, *A Fish Called Wanda*), after the Clinton-Lewinsky scandal

I've worked in England...it's cool. But I wouldn't want to live in a country that has such a right-wing institution as a monarchy. The royal family is foisted on everyone as role models, and it's so outdated! The eldest son inherits, and the youngest son is ahead of his older sister...they can't marry Catholics or Jews or anyone divorced...or Americans....And if you're Prince Edward and if you happen to be gay, you can never come out of the closet, though

I'm not sure why....It's all about straight, Protestant, medieval values and restrictions.

—**Brad Davis** (*Chariots Of Fire*)

I don't imagine the McCarthy witch-hunts could ever happen in Britain, no....They have more of a balance between liberal and conservative, politically and socially. In America, our two political parties balance out to conservative and more-conservative. Being liberal cost many of us our livelihoods...I don't think any conservative actor ever suffered for his convictions. Witch-hunters and their supporters only went on to greater glory—Nixon, John Wayne, Ronald Reagan, ... In the U.S., conservatives try to claim a monopoly on patriotism, and that is a dangerous habit.

—Oscar-winning and black-listed actress **Anne Revere** (she won for *National Velvet*)

Richard Chamberlain

I went to work and live in England to expand as an actor...to get away from (being stereotyped as) Dr. Kildare....I loved my time there, though most people eventually get homesick for wherever they come from....I didn't go to try and become the new Laurence Olivier or John Gielgud, but I didn't want to be trapped in a TV or movie character or image....One does feel more free to be oneself in Europe, sometimes.

—**Richard Chamberlain**, who allegedly came out in France

The American media's latest success story horror is radio shock-doc Laura Schlessinger...who is a bigoted moralist (who) proves that an orthodox Jew can be as intolerant and homophobic, etc., as a born-again Christian....Her rantings and fictions about homosexuality encourage the climate of hate and violence....She's also, almost inevitably for this type of person, a hypocrite, with those nude photos from her affair while she was married to another man....Her real mission is making money. Her result is more gay-bashings and divisiveness. She's bleached scum.

—**Mark Webster Chatfield**, Olympics swimmer and gold medalist at the 1994 Gay Games

These people who say God speaks to them are as pathetic as the ones who believe them. They speak to *themselves*, then claim it was God——they use God as a Good Housekeeping seal of approval.... Pat Robertson, who owns The Family Channel, said God was going to send destruction down Orlando's way, due to Disney's support of gays and lesbians. Well, instead, Jehovah, or the Big Weather Maker, sent Hurricane Bonnie right into Pat's part of Virginia, avoiding Orlando but causing power failures and flooding and property damage in the religious tycoon's area. In fact, Pat's *700 Club* TV program was temporarily halted; they had to air reruns two days in a row. That's what I call divine weather!

—**Walter Kendrick**, gay professor of English at Fordham University and expert on the Victorians (and Victorian attitudes)

What we need now is new energy, lots more straight folk coming out in support. Why doesn't Colin Powell or Sam Nunn get it? Barry Goldwater got it. Everyone needs to just get over it! We need all those famous Hollywood faces who lunch with gay people alone everyday to be vocal. I want my kids to see their heroes—Schwarzenegger and Cruise—march down Fifth Avenue in the Gay Pride Parade.

—**Phil Donahue**

They say if you know gay people, openly and honestly gay people, it'll diminish an individual's homophobia. Well, no. It depends on how greedy and hateful or ambitious or perverse somebody is.... Malcolm Forbes was gay, but his son wants to be a Republican president. Goldwater had a gay grandson, but Colin Powell is said to have a gay or lesbian kid, and this Republican senator, Knight, who is sponsoring California's anti-gay, straights-only marriage bill, has an openly gay son. It's disheartening, but it's human nature, and we all have to make sure the darker, meaner side of human nature doesn't affect our laws!

—veteran activist **Morris Kight**

Fundamentally, being gay is no more a choice than being or 'becoming' a heterosexual. But the valid answer to the invalid question of Is it a choice? is simply: so what if it were? So *what*? This is a fake controversy. The haters can't win against abortion, they can't rejoin church and state—thank goodness—and communism's too weak in Russia and too strong in China, so now the agitators' target is American citizens who happen to be homosexual. And you have pathetic, desperate characters like Jerry Falwell trying to stir up controversy and create misery just to line his pockets and harden American hearts! But our brains have to grow bigger and match our hearts—we have to ignore such hurtful hate-mongers. We can't let them make hatred spread....

—**Dr. Evelyn Hooker**, psychologist, author and grand marshall of West Hollywood's Gay Pride Parade

I have to admit I'm more comfortable with animal homosexuality than the human variety. But it's all a fact, and the media have kept the facts submerged....I recall a friend who used to work at Disney in the 1960s and '70s who said that those nature 'documentaries' which focused exclusively on animals mating and breeding were often using footage of animal homosexuality but re-labeling it as 'normal.' Who, then, are we to judge nature? I was very disturbed when I heard that.

—animal rights activist and author **Cleveland Amory**

There was this very popular preacher named Billy Sunday, a pre-Billy Graham, and he would slander what weren't even referred to then as homosexuals. There were many stupid names—but no name for homophobia, which was the normal state of affairs....Sunday was trying to link homosexuality with the usual biblical tales, the Sodom and Gomorrah story, etc. Also with bestiality. Which has no more to do with homosexuality than heterosexuality! Less so—nearly every farm boy I ever heard of who did it with an animal was a horny straight boy...and incest, what's that usually got to do with, but straight men and boys bothering the hell out of their daughters or sisters?

—fashion designer and gay rights activist (before he became famous for designing the topless swimsuit) **Rudy Gernreich**

It's not a great movie, and...the studio wanted 'more morality' injected into it. What can you do? Add more makeup to the villains....(Codirector) Sergio Leone suggested nudity, but this was a biblical thing, not some Greek or Roman saga.

—*Sodom & Gomorrah* (1962) codirector **Robert Aldrich** (*What Ever Happened To Baby Jane?*)

Mr. Aldrich is a puritan at heart....They wanted a Hollywood version, for American *and* European audiences, with little (sic) entertainment, much exotic spectacle, and lots of revenge and punishment.

—Italian *S&G* codirector **Sergio Leone**

I think it's a highly moral, instructive and an appealing film, which any daughter of mine is welcome to view at any time.

—*Sodom* star **Stewart Granger**, who was outed in the 1950s by Hedda Hopper over a reported affair with fellow Englishman and actor Michael Wilding (Elizabeth Taylor's second husband)

I agreed to work with Madonna and Steven Meisel on their book, *Sex*. At first I declined: 'I've got kids. I can't risk losing my Lancôme contract, as I learned from (doing the film) *Blue Velvet*.' Madonna and Steven insisted, and they sounded so interesting in their search to understand and illustrate all the varieties and shades sex could take. 'I don't want to appear nude or French-kiss you, Madonna.'

'Okay,' she answered, and off we went to Miami for the photos. We dressed up like men, playing around like girlfriends making fun of boys. When the photos came out, in the context of the book, it looked as if we were lesbians. Lancôme got upset, but it was easy to defend myself: 'What's the matter with being a lesbian?' That deflected any proceedings against me.

—**Isabella Rossellini**, European-raised model and actress

We can't name her, she asserts she's heterosexual, but she's a blonde superstar, totally bi, loves dark-haired women, and she's famous for her on-screen nudity which she's now a little old to keep doing, but her fantasy has always been to make love to Isabella Rossellini. Unfortunately for her, Isabella's pro-gay but apparently prefers male non-hunks like (Martin) Scorsese and Gary Oldman to your, um, basic blonde-bimbo sex symbol.

—Hollywood journalist and author **Paul Rosenfield**

Hollywood's most desirable gals.

—**Tallulah Bankhead**'s description of 1930s box office stars Greta Garbo, Cary Grant, Joan Crawford and Jean Harlow

I thought Bronson Pinchot was *out*. Excuse me! Not just because of all the gay roles, either. But next thing I read, he's telling the (mainstream) press about his latest role and how 'my girlfriend' told him she didn't mind sleeping with Stan Laurel, but blah-blah-blah. Then he says, 'But that's not why we broke up.' It's my opinion, but actors should stick to acting and leave imagination to the writers.

—West Hollywood Internet columnist **Henry Nicklin** (June, 1999)

I fell madly in love with (costar) Rock Hudson...in 1957. I had no idea he was gay—I had no idea anybody was gay. He dated me every night, but nothing happened....I chalked that up to the fact that he was married at the time and I'm Catholic. So I fell more in love with him because he was principled!

—film actor and Broadway star **Elaine Stritch**

I wasn't at all surprised. In fact, I was relieved. Now I don't feel like such a failure.

—**Brooke Shields**, discussing her reaction to news that former "date" George Michael is gay

He should never have broken up with David Bowie. This never would have happened.

—**Jay Leno**, on Mick Jagger being sued for divorce by his wife because his girlfriend was pregnant by him

When we found the place for our (heterosexual wedding) ceremony, it was absolutely perfect, except for these huge framed pictures of Nancy and Ronald Reagan. I had to cover those up. I didn't want Reagan's presence at my wedding. He added to the horror of AIDS by never addressing it. I watched him on television, speech after speech after speech, and he never even said the word. If we're in the middle of a plague and the leader of the country ignores it, it's encouraging people to be stupid, scared and put their heads in the sand.

—**Kathy Najimy** (*Sister Act*, *Veronica's Closet*)

It's all about how people insert the penis into the anus and they insert the fist into the anus, etc., etc. That was all very interesting, but it seemed to me that the most interesting question was how the people of Orange County came to insert an anus into the House of Representatives.

—U.S. Congressman **Barney Frank** (Dem.—MA), on misinformation passed on by William Dannemeyer (Rep.—CA) about how AIDS is transmitted

Can you beat it? Excuse the expression. Now Bob Dole, the man who clawed his way to the middle, is a spokesman for 'erectile dysfunction,' that is, impotence. I suppose the Viagra makers are trying to reach the under-100 crowd....Do you notice that gays never need these sex boosters? But then, we're not chained to butch wives, missionary positions, or for younger men, insecurity, fear of commitment and/or pregnancy, self-consciousness,.... and go forth and multiply like animals with an unlimited food supply....As one of the characters in *The Fantasticks* says, 'Please, God, don't let me be normal!'

—Internet columnist **Henry Nicklin**

Mark (Wahlberg, formerly Marky Mark) came to me and said, 'I've got an inch on Leo.' And he showed it to me, and then I hired him.

—*Boogie Nights* director **Paul Thomas Anderson**, on why he cast MW over Leonardo DiCaprio (apparently, no one asked Mark how he knew...)

People can sense what is real. Luther Vandross sings about loving girls and being the most romantic guy in the world, but he's a goddamn freak! He goes out and sniffs little boys' underwear and shit like that.

—Rap-rocker **Kid Rock**, to *Pop Smear* magazine, spreading stereotypical misinformation

Great coach. As a man, well, I've never slept with him.

—basketball star **Dennis Rodman,** on Chicago Bulls coach Phil Jackson (pre Carmen Electra...)

The attraction between us was instantaneous, electric, unforgettable....We met for romantic moments in his dressing-room apartment in the Star Building on the lot after work. We took long rides, speeding down Sunset (Blvd.) to Malibu, we shared dinners at the nondescript seaside diners that bordered the dark shimmer of the Pacific Ocean. Tyrone (Power) loved giving gifts: gold jewelry nestled in burgundy velvet boxes, white cashmere sweaters, leather-bound books—everything but the stability and commitment I needed most.

—designer **Mr. Blackwell**, whose memoirs also recounted affairs with Cary Grant and (Grant's lover) Randolph Scott

There's this whole circle of guys who were close to Sal Mineo in varying degrees....Don Johnson and Don's sister lived with Sal. Sal discovered Don—Don was his protégé, he starred Don in a gay-themed play with nudity in it....Another protégé was Bobby Sherman. ...Peter Bogdanovich was a good friend—other way around: Sal was a good friend, he found him properties to direct, but when Peter hit big-time, he didn't cast Sal. Then he went downhill anyway, but by then Sal was gone....Another pal was Desi Arnaz Jr....After Sal died, most of these guys pretended they barely knew him, or like Bogdanovich, who tells interviewers Sal wasn't really gay, yet Sal was one of the first to come out of the closet, and it cost him his career.

—actor turned novelist **Tom Tryon**, who died of AIDS

People have credited me with what I have created (a talk show). Well, I didn't create anything. I just copied Merv Griffin. It's that afternoon sit-down-with-your-grandmother kind of programming.

—Mervian host **Rosie O'Donnell**

Can I just say how pissed off I am at her? She canceled on me four fucking times...and now she doesn't even return my calls!... And I am so sick of hearing how bad they treated her in this town, because they treated me a million times worse than her, and now she's one of the ones who's doing it to me.

—talk show host **Roseanne**, on Ellen DeGeneres

When they found out I never mentioned homosexuality at all (in his one-man show), their love for me died in an instant. I'm afraid I also lost the love of the entire homosexual community when I said that Princess Diana was trash and got what she deserved.

—90-year-old author and sometime wit **Quentin Crisp**

I don't do political interviews, I just entertain. I'm not a deep thinker, dear, I'm a deep shopper. A teacher of mine used to say—are you listening, Quentin Crisp?—that it's one thing to seem a fool. It's another to open your mouth and remove all doubt.

—veteran drag divo **Charles Pierce**

How Quentin Crisp became an icon is a puzzlement. A self-destructive eccentric with no self-esteem, he did survive his hard times to emerge not a hero, just a martyr. Eventually a gay Uncle Tom, who not only feels we deserve no equal rights but not even the right to exist. He's going from bad to worse to senile...(and) is one of the worst cases of siding with one's oppressors.

—poet **Allen Ginsberg**

Laurence Olivier was a vindictive and vain man—and a man with a secret (bisexuality). He was jealous that Maggie (Smith, Stephens' then-wife) and I were becoming popular individually and as a couple. A *real* couple, might I add, not merely for show (Olivier's first of three wives was lesbian)....We once spent a friendly, I thought, weekend with the Oliviers in Brighton (England). What we found out later was that Larry had already posted us a letter in which he coolly informed us that he had dispensed with Maggie's services (at the National Theatre) twice over—he would be doing an all-male version of *As You Like It* with Ronald Pickup as Rosalind, and his revival of *The Way Of The World* would feature Geraldine McEwan in the role Maggie had sought.

—**Robert Stephens** (*The Prime Of Miss Jean Brodie*)

Nobody can be as defensive as some gays....I admire that (*Kid in the Hall*) Scott Thompson is out of the closet. But he can't seem to do a gay character that isn't a complete put-down. Then, when someone gay takes exception, (Thompson) takes umbrage, becomes all pissy and puts them down quite soundly, as he did a friend of mine....He's the sort of gay performer who's less popular with gay audiences than more average ones who don't mind, or even feel comforted by, those stereotypes that Thompson seems to dote on.

—**Dack Rambo**, *Dallas*

Far be it from me to say it, but I know he dearly loved his late wife. But many people dearly love a brother or sister, and sex has nothing to do with it....Readers tend to think that with actors, sex enters into each and every relationship. Not so, not so.

—apparently heterosexual **Robert Stephens**' way of noting the homo- or bisexuality of fellow Brit Jeremy Brett, best known as TV's *Sherlock Holmes*

(Jay) Leno was always able to come up with occasional good jokes during an interview—an incipient flair that Dick Cavett had spotted even as far back as Leno's first night as regular host of *The Tonight Show*. Tom Cruise, Cavett wrote in a review of the show, was talking about shooting a love scene: 'I just lay there naked with my eyes shut.'

Leno cut in with a quick one: 'That's how some actors get their jobs, but go on.'

—author **Jay Walker**, in *The Leno Wit*

The one I admire is Rufus Wainwright. His first album was a huge success, with critics too, and he came right out. The longer one leaves it, the harder it is to do....He has the same soulful good looks as Gilbert O'Sullivan ("Alone Again," "Naturally") did, but *he* had all that speculation of 'is he or isn't he', which alienated a lot of the gay fans and the more rigid straight ones...and Wainwright won't have to do all the posing and be as fearful as, say, George Michael. It saves so much crap to just come out at the start, let people know what's what, and get on with your career and making music.

—openly "bi" **Richard Fairbrass**, of the UK group Right Said Fred ("I'm Too Sexy")

In our patriarchal society, I think it's even more difficult to come out as gay than lesbian, though I applaud them both. But I'm really heartened by these young men, these attractive, commercially viable actors, especially from TV, who have come out... like Mitchell Anderson, Chad Allen, Dan Butler, Wilson Cruz and (from movies) Rupert Everett. They're really helping pave the way, and they're not just beautiful on the outside.

—actor **Brian Hurley**, who died at 49 of AIDS

He's like the sexiest gay man alive. If he were a movie star he could be openly gay because you'd still want to see him kissing women. He's that sexy.

—**Rita Wilson**, actress and Tom Hanks' wife, on designer Tom Ford, with whom she helped raise $1.2 million at a fashion show benefiting AIDS Project Los Angeles

Susan (Sarandon) is the ideal woman for me. I'm secretly in love with her. If anything ever happens to Tim (Robbins), I'm more than willing to step in.

—**Julia Roberts**, on her *Stepmom* costar, quoted in Australia's *Woman's Day* magazine

If, you know, straight women can be pro-lesbian, why can't Camille Paglia? What kind of gimmick is that? An anti-lesbian lesbian, an anti-feminist feminist? No wonder those self-righteous talk-show guys book her as a guest—she parrots the same prejudices. I think what occurred was Camille kept her bra but burned her brain.

—pro-lesbian feminist author
Audre Lord

It was obvious what (Ernest) Hemingway was doing, all those years he picked on Truman Capote...(Hemingway's) whole literary style was the wearing of fake hair on his chest...attacking from the closet, from a position of insecurity....Beware the fellow who's so frequently anti-homosexual; he most likely has more than a skeleton tucked in his closet.

—actress turned author
Louise Brooks

Clifton Webb

Devout!

—actor **Clifton Webb** (*Laura*, *The Razor's Edge*), when asked if he were homosexual

Please! Miss Mansfield, we're all *wine* drinkers at this table.

—**Clifton Webb**, at a 1950s party welcoming Sophia Loren to Hollywood, crashed by Jayne Mansfield, who stood next to a seated Webb, her extra-large bosom almost spilling into his face

Roseanne: "I think women can be much nastier than men. I think women should go to the wars."

k.d. lang: "Oh, no, Roseanne. That's ridiculous. Women don't have an overwhelming compunction to kill."

Roseanne: "Don't they? Perhaps it's just me."

—talk show host **Roseanne** and lesbian guest **k.d .lang**

Some of my best friends are lesbians! What's new?

—**Tallulah Bankhead** (bi), not denying her non-platonic relationship with comic actress Patsy Kelly

I was rather surprised when I found out Jodie Foster apparently isn't a feminist, or not admittedly so, unlike a straight actress like Barbra Streisand....I have a friend, a lesbian from Spain, an older, very butch woman, and I was aghast when she explained that she revered (late fascist dictator Francisco) Franco—a man who abhorred male and female homosexuals. But I gradually learned that there's a certain type of tough lesbian who identifies with ultra-male, or ultra-chauvinist, authority figures...a strain of lesbian that, like a lot of straight men, has no real use for women except as sex objects.

—**Ron Vawter** (*Silence Of The Lambs*)

I think it's gone to her head—the success, the pressure, the covering up....In her first season, I heard (Rosie O'Donnell) hired Kate Clinton, a lesbian comedienne, as a writer for her talk show. Then came all the stories about tantrums and firings, the temperament, etc. I don't know anything about that....But once her show creamed the competition and got renewed and went very mainstream, etc., there didn't seem to be room on her show for an openly lesbian writer—rumor potential and too close to home, etc.

—Beat poet laureate
Allen Ginsberg

Out magazine: "Do you think (Rosie O'Donnell) will ever marry Tom Cruise if Nicole (Kidman) leaves him?"

Sandra Bernhard: "Honey, you know what? If people want to get lost in their illusions, let 'em. That's all I can say."

Out: "It's gotta be a painful existence."

Bernhard: "Honey, not when you're depositing those million-dollar checks into your account. I think it's a pretty fucking cushy existence. I don't think anybody's feeling any pain."

—Sandra Bernhard

Whether or not we're big fans of Ellen (DeGeneres) or Anne (Heche), these gals put their careers on the line. Therefore we should root for them, because they bravely and openly represent all same-sex couples and all gay people who come out at work and take the consequences of not lying or being ashamed.

—Mart Dayne McChesney (*The Guiding Light*)

Chastity Bono started it—she asked if Ellen was too gay? So I want to ask: Was Bill Cosby too black? Was Ricky Ricardo (sic) too Cuban? Was Seinfeld too whiny? Is Dan Butler's character (on *Frasier*) too straight? Was Dr. Smith on *Lost In Space* too gay? I ask you....

—artist **Vernon "Copy" Berg**, who in 1975 successfully sued the Navy to challenge his "other than honorable" discharge on the grounds of homosexuality—the result was that the U.S. armed forces finally began granting *honorable* discharges to gay personnel

. . . final words

There is a certain silence which appears to be mysterious, but which is only weakness.

—**Christina**, Sweden's lesbian monarch

When I was in the military they gave me a medal for killing two men, and a discharge for loving one.

—on the tombstone, in Congressional Cemetery, of Sergeant **Leonard Matlovich**

The voice of the intellect is a soft one, but it does not rest until it has gained a hearing. Ultimately, after endlessly repeated rebuffs, it succeeds. This is one of the viewpoints in which one may be optimistic about the future of mankind.

—**Freud**, in 1928

-30-

Index

A.M. America, 200
Abrams, Jill, 170
Abzug, Bella, 276
Adams, Michael, 242
Adams, Nick, 259
Addams Family Values, 69
Adrian, Iris, 195
Adventures of Priscilla, Queen Of The Desert, The, 29, 46, 133, 246, 283
Advocate, 64, 82, 152, 154,, 155, 156, 158, 161, 168
Affleck, Ben, 291
African Queen, The, 295
Ager, Susan, 29
Agony And The Ecstasy, The, 275
Aikman, Troy, 63
Albee, Edward, 222
Aldrich, Robert, 303
Alec Baldwin Doesn't Love Me, 285
Alexander, Jason, 15, 252
Alive And Kicking, 15, 252
All-American Girl, 95
Allen, Chad, 43, 63, 71, 118, 309
Allen, Fred, 24
Allen, Gracie, 130
Allen, Peter, 99, 104, 107, 108, 114, 135, 136, 297
Allen, Steve, 250
Allen, Tim, 163
Allen, Woody, 107
Allison, Dorothy, 158, 222
Allred, Gloria, 242
Ally McBeal, 213
Almendros, Nestor, 28
Almost Golden, 197
Alsop, Angus, 61
Altman, Dennis, 284
Altman, Robert, 139
Amadeus, 108
Amanda, Donohoe, 173, 195
Amburn, Ellis, 142
Ammiano, Tom, 62,249, 254, 257
Amory, Cleveland, 302
An American Family, 121
And The Band Played On, 68, 275
Andelson, Sheldon, 230
Anderson, Gillian, 212, 215
Anderson, Judith, 284
Anderson, Mitchell, 43, 47, 108, 127, 309
Anderson, Paul Thomas, 305
Andresen, Bjorn, 124
Andress, Ursula, 253
Andrews, Harry, 264
Andrews, Julie, 173, 221
Andy Warhol Diaries, The, 125
Andy Warhol's 'Bad', 213
Angeli, Pier, 32
Anger, Kenneth, 241
Animals Are People Too, 220
Annie, 69
Another Country, 262
Another World, 19, 87, 244, 267
Any Mother's Child, 198
Arden, Eve, 230
Ardolino, Emile, 30, 84, 149, 194
Are You Being Served?, 261
Ariel, Mark, 89
Armani, Giorgio, 253, 280
Armey, Richard, 57, 221
Arnaz, Desi Jr., 306
Arne, Peter, 276, 298
Arquette, Alexis, 14, 16, 56, 112, 113, 175, 232
Arquette, Rossana, 113
Arthur, Bea, 170, 174, 237
Arvin, Newton, 191, 278
Arzner, Dorothy, 284
As Good As It Gets, 56, 266
As The World Turns, 237
As You Like It, 308
Ashcroft, Peggy, 219
Ashman, Howard, 62, 221, 269
Asner, Ed, 128
Astaire, Fred, 184
Atherton, William, 279
Auntie Mame, 127, 261
Aurelious, Marcus, 177
Austen, Howard, 140, 192
Backus, Jim, 40, 258
Bacon, James, 193, 295
Bacon, Sir Francis, 255
Baer, Max Jr., 38
Bagley, Ben, 31, 67, 83, 125, 157, 160, 229, 237, 242, 282, 297
Bahnsen, George, 62
Baio, Scott, 273
Baldwin, Alec, 121, 285
Baldwin, Billy, 197, 285
Baldwin, James, 238
Baldwin, Stephen, 127
Ball, Lucille, 47, 148
Banderas, Antonio, 17, 262
Bandy, Way, 191
Bankhead, Tallulah, 91, 205, 206, 286, 304, 310
Barbarella, 224
Barker, Clive, 136
Barney, Natalie, 189
Barr, Richard, 21
Barr, Roseanne, 55, 87, 93, 97, 169, 181, 209, 242, 243, 266, 307, 310
Barresi, Paul, 272
Barrowed Time, 22
Barry, Gene, 52
Barry, Stephen, 201
Barrymore, Drew, 103, 179, 195, 251
Barrymore, John, 251
Bart, Lionel, 85, 218, 235
Bart, Peter, 294
Bartel, Paul, 138, 225
Basinger, Kim, 121
Bastard Out Of Carolina, 222
Batchelor, Ruth, 200
Batman, 12, 179, 261
Bay Windows, 297
Baywatch, 145
Beard, Peter, 261
Beardsley, Aubrey, 153
Bearse, Amanda, 103, 262
Beastie Boys, 43
Beatles, The, 117
Beaton, Sir Cecil, 17, 41, 273
Beauty And The Beast, 90
Beeman, Tony, 67, 71, 147
Bell, Arthur, 121
Bell, Cei, 238
Bellamy, Ralph, 60
Benner, Richard, 18
Bennet, Michael, 184
Benshoff, Dr. Harry, 179
Berg, Vernon "Copy", 312
Bergen, Frances, 32
Berger, Helmut, 127, 146
Bergman, Ingmar, 82, 272
Berle, Milton, 23
Bernhard, Cydney, 30, 243-244
Bernhard, Sandra, 80, 105, 224, 253, 262, 281, 294, 311
Bernstein, Leonard, 39, 46, 105
Bertolucci, Bernardo, 272
Bertugli, David, 247
Berzon, Betty, 144
Besser, Joe, 131
Betz, Edward, 48
Beverly Hillbillies, The, 38, 116, 189
Beverly Hills 90210, 119
Bewitched, 12, 22, 94, 120, 218, 256, 269, 280
Big Valley, The, 197
Billy's Hollywood Screen Kiss, 138
Birdcage, The, 33, 183
Birdwell, Russell, 40
Bixby, Bill, 20, 130
Black Out, 262
Blair, Selma, 212
Bleeth, Yasmine, 285
Blondie, 257
Bloodhounds Of Broadway, 224
Blue Velvet, 303
Blyth, Ann, 176
Bogarde, Sir Dirk, 64
Bogart, Humphrey, 295
Bogdanovitch, Peter, 306
Bolan, Marc, 109
Bonaduce, Danny, 294
Bond, James, 226, 253
Bono, Chastity, 23, 25-26, 60, 108, 114, 146, 210, 312
Bono, Sonny, 19, 60, 176, 256, 257
Boogie Nights, 305
Boosler, Elayne, 182, 223
Boswell, John, 296
Bottoms, Joseph, 39
Bound, 18, 204
Bourré, Jean-Paul, 265
Bouvier, Jack, 270
Bowie, David, 109, 123, 218, 304
Bowra, Sir Maurice, 186
Boy George, 13, 36, 44, 80, 106, 113, 172, 175, 183, 187, 223, 262, 298
Boyfriend, The, 66, 156, 293
Boys In The Band, The, 28, 53, 72, 177, 289, 299
Boys On The Side, 52, 179, 271
Boyzone, 98
Brady Bunch Movie, The, 174
Brady Bunch, The, 118
Bragman, Howard, 68, 76, 162, 163, 164, 238
Brain Candy, 94
Branagh, Kenneth, 245
Brando, Christian, 270
Brando, Marlon, 119, 205, 251, 260, 271-272, 288, 292-293
Braveheart, 56
Breakfast At Tiffany's, 134, 245
Breaking Away, 81
Breckingridge, Myra, 265
Bressan, Arthur, 279
Brett, Beasly, 78, 289
Brett, Jeremy, 308
Brideshead Revisited, 299
Bridges, James, 225
Bright, Susie, 84
Bristow, Patrick, 96
Brochtrup, Bill 56
Broderick, Matthew, 55
Brokaw, Tom, 282
Brolin, Jim, 121
Bronski Beat, 73
Bronski, Michael, 153, 208
Bronson, Charles, 39
Brooke, Rupert, 205
Brookner, Howard, 224
Brooks, Louise, 310
Brophy, Brigid, 153, 154
Brothers, Dr. Joyce, 191
Brown, Forman, 214
Brown, Jerry, 118, 124, 256
Brown, Johnny Mack, 279
Brown, Rita Mae, 224, 240, 245, 248, 277
Brown, Willie, 90
Browne, Coral, 263
Browne, Lance, 25, 72, 183
Brownell, John Peter, 167
Brownworth, Victoria, 161
Bryant, Anita, 57, 118, 139, 154, 275
Buchanan, James, 256
Buchanan, Pat, 264
Buddies, 279
Buffy The Vampire Slayer, 179
Bullock, Jim J., 33
Burgess, Anthony, 117, 207, 276
Burnett, Carol, 182
Burns, George, 21, 130
Burr, Raymond, 42, 185
Burridge, Geoffrey, 190
Burroughs, William S., 101
Burton, Phillip, 188
Burton, Richard, 14, 188, 190
Burton, Tim, 179
Butler, Dan, 103, 131, 280, 309, 312

Caan, James, 71
Caan, Scott, 71
Cable Guy, 95
Caen, Herb, 240
Cagney And Lacey, 269
Caine, Michael, 66, 264, 278
Cale Porter, 229
Callen, Michael, 21, 57, 62, 99, 105, 125, 211, 212, 257, 287
Callow, Simon, 228
Cameron, Sue, 95, 124, 277
Campbell, Naomi, 201
Candice, Bergen, 32
Cannon, Dyan, 66
Cantinflas, 140
Capote, Truman, 11, 35, 41, 45, 50, 75, 85, 103, 106, 112, 114, 119, 135, 137, 140, 144, 184, 189, 191, 198, 201, 202, 213, 215, 216, 228, 247, 250, 255, 260-261, 263-264, 265, 266-267, 268, 270, 274, 278, 287, 288, 292, 310
Capucine, 64
Capurro, Scott, 67
Cardinal, The, 51, 229
Carey, Phil, 40
Carlson, Kenneth Joseph, 68
Carne, Judy, 193
Carrey, Jim, 95
Carroll, David, 139
Carson, Joanne, 268
Carson, Johnny, 112, 268
Casares, Ingrid, 253
Casey, Warren, 227
Cashman, Michael, 29
Cat Creature, The, 17
Cats, 70
Cavett, Dick, 266, 308
Celebrity, 38
Celluloid Closet, The, 84
Cervantes, 8
Chakiris, George, 63
Chamberlain, Richard, 300
Change Lobsters And Dance, 181
Channing, Carol, 192-193, 273, 294
Channing, Stockard, 98
Chapman, Graham, 28, 45, 135, 171, 177, 201, 216, 256
Chariots Of Fire, 276, 300
Charleson, Ian, 276
Charlie's Angels, 277
Charlton, Janet, 94,110
Chasing Amy, 291
Chatfield, Mark Webster, 300
Cheers, 68, 127
Cheever, Susan, 142
Chekhov, 145
Cher, 19, 179, 210, 230, 249, 256, 257, 291
Chester, Craig, 25, 115
Chicago Tribune, 71
Children's Hour, The, 275
China Syndrome, The, 225
Chinatown, 204
Cho, Margaret, 95
Choice Of Evil, 238
Chorus Line, A, 184
Christie, Julie, 254
Christina, 313
Christopher Street, 225
Christopher Strong, 284
Christopher, Keith, 19, 56, 87, 141, 244, 267, 270
Churchill, Winston, 80, 171
Ciccone, Christopher, 187
City Of Night, 235
Claire Of The Moon, 16, 114
Clancy, Tom, 85
Clarens, Carlos, 57, 61, 218, 275, 279, 295
Clark, Al, 283
Clarke, Arthur C., 174
Clary, Robert, 247
Clausen, Connie, 29, 40, 185
Clay, Andrew Dice, 266
Cleese, John, 299
Cleopatra, 22, 126
Cleveland, Mark, 77
Clift, Montgomery, 37, 178, 205, 206, 287
Clinton, Bill, 22, 35, 67, 76, 86, 220, 226, 299
Clinton, Chelsea, 57
Clinton, Hillary, 150, 256
Clinton, Kate, 311
Cloclwork Orange, A, 207, 276
Clooney, George, 188
Club Rules, The, 18, 255
Cobain, Kurt, 123, 240
Cocteau, Jean, 90
Cohn, Roy, 62
Colette, 172
Collard, Cyril, 272
Collins, Jackie, 249
Collins, Joan, 215
Colton, Adam, 76
Como, William, 218
Con Air, 54
Condon, Richard, 11, 32, 40, 271
Conn, Nicole, 16, 114
Connery, Sean, 278
Constantinides, Olga, 95
Contact, 27
Cook, Terence Cardinal, 113-114
Cooper, Gary, 238
Copland, Aaron, 105
Copperfield, David, 105, 290
Corby, Ellen, 159
Corydon, 226
Cosby, Bill, 312
Cosell, Howard, 131
Cosmopolitan, 187
Courtship Of Eddie's Father, The, 20
Cousteau, Jacques, 208
Cover Up, 76
Coward, Sir Noel, 17, 48, 64, 255
Cox, Wally, 119, 205
Crabtree, Howard, 74, 230
Cramer, Doug, 131
Crawford, Cindy, 174, 253, 285
Crawford, Joan, 202, 279, 304
Crisp, Quentin, 103, 104, 223, 307
Cromwell, Richard, 53
Crosby, David, 86
Crosby, Stills, Nash & Young, 86
Crossfire, 17
Crothers, Joel, 141
Crowley, Mart, 289
Cruel Intentions, 212
Cruise, Tom, 53, 63, 107, 158, 168, 188, 285, 301, 308, 311
Cruising, 54
Cruz, Wilson, 13, 14, 47, 99, 111, 232, 267, 273, 309
Crystal, Billy, 98, 103
Cukor, George, 12, 48, 79, 200, 204, 295
Culture Clash, 153
Culture Club, 241
Cummings, Robert, 24
Cunanan, Andrew, 109, 185, 282
Cuomo, Andrew, 79
Curran, Keith, 69, 71, 94
Curry, John, 19, 245
Curry, Tim, 129
Curtis, Jamie Lee, 64
Curtis, Tony, 119, 291
Cybill, 34
Cynara, 16
D'Amico, Antonio, 185, 202
Dailey, Dan, 130, 278
Daily Express, 247
Daily Mail, 207
Daily Show, The, 252, 285
Dakota, Bill, 124
Dall, John, 35
Dallas, 20, 44, 114, 172, 308
Dalle, Beatrice, 262
Dallesandro, Joe, 124, 215, 240
Dalton, Timothy, 226
Daly, James, 269
Daly, Tyne, 269
Damned, The, 127
Damon, Matt, 254
Dance, 218
Dangerfield, Rodney, 36, 111, 249, 291
Dannemeyer, William, 305
Danova, Cesare, 126
Darling, 60
Darrow, Clarence, 239
Davenport, Lindsay, 146
Davies, Gwyneth, 248
DaVinci, Leonardo, 134
Davis, Bette, 231, 254, 287, 291
Davis, Brad, 66, 97, 115, 117, 161, 276, 300
Davis, Sammy Jr., 12, 135, 258
Day Of The Locust, 279
Day-Lewis, Daniel, 54
Deacon, Richard, 130, 224
Dean, James, 32, 37, 38, 40, 123, 128, 193, 203, 251, 257-258, 259, 260, 265-266, 274, 291
Dear Abby, 217
Death Becomes Her, 149
Death In Venice, 64, 124
Deathtrap, 66
DeBrier, Samson, 32, 112, 134, 135, 297
DeGeneres, Betty, 163, 233
DeGeneres, Ellen, 15, 16, 25, 27, 29, 31, 35-36, 44, 45, 51, 55, 56, 61, 71, 92, 104, 105, 110, 122, 134, 136, 146, 162, 163, 169-170, 172, 176, 183, 192, 199, 206, 227, 235, 243, 249, 253, 254, 281, 282, 294, 307, 311, 312
Del Rio, Dolores, 65
DeLaria, Lea, 35, 61, 88, 140, 182, 191
Delon, Alain, 11, 70
Demy, Jacques, 157
Deneuve, Catherine, 14
Dennis, Patrick, 261
Dennis, Sandy, 110, 118
Depp, Johnny, 23, 178
Dern, Laura, 16
Designing Women, 139, 216
Detroit Free Press, 29
Deutsch, Helen, 121
Dewhurst, Colleen, 141
Diamond, Dave, 188
DiCaprio, Leonardo, 14, 31, 133-134, 291, 294, 305
Dick Van Dyke Show, The, 130, 224
Dick, Andy, 19, 187
Dickinson, Janice, 181
Dietrich, Garbo, 63
Dietrich, Marlene, 189, 206
Diff'rent Strokes, 144, 192, 206, 212
Different Story, A, 53
Dillard, Gavin Geoffrey, 82
Diller, Phyllis, 119, 293
Dillon, Matt, 175
Dion, Celine, 90
Dior, Karen, 205
Dirty Dancing, 84, 132, 194
Disney, 301, 302
Divine, 128, 257, 292
Dobie Gillis, 23, 44, 234
Dodds, John, 219
Dole, Bob, 170, 305
Dole, Elizabeth, 170
Dollard, Ann, 72
Donahue, Phil, 244, 301
Donahue, Troy, 278, 292
Donnelly, Patrice, 199
Donovan, Casey, 130
Dougie Howser, M.D., 254
Dove, Ulysses, 117
Downey, Robert Jr., 123, 140, 232
Doyle, Conan, 269
Doyle, Tim, 99
Dr. No, 264
Dr. Quinn, Medicine Woman, 43, 63, 71, 118
Dr. Seuss, 160
Dr. Zhivago, 88
Dracula, 148, 284
Dragazine, 133
Drake, Robert, 78-79, 100, 226
Dreamgirls, 184
Dreyfuss, Gerry, 133
Dreyfuss, Richard, 133
Drivas, Robert, 190
Dukes Of Hazard, The, 285
Dunaway, Faye, 14
Dunn, Nora, 30, 31
Dunne, Phillip, 126
Dunphy, Jack, 140, 184, 201, 246
Earle, Charlie, 55
Eastwood, Clint, 34, 121, 225
Eating Raul, 225
Ebert, Roger, 254
Ebsen, Buddy, 189
Edge, 63, 75, 77, 234
Edholm, Geoffrey, 279
Edwards, Blake, 134, 245
84 Charing Cross Road, 199
Electra, Carmen, 306
Eliot, George, 248

Elizabeth, 58
Ellen, 15, 27, 44, 96, 99, 104, 110, 132, 199
Ellington, Duke, 138
Ellington, Mercer, 138
Elliott, Stephen, 29, 283
Ellis, Brett Easton, 156
Elvira, 105
Elwes, Cary, 262
Encore! Encore!, 137, 149
Enough Is Enough, 126
Entertainment Tonight, 50
Epperly, Jeff, 297
Estefan, Gloria, 217
Etheridge, George, 34, 104
Etheridge, Melissa, 34, 104, 105, 137, 164, 209
Evans, Linda, 197
Evening Shade, 115, 139
Everett, Rupert, 16, 31, 56, 89, 139, 158, 169, 172, 180, 253, 262, 286, 309
Evil Under The Sun, 286
Evita, 257
Eye Of The Storm, The, 185
F Troop, 127
Fab!, 28, 43, 73, 88, 220, 242, 285
Fabio, 125
Fairbanks, Harold, 33, 165
Fairbanks, Howard, 275
Fairbass, Richard, 309
Fairchild, Morgan, 182
Falwell, Jerry, 78, 83, 208, 235, 289, 302
Family Channel, The, 301
Family Ties, 39, 231
Family, 202
Fan, The, 261
Fantasticks, The, 305
Farrell, Charles, 60, 291
Fassbinder, Rainer Werner, 80, 227
Fawlty Towers, 299
Feinberg, David, 145, 231, 245, 280
Feinstein, Michael, 104
Fenn, Sherilyn, 197
Ferguson, Ken, 58, 70, 74, 158
Ferrer, Miguel, 61
Feury, Peggy, 53
Fiddler On The Roof, 177
Fierstein, Harvey, 56, 158, 169, 170, 239, 250, 264, 267
Finch, Peter, 16, 54, 183
Finney, Albert, 60
Firbank, Ronald, 153
Fischer, Kate, 30
Fish Called Wanda, A, 299
Fisher, Carrie, 197, 202
Fisher, Clive, 255
Fisher, Eddie, 197
Fitzpatrick, Larry, 143
Flack, Tim, 59, 97, 107, 122
Flemying, Jason, 15
Flirtations, The, 287
Flynn, Errol, 32, 261, 274, 288
Foch, Nina, 39
Fonda, Jane, 118, 224, 252, 293
Fontanne, Lynne, 48, 64
Footnotes, 215
Forbes, Malcolm, 301
Ford, Gerald, 60, 117
Ford, Harrison, 26, 251, 295
Ford, Leo, 293
Ford, Michael Thomas, 285
Ford, Tom, 309
Forrester, Cody, 89-90
Forster, E.M., 195
Forwood, Anthony, 64
Foster Child, 20
Foster, Buddy, 20, 116-117
Foster, Charles, 243-244
Foster, Jodie, 16, 20, 27, 29-30, 62, 110, 116-117, 160, 175, 181, 243, 244, 263, 281, 311
Foul Play, 149
Four Weddings And A Funeral, 64
4-Front, 232
Fox, The, 118
France, Pierre Mendes, 200
Franco, Francisco, 311
Frank, Barney, 57, 92, 96, 233, 305
Frankfather, William, 149
Frankie Goes To Hollywood, 126
Franklin, Ben, 143
Fraser, Brendan, 103
Frasier, 103, 131, 280, 312
Freud, Sigmund, 124, 226, 299, 313
Frey, Leonard, 72, 177
Friday The 13th Part 2, 58
Frisk, 25
From Here To Eternity, 37
From Shirley Temple To Aimee Semple, 881
Front Runner, The, 52, 65
Frontiers, 77, 89, 237
Fry, Stephen, 82, 262
Fuller, Samuel, 253
Funes, Jessie, 75
Funicello, Annete, 50
Funny Girl, 289
Furnish, David, 185
Fying Nun, The, 127
Gable, Christopher, 66, 156, 293
Gable, Clark, 251, 279
Gabor, Eva, 33, 240, 254-255, 298
Gabor, Zsa Zsa, 196, 291, 298
Galindo, Rudy, 230
Gallo, Clifford, 150
Gallo, Vincent, 180, 273
Garbo, Greta, 84, 196, 224, 273, 304
Gardner, Ava, 240
Garland, Judy, 135, 203
Gately, Stephen, 98
Gauguin, 290
Gay And Lesbian Times, 73, 85
Gay Book Of Days, The, 197
Gay Canon, The, 78, 100, 226
Gaynor, Gloria, 57
Gaynor, Janet, 254
Geer, Herta, 159
Geer, Will, 159
Geffen, David, 137, 263
Geisel, Theodore, 160
Gelin, Daniel, 268
Gellar, Sarah Michelle, 212
General Electric Theatre, 258
General Gordon, 58, 275
Genre, 37, 133, 167, 236
Gere, Richard, 105, 199, 264
Gernreich, Rudy, 302
Giant, 251, 259, 291
Gibbons, Cedric, 65
Gibbons, Elliot, 65
Gibson, Mel, 56, 205, 283
Gide, Andre, 226
Gielgud, Sir John, 250, 286, 292, 299, 300
Gilbert, Sara, 43
Gilligan's Island, 15, 258, 280
Gilmore, John, 39, 193, 203, 259, 266
Gingrich, Candace, 269
Ginsberg, Allen, 15, 35, 96, 118, 136, 192, 266, 307
Giraudoux, Jean, 168
Gish, Lillian, 181
Gleason, Jackie, 33
Glendening, Bruce, 165
Glendening, Paris, 165
Globe, 43, 149, 205
Gods And Monsters, 208
Gogol, Nikoli, 78
Goldberg, Whoopi, 109, 271
Goldwater, Barry, 47, 301
Goldwyn, Francis, 176
Goldwyn, Sam, 176
Good Will Hunting, 51, 246, 291
Goodbye Girl, The, 133
Goodman, John, 137
Goodstein, David B., 154
Gordon, Gale, 149
Gore, Al, 67, 75, 186
Gore, Tipper, 186
Gould, Elliot, 111
Gould, Jason, 111
Grable, Betty, 130
Graham, Billy, 78, 250, 302
Graham, Lee, 13, 23, 36, 43, 60, 94, 120
Graham, Sheilah, 12, 122
Graham, Stedman, 277
Graham, Virginia, 97, 291
Grand Hotel, 139
Granger, Farley, 176
Granger, Stewart, 24, 303
Grant, Amy, 85, 282
Grant, Cary, 24, 42, 66, 130, 148, 151, 157, 158, 184, 211, 219-220, 224, 255, 269, 295, 304, 306
Grant, David Marshall, 51, 164
Grant, Hugh, 32, 64, 139
Grease, 98, 227
Great Romances, 221, 269
Greater Tuna, 84
Green Berets, The, 290
Greif, Martin, 18, 49, 72, 197
Grief, 25, 32
Grier, Pam, 264
Griffin, Merv, 33, 146, 240, 265, 307
Griffith, Stan, 241
Grimes, Tammy, 237
Guest, Christopher, 64
Guiding Light, 16, 60, 87, 244, 270, 311
Guilaroff, Sidney, 40-41, 84
Gypsy, 30, 49, 270
Haas, Lukas, 273
Haber, Joyce, 131, 219
Hackman, Gene, 183
Hagman, Larry, 19-20
Haile, Mark, 221
Haines, William, 152, 202
Hairspray, 16, 257
Hajdis-Holman, Dorothy, 198, 233
Haley, Alex, 286
Halloween, 277
Hamilton, Tony, 76
Hamlin, Harry, 55
Hanff, Helene, 199, 200, 213
Hanks, Tom, 16, 17, 209, 263, 309
Hard Copy, 71
Haren, Christian, 274, 278
Hargreaves, John, 45
Harlow, Jean, 304
Harold And Maude, 20
Harper, Valerie, 128
Harrington, Curtis, 17
Harris, Julie, 231
Harris, Neil Patrick, 254
Harry, Debbie, 257
Hart, Larry, 48
Hartman, Phil, 134, 232
Hartzell, Russell John II, 209, 221
Harvey, Laurence, 172
Hatcher, Tom, 186
Hawkins, Sophie B., 189
Hawthorne, Sir Nigel, 140, 194
Hay, Harry, 159
Hayden, Tom, 118
Hayes, Robert, 27
Hayward, Leland, 295
Hayworth, Rita, 273-274
Head, Edith, 64, 65
Head, Murray, 16
Heche, Anne, 26, 29, 36, 38, 55, 71, 89, 92-93, 105, 110, 136, 142, 158, 162, 169-170, 176, 183, 192, 206, 222, 227, 249, 251, 294, 295, 311
Heffer, Simon, 207
Hefner, Hugh, 128, 210
Hellman, Lillian, 163, 275
Hello Dolly!, 26
Helms, Jesse, 46
Hemingway, Ernest, 267, 310
Hemingway, Mariel, 55
Hemphill, Essex, 187
Henderson, Florence, 118
Henderson, Rick, 68
Hepburn, Audrey, 84
Hepburn, Katharine, 284, 295
Herlihy, James Leo, 288
Heston, Charlton, 58, 275, 283
Hexum, Jon-Erik, 123
Hickey, William, 280
Higgins, Colin, 20
Hill, Benny, 132, 252
Hill, Josephine Dominguez, 117
Hingis, Martina, 146
Hitler, Adolf, 77, 83
Hoffman, Dustin, 51
Hogan's Heroes, 247
Holland, Tim, 268
Holliman, Earl, 59
Hollywood Babylon, 241
Hollywood Kids, The, 25, 72, 183
Hollywood Lesbians, 64, 116
Hollywood Reporter, 152
Hollywood Squares, 33, 166
Hollywood Star, 128
Hollywood Studio, 120

Holmes, James, 144
Holmes, Phillips, 63
Holmes, Sherlock, 269, 308
Home Before Dark, 142
Honeymooner's, 33
Hooker, Dr. Evelyn, 302
Hooper, Forrest G., 116
Hoover, J. Edgar, 117, 296
Hope, Bob, 46, 234
Hopper, Dennis, 259
Hopper, Hedda, 24, 284, 303
Hopper, William, 24
Hormel, James, 226
House Of Flowers, 119
Houston, Cissy, 216
Houston, Whitney, 156, 216
How To Marry A Millionaire, 17
How To Murder Your Wife, 12
Howar, Barbara, 156
Howard's End, 194
Howerd, Frankie, 254
Huckleberry Finn, 85
Hudson, Rock, 37, 117, 122, 123, 125, 128, 194, 210, 211, 224, 266, 273, 278, 304
Hughes, Howard, 295
Hulce, Tom, 108
Hume, Benita, 181
Humphries, Barry, 132
Hunger, The, 14
Hunter, Gregg, 265
Hunter, Ross, 221
Hunter, Tab, 128, 278, 286, 292
Huntley, Raymond, 148
Hurley, Brian, 57, 96, 222, 309
Huston, John, 251, 267
Huston, Skip, 208
Hutchence, Michael, 79, 109-110
Hutton, Barbara, 219-220
Hutton, E.F., 219
Hutton, Lauren, 197, 254
I Am A Camera, Bell, Book And Candle, 49
I Left My Heart In San Francisco, 218
I Love Lucy, 19, 149, 219
I Shot Andy Warhol, 173
I Think I Do, 14
Ian, Janis, 46
Ideal Husband, An, 158
Iger, Bob, 15
Illustrated Man, The, 190
In And Out, 69, 251
In Her Sister's Shadow, 271
In Living Color, 45
In The Heat Of The Night, 238, 286
Inman, John, 261
Interview, 27, 133
INXS, 109
Irons, Jeremy, 299
Irving, Henry, 148
Isherwood, Christopher, 70, 186, 215, 260
Jabara, Paul, 45, 105, 126, 180, 279
Jackie Brown, 264
Jackson, Glenda, 42, 98
Jackson, Kato, 276
Jackson, Michael, 156, 252, 265, 277
Jackson, Phil, 306
Jagger, Bianca, 230
Jagger, Mick, 124, 180, 199, 290, 304
James, Henry, 298
Jar Jar Binks, 95
Jarrico, Paul, 33
Jasmine, Paul, 136
Jay, Karla, 207
Jeffrey, 56, 87
Jeni, Richard, 213
Jeter, Michael, 115, 136, 139, 287, 292
Jinxed, 24
Jobriath, 218
John Larroquette Show, The, 128
John, Elton, 58, 76, 90, 100, 103, 107, 123, 146, 155, 164, 185, 253, 264, 286, 282, 293, 299
Johnson, Don, 306
Johnson, Holly, 126
Johnson, Jed, 199, 213, 283
Johnson, Richard, 71
Johnson, Van, 136
Jones, Cherry, 144
Jones, Grace, 173, 253
Jones, Jimmy, 265
Jones, Merlin, 50
Jones, Tom, 255
Joplin, Janis, 103, 263
Kaczor, Bill, 89
Kamen, Stan, 39, 123
Karloff, Boris, 148
Kasha, Larry, 61
Kattan, Chris, 250
Kazan, Elia, 206
Kearns, Michael, 68, 112, 127
Kelly, Gene, 26, 230
Kelly, George, 154
Kelly, Grace, 154
Kelly, Patsy, 310
Kendrick, Walter, 80, 151, 301
Kepner, Jim, 30, 38, 41, 49, 84, 111, 119, 174, 176, 254
Kerouac, Jack, 142
Kerwin, Brian, 53
Khartoum, 58, 275-276
Kid Rock, 306
Kidman, Nicole, 107, 285, 311
Kids In The Hall, The, 54, 109, 132, 308
Kier, Udo, 116
Kight, Morris, 301
Kilborn, Craig, 57-58, 252
Killing Of Sister George, The, 72, 112, 254
Kind Hearts And Coronets, 190
King, Billie Jean, 138, 146, 173
King, Perry, 53
Kinison, Sam, 45, 161
Kinnear, Greg, 31, 56, 266
Kinsey, Dr. Alfred, 194
Kirk, Tim, 50
Kirkman, Tim, 47
Kirkwood, James Sr., 268
Kirkwood, James, 268
KISS, 58
Kitchener, Lord, 276
Kitt, Eartha, 258
Klein, Calvin, 292
Klein, Howie, 163
Kline, Kevin, 251-252
Kmetko, Steve, 152-153, 168
Knots Landing, 61, 231
Koch, Ed, 108, 135
Komack, James, 26
Kopay, David, 139, 147
Kopelson, Arnold, 127
Kramer, Larry, 99, 101, 108, 135, 137, 170, 177
Krupa, Gene, 286
Kuehl, Sheila James, 23, 44, 92, 234, 290
Kulp, Nancy, 116
Kushner, Tony, 137
L.A. Confidential, 133
L.A. Law, 25, 55, 173, 195
L.A. Reader, 150
L.A. Weekly, 270
La Cage Aux Folles, 27, 52, 74, 228
Lachs, Stephen, 99
Ladd, Alan, 278
Ladies Home Journal, 203
LaGuardia, Robert, 37, 205
Lair Of The White Worm, 173
Lake, Ricki, 283
Lake, Veronica, 181
Lambert, Douglas, 194
Lambert, Gavin, 125
Lancaster, Burt, 174
Lanchester, Elsa, 254, 284
Landers, Ann, 217
Lane, Nathan, 30, 43, 46, 137, 143, 149, 158, 168, 213, 252
lang, k.d., 25, 30, 43, 76, 104, 106, 111, 179, 209, 210, 249, 310
Langtry, Lillie, 133
Lansbury, Angela, 53, 182, 195
Larry Sanders Show, The, 132, 281
Larson, Jack, 225
Last Dance, 180
Last Of The Mohicans, The, 179
Last Tango In Paris, 50, 178, 272
LaTourneaux, Robert, 28, 53, 72, 141
Laugh Factory, 59
Laugh-In, 131, 193
Laughing Sinners, 279
Laughton, Charles, 53, 284
Lauper, Cyndi, 187, 239
Laura, 310
Laurel, Stan, 304
Lauren, Ralph, 131, 280
Laurent, Saint, 199
Laurents, Arthur, 176, 186
Laurie, Piper, 41
Lavant, Oscar, 39
Law, John Phillip, 224
Lawless, Lucy, 201, 243
Lawrence Of Arabia, 88
Layton, Joe, 221, 255, 273
Le Monde, 208
Leaving Las Vegas, 14
Leavitt, David, 248
Lee, Gypsy Rose, 270
Lee, Lila, 268
Lee, Linda, 119
Left-Handed Gun, The, 78
Leigh, Vivien, 251
Lemmon, Jack, 128
Lennox, Annie, 146
Leno Wit, The, 308
Leno, Jay, 282, 304, 308
Leone, Sergio, 303
Lerner, Karen, 271
Les Miserables, 70
Les Nuits Fauves, 272
Lesbian News, 26, 204, 295
Lesbians On The Loose, 26, 189, 243
Letterman, David, 128
Lettice, Hedda, 162
Lettow, Jeffrey, 153, 155
Levene, Sam, 17
Lewinsky, Monica, 76, 91, 210, 288, 299
Liberace, 13, 22, 28, 106, 117, 171, 198, 257, 261, 267, 287
Liberace, George, 287
Liberace, Ina, 202, 287
Liberace, Lester Lee, 287
Lichtenstein, Mitchell, 130
Lichtenstein, Roy, 130
Life Of Brian, The, 256
Limbaugh, Rush, 77
Lindfors, Viveca, 30
Link, Ron, 220, 235, 243, 299
Little Mermaid, The, 62, 221, 269
Little Richard, 286-287
Liu, Lucy, 213
Live Fast—Die Young, 38, 203
Liza, 196
Locke, Sondra, 225
London Daily Mirror, 165
Lone Ranger, 125
Lonely Passion Of Judith Hearne, The, 151
Longtime Companion, 8, 229
Loos, Anita, 8, 229
Lorca, Federico Garcia, 100
Lord, Audre, 224, 310
Lords, Traci, 196
Loren, Sophia, 14, 178, 310
Los Angeles Times, 167, 219
Lost Horizon, 170
Lost In Space, 312
Lost Language Of Cranes, The, 150
Loud, Lance, 121
Louganis, Greg, 23, 93, 223, 247
Louise, Tina, 15, 280
Love! Valor! Compassion!, 15, 252
Love, American Style, 54
Loved One, The, 28, 268
Loving, 237
Lovitz, Jon, 172
Lowe, Charles, 192-193, 273
Lowe, Rob, 51
Lubin, Arthur, 225
Lucas, George, 95
Luce, Clare Booth, 260-261
Ludwig, 127
Lugosi, Bela, 148
Lunt, Alfred, 48, 64
Lupino, Ida, 260
Lust For Life, 290
Lust In The Dust, 128
Lynch, Kelly, 197
Lynde, Paul, 54, 267
Lytess, Natasha, 63
MacDonald, Joe, 181
MacDonald, Norm, 237, 250
MacDowall, Roddy, 30, 143, 286
Machiavelli, 11
Mackintosh, Cameron, 70
MacLaine, Shirley, 276

Maderitz, James, 71, 76
Madison, Guy, 126
Madness Of King George, The, 139, 194
Madonna, 105, 174, 187, 196, 249, 253, 257, 262, 281, 303
Maelen, Christian, 14
Maggenti, Maria, 240
Maher, Bill, 46
Mailer, Norman, 265
Main, Marjorie "Ma Kettle", 26
Majority Of One, A, 49
Make Room For Daddy, 294
Making Love, 27, 55
Making Of A Monster, The, 265
Malatesta, Peter, 234
Malden, Karl, 247
Mama Rose, 270
Man In The Iron Mask, The, 291
Man Who Would Be King, The, 278
Manilow, Barry, 128-129, 254
Manner, David, 284
Mansfield, Jayne, 310
Mansfield, Katherine, 143
Manson, Marilyn, 266
Mantel, Henriette, 174
Marais, Jean, 90, 91
Margolyes, Miriam, 164
Marin Independent Journal, 153, 155
Marlboro Man, 274, 278
Marquand, Christian, 270
Marriage Of Maria Braun, The, 227
Married With Children, 103, 262
Martin, Dean, 128
Martin, Mary, 20, 250, 254
Martin, Ricky, 149
Marvin, Lee, 276
Marx, Groucho, 112, 250
Mary Tyler Moore Show, The, 128
Mary, John B., 90
Mason, Perry, 24, 42
Masters, Billy, 28, 31
Masters, George, 283
Matalon, Vivian, 190
Mathis, Johnny, 106, 116, 128, 171, 177, 178
Matlovich, Leonard, 313
Matthau, Carol, 202
Matthau, Walter, 202
Mature, Victor, 195
Matuszak, John, 110, 266
Maugham, Somerset, 48
Maupin, Armistead, 65, 67-68, 113, 116, 125, 129, 165, 272
Mauresmo, Amelie, 146
Maya, Frank, 66, 191, 217, 219
Mayberry R.F.D., 116
Mayo, Virginia, 120
McCain, John, 57
McCambridge, Mercedes, 291
McCarthy, Joseph, 300
McChesny, Mart Dayne, 58, 60, 61, 143, 146, 158, 247, 289, 311
McCowen, Alec, 190
McCracken, Joan, 247
McCullers, Carson, 260
McDonald, Boyd, 159, 184, 200, 264
McDonald, Buddy, 58
McEwan, Geraldine, 308
McKechnie, Donna, 184
McKellan, Sir Ian, 67-68, 69, 109, 140, 142, 158, 162, 164, 178, 209, 210, 215
McKuen, Rod, 173
McNichol, Kristy, 202, 287
McRae, Carmen, 231
McWilliams, Pat, 43
Meade, Dr. Margaret, 239
Medical Center, 269
Meisel, Steven, 303
Melrose Place, 136
Mercury, Freddie, 207
Merman, Ethel, 224
Merrill, Gary, 287
Michael, George, 21, 28-29, 36-37, 43, 48, 106, 113, 118, 141, 144, 165, 175, 227-228, 247, 262, 273, 298, 304, 309
Michaels, David, 128
Michelangelo, 58, 275
Michener, James, 148
Midler, Bette, 24, 69
Midnight Cowboy, 72, 225, 288
Midnight Express, 161
Midnight In The Garden Of Good And Evil, 264
Mildred Pierce, 230
Milford, Erik, 120
Milk Train Doesn't Stop Here Anymore, The, 286
Milk, Harvey, 34, 60, 100, 166
Miller, George, 84
Miller, Joseph, 83, 205
Miller, Stuart, 211
Millet, Kate, 219
Mineo, Sal, 124, 251, 259, 265-266, 274, 286, 306
Minnelli, Liza, 97, 135-136, 172, 173
Minnelli, Vincente, 203
Mishima, Yukio, 260
Mitchum, Robert, 258
Monette, Paul, 22, 41, 43, 59, 106, 108, 125, 129, 198, 211, 296
Monkey's Uncle, The, 50
Monroe, Marilyn, 63, 91, 255, 283, 287
Montgomery, Elizabeth, 218
Monty Python, 28, 45, 135, 171, 216
Moonlighting, 34
Moore, Brian, 151
Moore, Robert, 72, 184
Moore, Sara Jane, 60
Morley, Sir Robert, 54
Moscone, George, 166
Moscone, Jonathan, 166
Moss, Jon, 223, 241
Moss, Kate, 137
Most Fabulous Story Ever Told, The, 87
Mother Teresa, 56, 79
Mouse Hunt, 149
Mozart, 108, 220
Mr. Ed, 225
Mr. Peepers, 119
Mr. Wrong, 254, 282
Mrs. Doubtfire, 12, 22, 56
Mummy, The, 284
Murder By Death, 45, 184, 265
Murder On The Orient Express, 60
Murdoch, Rupert, 61
Murnau, F.W., 38
Murphy, Diane, 120
Murphy, Eddie, 45, 187, 205, 264, 270
Murphy, Timothy Patrick, 44
Musto, Michael, 13, 109, 286, 290, 299
My Best Friend's Wedding, 16, 31, 56, 89, 169, 172
My Fair Lady, 12
My Favorite Martian, 130
My Little Margie, 61
My Mother, My Father And Me, 163
My Own Private Idaho, 51, 116
My So Called Life, 13, 47, 111, 232
Nabors, Jim, 220
Najimy, Kathy, 93, 248, 305
Nakagawa, Ryan, 222
Napier, Alan, 261
National Enquirer, 56, 115, 253
National Geographic, 70
National Insider, 121
National Velvet, 300
Navarro, Ramon, 100, 171
Navratilova, Martina, 29, 137, 149, 164, 196
Negulesco, Jean, 17
Nelson, Gene, 128
Nelson, Kenneth, 299
Nelson, Ricky, 65
Nelson, Willie, 246
Nesbitt, Cathleen, 205
Network, 54
New Weekly, 30, 249
New York Post, 229
New York Times, 282
Newman, Paul, 52, 65
NewsRadio, 19, 134, 187, 232
Newsweek, 89
Newton, Helmut, 181
Nicholson, Jack, 33, 251
Nicklin, Henry, 304, 305
Night Of The Iguana, 267
Nimmo, Derek, 156
Nine To Five, 20
Nirvana, 123
Nixon Off The Record, 47
Nixon, Richard, 47, 300
Norman, Connie, 59, 151
Novello, Ivor, 171
Nunn, Sam, 301
Nureyev, Rudolf, 160
Nye, Matt, 220
NYPD Blue, 56
Nyswaner, Ron, 54
O'Brien, Conan, 67
O'Donnell, Rosie, 20, 54, 67, 96, 107, 137, 140, 152, 162, 175,176, 254, 307, 311
O'Dowd, Brian, 203
O'Hara, Scott, 58
O'Haver, Tommy, 138
O'Sullivan, Gilbert, 309
O'Toole, Darian, 91
Ober, Phil, 219
Ocamb, Karen, 236
Off P'tree, 152
Oklahoma!, 128
Oldman, Gary, 304
Oliver!, 85, 218, 235
Oliver, Larry, 250
Olivier, Laurence, 129, 215, 300, 307-308
On The Town, 88
Onassis, Jackie Kennedy, 270, 271
Operation Petticoat, 211, 269
Opposite Of Sex, The, 52, 236, 237
Orloff, John, 87
Orser, Brian, 147
Osborne, Joan, 229
Osborne, Robert, 152
Osmond, Donny, 59
Osmond, Marie, 59
Other Voices, Other Rooms, 85, 267
Our Miss Brooks, 229
Out And About, 147
Out, 311
Outrageous!, 18
Ovitz, Mike, 170
Owens, Dana "Queen Latifah", 137
Page, Geraldine, 32, 259
Paglia, Camille, 41, 284, 296, 297, 309-310
Palmer, Lilli, 181
Pan, Hermes, 274
Pangborn, Franklin, 120
Parker, Dorothy, 223, 260-261
Parker, Jean, 250
Parker, Sarah Jessica, 123
Partridge Family, The, 294
Party Of Five, 43, 47, 108, 127
Pasolini, Pier Paolo, 246
Passage To India, A, 219
Pastrano, Andres, 220
Patrick, Robert, 184
Paulk, Anne, 88-89
Paulk, John, 88
Paulsen, Pat, 256
Pearce, Guy, 133
Peck, Gregory, 97
Pee Wee's Big Adventure, 179
People, 136, 145, 196
Perez, Charles, 63
Perkins, Anthony, 62, 117, 136, 203, 296, 297
Perry, Eleanor, 140, 188
Perry, Luke, 119, 124
Personal Best, 55, 199
Peters, Michael, 252
Petersen, Wolfgang, 155
Peterson, Cassandra "Elvira", 105
Peterson, Paul, 284
Pfeiffer, Michelle, 176, 193
Phantom Menace, 95
Phantom Of The Opera, The, 70
Philadelphia Daily News, 238
Philadelphia, 16, 17, 33, 44, 54, 262
Phillips, Julia, 273
Phoenix, Joaquin, 175
Phoenix, River, 202
Pickup, Ronald, 308
Picture Of Dorian Gray, The, 227
Pierce, Charles, 216, 307
Pierce, David Hyde, 280
Pillow Talk, 211
Pinchot, Bronson, 304
Pintauro, Danny, 56
Piper, Bill Jr., 295
Pitt, Brad, 50, 127, 249, 262
Plato, Dana, 144, 192, 206, 212
Playboy, 96, 210
Playgirl, 123, 262

Pleasure Principle, The, 208
Plesence, Donald, 277
Plimpton, George, 261
Poitier, Sidney, 134
Poker, Anne, 89
Polanski, Roman, 204
Politically Incorrect, 46, 86, 250, 285
Ponti, Carlo, 178
Pop Smear, 306
Pope John Paul II, 250
Porter, Cole, 48, 119, 270
Poundstone, Paula, 145, 174
Powell, Colin, 19, 301
Power, Tyrone, 8, 100, 186, 203, 270, 273, 297, 306
POZ, 205, 282
Prayer Warriors, 211
Prelude To A Kiss, 247
Preminger, Eric, 270
Preminger, Otto, 270
Prentice, Keith
Presley, Elvis, 117-118, 191, 257, 258, 274, 285, 286
Presley, Lisa Marie, 277
Preston, John, 66
Preston, Robert, 53
Price, Dennis, 190
Price, Vincent, 160, 263
Pride And The Passion, The, 255
Priest, 62
Priestley, Jason, 118
Prime Of Miss Jean Brodie, The, 308
Prince Albert Of Monaco, 154
Prince Charles, 200-201
Prince Edward, 156, 299
Prince Of Foxes, The, 57
Prince, 121
Princess Diana, 58, 79, 169, 185, 200-201, 249, 277, 281-282, 299, 307
Principal, Victoria, 172
Private Life Of Sherlock Holmes, The, 269
Private On Parade, 188
Prizzi's Honor, 32, 251, 280
Proof, 95
Pruitt, Keith, 237
Psycho (1960), 136
Psycho (1999), 142
Quayle, Dan, 195, 256
Queen, 207, 234
Quilley, Denis, 188
Quine, Richard, 12
Quinn, Anthony, 205
R.E.M., 150
Rabbi Hillel, 47
Radziwill, Lee, 271
Ragtime, 58
Rambo, Dack, 19-21, 114, 256, 297, 308
Randall, Bob, 196, 261
Randall, Tony, 131
Raphael, Frederic, 60
Ray, Johnnie, 119
Ray, Johnny, 36, 287
Ray, Nicholas, 259
Razor's Edge, The, 310
Ready To Wear, 139
Reagan, Michael, 250
Reagan, Nancy, 256-257, 275, 305
Reagan, Ronald Jr., 137
Reagan, Ronald, 229, 249, 256-258, 300, 305
Real World, The, 82, 141, 214, 236
Rebel Without A Cause, 40, 251, 258, 259
Rechy, John, 109, 235
Reddy, Helen, 67, 241, 297
Redford, Robert, 65, 278
Redgrave, Sir Michael, 80
Redgrave, Vanessa, 268
Reed, Rex, 264
Reed, Robert, 118
Reeve, Christopher, 66
Reeves, Keanu, 63, 263
Reid, Beryl, 112, 254
Reitman, Ivan, 251
Rene, Norman, 13, 150, 192, 199, 247
Reno, Hunter, 196
Reno, Janet, 57, 196
Resnick, Faye, 275
Reubens, Paul, 32, 252
Revere, Anne, 300
Rey, Alejandro, 127
Reynolds, Burt, 193
Reynolds, Dale, 21
Rhoda, 128
Ricardo, Ricky, 312
Rice, Anne, 180
Richards, Keith, 58
Richards, Michael, 263
Richardson, Joely, 268
Richardson, Natasha, 268
Richardson, Tony, 28, 268, 286
Ridgely, Andrew, 28
Right Said Fred, 309
Rimbaud, Arthur, 31, 145, 299
Rivera, Chita, 237, 267
Rivera, Geraldo, 44
Rivers, Joan, 275
Robbins, Tim, 309
Roberts, Julia, 309
Roberts, Oral, 288
Roberts, Tom, 75
Robertson, Pat, 71, 78, 182, 211, 264, 301
Robson, Flora, 175
Rocky Horror Picture Show, The, 129
Rodman, Dennis, 59, 145, 306
Rolling Stone, 112, 135, 220
Rollins, Henry, 126
Rollins, Howard, 83, 131, 238, 250, 286
Romero, Cesar, 12, 42, 100, 126, 130, 195, 204, 251, 271
Room At The Top, 148
Room Of One's Own, A, 220
Room With A View, A, 228
Roos, Don, 52, 236, 267, 271
Roosevelt, Eleanor, 101, 150-151
Roosevelt, Elliott, 151
Roosevelt, Franklin D., 151
Rope, 35
Rorem, Ned, 144
Rosas, Jacques, 237
Rosay, Delphine, 91, 154, 156
Rosenberg, Leonard, 131
Rosenblum, Nancy, 26
Rosenfield, Paul, 18, 197, 219, 255, 295, 304
Ross, Herb, 271
Ross, William Edward Daniel, 77, 160
Rossellini, Isabella, 303-304
Rossi, Leonardo, 79
Rouilard, Richard, 152, 161
Rubin, Benjamin, 70
Rubyfruit Jungle, 277
Rudnick, Paul, 69, 87
RuPaul, 170, 250, 252, 291
Rushton, Matthew, 22
Russell, Katharine, 295
Russell, Kurt, 38
Russo, Vito, 117, 122, 159, 226
Rusty, Hamer, 294
Ryan's Daughter, 88
Sabato, Antonio, 266
Sagan, Dr. Carl, 27
Salome, 112
Samson And Delilah, 76
San Francisco Chronicle, 65
San Jose Mercury News, 238
San Vicente, Romeo, 43, 137, 263, 285
Sandler, Barry, 27
Sanello, Frank, 139, 142, 168
Santoro, Dean, 201
Sarandon, Susan, 14, 152, 309
Sargent, Dick, 12, 22, 94, 190, 256, 269, 280
Sartre, Jean-Paul, 208
Saturday Night Live, 19, 31, 134, 250
Savage, Dan, 137
Savant, Doug, 136
Savitch, Jessica, 197
Say Anything, 43
Scarlet Street, 208
Scavullo, Francesco, 263
Schaech, Johnathon, 254
Schaefer, George, 27, 185
Schiffer, Claudia, 262, 290
Schindler, Allen, 233
Schlafly, Phyllis, 19
Schlesinger, John, 225, 279
Schlessinger, Dr. Laura, 77, 300
Schmidt, Paul, 145, 217
Schneider, John, 285
Schneider, Maria, 50, 178, 268, 271-272
Schwarzenegger, Arnold, 301
Scorsese, Martin, 304
Scott, Lizabeth, 227
Scott, Randolph, 184, 306
Screening The Sexes, 120
Seagal, Steven, 280
Secrest, Meryle, 210
Sedaris, David, 67
Seinfeld, 15, 252, 263
Seinfeld, Jerry, 15, 263, 312
Seiuli, Atison, 270
Selleck, Tom, 251-252
Sergeant, The, 224
Serrault, Michel, 228
Setting Them Straight, 144
700 Club, 301
Seven, 127
Sex, Lies And Videotape, 46
Shadow, The, 26
Shakespeare, Anne, 120
Shakespeare, William, 58, 120, 241, 255, 298, 299
Shalit, Gene, 187
Shandling, Gary, 132
Shapiro, Stanley, 211
Sharif, Omar, 50
Shaw, Artie, 240
Shaw, Irwin, 265
Sheedy, Ally, 138
Sheedy, Charlotte, 138
Sheldon, Lou, 290
Shepard, Eric, 24, 239, 281
Shepard, Matthew, 100, 168, 208, 233, 248
Shepherd, Cybill, 28, 34, 96, 98, 179, 204
Sher, Anthony, 164
Sherman, Bobby, 306
Sheybal, Vladek, 264
Shields, Brooke, 304
Shields, Jimmy, 202
Shilts, Randy, 275
Shimbun, Asahi, 236
Shimizu, Jenny, 189, 212
Shipman, David, 149
Shoestring Revue, The, 67
Shore, Dinah, 30, 280
Shore, Pauly, 263
Shown, Ed Joe, 152
Shue, Elizabeth, 14S
Siegfried And Roy, 290
Signorile, Michelangelo, 22
Silence Of The Lambs, 311
Silver, Joel, 142
Silverman, Mark, 70
Simmons, Gene, 58
Simpson, Nicole Brown, 272
Simpson, O.J., 125, 151, 270
Sinatra, Frank, 45, 128, 255
Single White Female, 52
Sipple, Oliver, 117
Sister Act, 84, 149, 305
Sisters, 31
Six Days/Seven Nights, 26, 55, 251, 295
Six Degrees Of Separation, 252
Skal, David, 263
Skolsky, Sidney, 255
Skye, Ione, 43, 212
Smith, Alexis, 32, 224
Smith, Anna Nicole, 196
Smith, Jerry, 139
Smith, Kevin, 291
Smith, Liz, 12, 105, 121, 158, 210, 294
Smith, Maggie, 307-308
Smith, Steve, 157, 214
Smith, Will, 252
Smothers, Tommy, 293
Snider, Dee, 241
Snyder, Tom, 58, 72, 136, 287
Soap, 98, 103
Sobule, Jill, 107, 170, 171, 193
Socrates, 11
Sodom And Gomorrah, 303
Somers, Suzanne, 28
Somerville, Jimmy, 21, 36, 49, 73, 114, 128, 262, 298
Sommersby, 244
Sondheim, Stephen, 160, 210
Soul, David, 204
Space Camp, 47
Spartacus, 35, 129, 290
Spelling, Tori, 285
Spigelgass, Leonard, 49, 259-260
Spilsbury, Klinton, 125
Sports Illustrated, 224

Springfield, Dusty, 132, 155, 156
Springstein, Bruce, 246
Spy, 197
Spyulberg, Budd, 189
Stallone, Sylvester, 53, 94, 158, 299
Stamos, John, 266
Stamp, Terence, 46, 246
Stank-In, The, 71
Stanwyck, Barbara, 197
Star Brothers, 132
Star Wars, 95
Star, 94
Starsky And Hutch, 204
Steel, Dawn, 271
Steiger, Rod, 224, 268
Steinem, Gloria, 276
Stephens, Robert, 307, 308
Stepmom, 152, 309
Stern, Howard, 266, 282
Stevens, Craig, 32
Steward, Samuel M., 194
Stewart, James, 157
Stewart, Jon, 285
Stipe, Michael, 150
Stoddard, Tom, 73, 216, 288
Stoker, Bram, 148
Stone, Oliver, 246
Stone, Sharon, 87, 142, 168
Stosine, William C., 223
Stowe, Madeleine, 179
Strasberg, Susan, 91, 225
Strayhorn, Billy, 138
Streamers, 130
Streetcar Named Desire, A, 292
Streisand, Barbara, 19, 111, 199, 311
Stritch, Elaine, 304
Strode, Woody, 134-135
Strub, Sean, 282
Stryker, Jeff, 293
Stuart, Jason, 44, 191
Stubbs, Michael, 37
Subber, Saint, 115, 119
Suddenly, Last Summer, 78
Sues, Alan, 131
Sullavan, Margaret, 295
Sullivan, Andrew, 284
Sullivan, Ed, 274
Summer, Donna, 57, 275
Sunday, Billy, 302
Sunday, Bloody Sunday, 16, 183
Sunset Boulevard, 269
Superman, 66, 225
Supernova, 14
Sutherland, Donald, 174
Swanson, Kristy, 179
Swayer, Diane, 277
Swayze, Patrick, 132
Sweeney, Terry, 19
Swoon, 25
Sylvia Scarlett, 295
Tagore, Rabindranath, 175
Take Two, 126
Tales Of The City, 113, 165
Tales Of The Lavender Menace: A Memoir Of Liberation, 207
Talk Soup, 266
Tarantino, Quentin, 264
Tassano, Rudy, 76
Taylor, Elizabeth, 22, 23, 24, 37, 45, 93, 178, 190, 303
Taylor, Lili, 173
Taylor, Robert, 274
Tchaikovsky, Peter, 32
Teletubbies, 78, 289
Teorema, 246
Tesh, John, 252
Tesich, Steve, 81
Tewksbury, Mark, 147
That Touch Of Mink, 211, 269
Thatcher, Margaret, 256
Thewlis, David, 14, 31
Thirtysomething, 51, 164
This Is Your Life, 190
Thomas, Jonathan, 222
Thomas, Marlo, 276
Thompson, Emma,132, 193, 194, 201
Thompson, Scott, 54, 94, 109, 132, 281, 308
Thoroughly Modern Millie, 221
Three Of Hearts, 197
Three Stooges, The, 131
Threesome, 127
Tilton, Charlene, 44
Time, 46, 88, 89, 186, 214, 281
Times Of London, 164
Titanic, 31, 33
To Wong Foo..., 98, 132
Tobias, George, 279
Today Show, The, 187
Tognazzi, Ugo, 228
Tolson, Clyde, 296
Tom Jones, 60
Tomlin, Lily, 52, 67, 116, 160,161-162, 185, 272
Tonight Show, The, 308
Torch Song Trilogy, 55, 56, 267
Total Eclipse, 14, 31
Touch Of Evil, 291
Townsend, Jill, 178
Townshend, Peter, 290
Tracy, Spencer, 295
Trantalis, Dean, 234
Travels With My Aunt, 190
Travis, Randy, 62
Travolta, John, 132, 158, 272, 299
Trials Of Oscar Wilde, The, 183
Truman Capote, 261
Truman, Harry S., 151
Truman, Margaret, 151
Trumbo, Dalton, 290
Tryon, Tom, 51, 229, 306
Tucker, Forrest, 127
Tune, Tommy, 26, 42, 136, 198, 215, 239, 293, 296
Turner, Kathleen, 251
Turner, Lana, 240
Tutu, Desmond, 229
TV Guide, 53, 59, 145, 206, 223, 181
Twain, Mark, 8, 299
Twilight Of The Gods, 96
Twisted Sister, 241
2001, 174
Tyler, Parker, 129, 255
Tyler, Robin, 111, 256
Tyson, Mike, 110
Umbrellas Of Cherburg, The, 157
Up The Down Staircase, 118
Updike, John, 109, 250
US, 135
USA Today, 174
Vachss, Andrew, 238
Valentine, Scott, 39, 124, 231
Valentino, Rudoloh, 40
Vallee, Rudy, 198
Valley Of The Dolls, 121
Valli, Virginia, 291
Vampira, 40
Van Buren, Abigail, 217
Van Druten, John, 49
Van Gogh, Vincent, 290
Van Sant, Gus, 51, 246
Vance, Vivien, 219
Vandross, Luther, 306
Vanity Fair, 210, 239
Variety, 185, 294
Vawter, Ron, 33, 44, 46, 311
Velasquez, Patricia, 224
Verlaine, Paul, 31
Veronica's Closet, 305
Versace, Donatella, 185, 202
Versace, Gianni, 185, 201, 202, 224, 253, 280-283, 299
Victim, 64
Victor/Victoria, 53, 134, 173, 245
Vidal, Gore, 13, 35, 41, 59, 78, 118, 126, 140, 171, 184, 192, 214, 260, 263, 265, 267, 287, 288-289
View, The, 249
Vilanch, Bruce, 84, 166, 167, 291
Vincent, Jan Michael, 125
Vincent, Nora, 137
Vior, Shirley, 86, 146
Visconti, Luchino, 63, 124
Vivier, Roger, 85
Voight, Jon, 225
Volcano, 55, 92, 142
Von Praunheim, Rosa, 28
Wachowski, Andy, 18
Wachowski, Larry, 18
Wagner, Jane, 185
Wahl, Ken, 24
Wahlberg, Mark, 134, 204, 305
Wainwright, Rufus, 309
Walk On The Wild Side, 172
Walker, Jay, 308
Walker, Lee, 69
Walsh, Arlene, 133, 134, 195, 244, 294
Walston, Ray, 130
Walters, Barbara, 243, 249
Waltons, The, 68, 127, 159
Warga, Wayne, 50
Warhol, Andy, 124, 125, 199, 215, 228, 240, 265, 283, 293
Warner, Jack, 32, 259
Washington Post, 46
Washington, Denzel, 252
Waters, John, 16, 178
Wattis, Richard, 31
Way Of The World, The, 308
Way We Were, The, 176
Wayans, Damon, 45, 59
Wayne, John, 15, 128, 206, 283, 290, 300
Weatherby, W.J., 287
Webb, Clifton, 310
Wedding Banquet, The, 130
Wedding Singer, The, 16
Weil, Brian, 134
Weir, John, 211
Weismuller, Johnny, 181
Welcome Back, Kotter, 26
Welles, Orson, 57, 133
Wenner, Jane, 220
Wenner, Jann, 112, 135, 220
Wescott, Glenway, 292, 298
West Side Story, 63
West, Mae, 84, 293
Westenhoefer, Suzanne, 25, 136
Westheimer, Dr. Ruth, 169
Wham!, 28, 141, 298
What Ever Happened To Baby Jane, 303
Wheeler, Jerry B., 24, 52
When Pigs Fly, 74
White, Dan, 60
White, Edmund, 231
White, Mel, 78
White, Patrick, 186, 283
White, Vanna, 196
Who, The, 290
Who's Afraid Of Virginia Woolf?, 21, 222
Who's The Boss, 56
Wilde, 262
Wilde, Oscar, 11, 12, 37, 69, 223, 227, 241
Wilder, Billy, 269, 291
Wilding, Michael, 24, 303
Will And Grace, 61
Williams, David, 88
Williams, Pete, 154
Williams, Robin, 16, 33
Williams, Tennessee, 154, 192, 198, 264, 267, 278, 286, 292-293
Willis, Bruce, 158
Wilson, Pete, 174
Wilson, Rita, 309
Winfrey, Oprah, 128-129, 277
Wings, 269
Winters, Shelley, 176, 252
Wiseguy, 24
Wojnarowicz, David, 227
Woman's Day, 309
Women In Love, 170, 264
Wood, Natalie, 259
Woolf, Virginia, 220
Woronov, Mary, 225
Wright, William, 163
Xena, 201, 243
X-Files, The, 212, 215
You'll Never Make Love In This Town Again, 196
Young, Andrew, 141
Young, Freddie, 88
Young, Loretta, 20
Young, Winston, 148
Zamora, Pedro, 82, 141, 214, 236
Zappa, Frank, 207
Zinneman, Fred, 37